# PRAISE FOR *WE WANT*

*Choice* Magazine Outstanding Acade

"Mumia Abu-Jamal has forged from incisive and thorough history of th ........y ... ...... is required reading for any who would seek to understand race, revolution, and repression in the United States....[G]iven the resurgence of overt and covert government suppression of dissent, true accounts of the popular struggles of the late 60s and early 70s are needed now more than ever. Abu-Jamal carefully imparts the history as passionate participant, skilled journalist, and critical historian."
—Amy Goodman, journalist, *Democracy Now!*

"An important and timely read, now as much as ever. In this new edition of *We Want Freedom*, Mumia provides with clarity and force the historical context for the Black Lives Matter movement—anchoring Black struggle in a long history of militant self-defense. This book is both a guide and a light: full of hope, lessons, challenges, and profound insight into our collective struggle for freedom. I encourage all organizers, new and seasoned, to read and discuss with your people."
—Page May, cofounder of Assata's Daughters

"Mumia is a soldier in the war for the soul of America. He is fighting the good fight with the same weapons his ancestors fought with: words. He sings with his words; he sings with his heart; he sings with the truth. Mumia is a free man, no matter what his address because he is a man who knows who he is: a child of challenging God."
—Nikki Giovanni, Poet

"Mumia Abu-Jamal speaks in a voice as timeless as the resistance to oppression he personifies. His words, his mind—indeed, his life itself— stand as inspirations to all of us who yearn for liberation, exemplifying the continuities of struggle joining one generation to the next in our common effort to attain the dignity of human freedom. This book is as necessary as it is unavoidable. It simply *must* be read by everyone endowed with the least twinge of social conscience."
—Ward Churchill, author of *Agents of Repression: The FBI's Secret Wars Against the Black Panther Party and the American Indian Movement*

"Writing eloquently from his prison cell, Mumia Abu-Jamal gives us a fascinating and unusual history of the Black Panther Party. His chapters 'A Woman's Party' and 'COINTELPRO' would be enough to make this book an invaluable addition to anyone's reading list."
—Howard Zinn, author of *A People's History of the United States*

"This book amazed and delighted me. I'm still not sure how Mumia has managed—from a maximum-security prison cell—to encompass in one book the broad scope of US history, a global perspective, and many intimate, first-hand accounts of life, love, and politics in the Black Panther Party. Mumia tells this story with such energy and passion that reading it, I felt I'd returned to the storefronts and battlefronts of the 60s and 70s. This is the Black Panther Party—and the social movements to which it was connected—in its historical context, its hopes and triumphs, as well as its tragedies and limitations. It is a story fundamental to understanding the US of the 20th and 21st centuries, and I am eternally grateful to Mumia Abu-Jamal for having written it."
—Laura Whitehorn, former political prisoner and editor of *The War Before*

"The republication of Mumia Abu Jamal's *We Want Freedom* has come right on time. Mumia's wonderful book is not only about the Black Panther Party and his experiences within it, but it is an urgent exposition of the long history of the Black Radical Tradition. Rich in historical detail and still attuned to ongoing contemporary discussions concerning Black liberation, *We Want Freedom* provides a new generation of activists, radicals, and revolutionaries with the politics and clarity necessary to sustain today's movement. Mumia's critical voice, experience, and analysis in *We Want Freedom*—written originally from death row—embody the courage and commitment necessary for any social movement to succeed."
—Keeanga-Yamahtta Taylor, author of *From #BlackLivesMatter to Black Liberation*

"Weaving his experiences in the Black Panther Party into the tapestry of Africans' history in America, Mumia Abu-Jamal's book is essential reading for all of us involved in the struggle for freedom."
—George Katsiaficas, editor of *Liberation, Imagination, and the Black Panther Party*

"Written from prison, this well-researched history of the Black Panther Party begins with a timely insight: the Black radical tradition matters if we are to win Black freedom. Originally published in 2004, this is Mumia's greatest gift to today's young activists who are reigniting the demand for Black freedom. One of its most incisive chapters, on the women of the Party, argues compellingly that they were its life-blood. Mumia's close examination of COINTELPRO's destructive strategies in the Party offers perspective on the policies of incarceration and police militarization that came later: the deployment of violent repression against Black radicals in the Sixties emboldened state violence and broadened it to the Black community. In this beautifully written political memoir, Mumia conveys the power that is unleashed when young Black people in the US are mobilized with a mission and grounded in a revolutionary political platform."

—Johanna Fernández, Department of History, Baruch College, editor of *Writing on the Wall*, and author of the forthcoming *When the World Was Their Stage: A History of the Young Lords Party, 1968–1974*

"*We Want Freedom* is a welcome addition to the Oakland centered accounts of the Black Panther Party. Mumia Abu-Jamal provides a provocative and insightful narrative of local Panther activism in Philadelphia. He presents a superb and thoughtful critique of a myriad of organizational dynamics, including tensions between local Party affiliates and national headquarters, gender relations, and intrafactional conflict within the BPP. Mumia's *We Want Freedom* enriches our understanding and appreciation of the Black Panther Party. His work will undoubtedly inspire his former Party comrades to document their experience of local Panther activism in the various communities across the United States."

—Charles E. Jones, chair of the Department of African American Studies, Georgia State University and editor of *The Black Panther Party Reconsidered*

"[*We Want Freedom*] will have an important place in the literature of the Black Panther Party. ... Abu-Jamal has written a book which amplifies the voices and experiences of rank-and-file members and attempts to ground their stories in a local context. In the final analysis, *We Want Freedom* forces scholars to reframe their assumptions about the Panthers' internal political culture, bottom-up realities, gender politics, and organizational history."

—Robyn C. Spencer, author of *The Revolution Has Come: Black Power, Gender, and the Black Panther Party in Oakland*

"Mumia's keen analysis of the Panthers provides readers with a unique understanding of an organization J. Edgar Hoover deemed the 'greatest threat to the internal security in the country.' Rewarding too is his fresh assessment of the role of women in the Party, which thoughtfully draws on the work of the late Safiya Bukhari."

—Herb Boyd, author of *Brotherman* and *Black Panthers for Beginners*

*"We Want Freedom* demonstrates once again Mumia Abu Jamal's leadership and commitment to activism and social change. Abu Jamal's accounts of the strengths and triumphs of the Black Panther Party give readers hope. However, for those who view the governments' repression of the Black Panther Party as unique, the book also gives an opportunity to see what the USA PATRIOT Act portends for social justice activists of today."

—Tonya McClary, American Friends Service Committee National Criminal Justice Program

## PRAISE FOR MUMIA ABU-JAMAL

"Revolutionary love, revolutionary memory, and revolutionary analysis are at work in every page written by Mumia Abu-Jamal ... His writings are a wake-up call. He is a voice from our prophetic tradition, speaking to us here, now, lovingly, urgently."

—Cornel West

"When you listen to Mumia Abu-Jamal you hear the echoes of David Walker, Frederick Douglass, W.E.B. Du Bois, Paul Robeson, and the sisters and brothers who kept the faith with struggle, who kept the faith with resistance."

—Manning Marable

"Mumia Abu-Jamal is one of the most important public intellectuals of our time ... He offers us new ways of thinking about law, democracy and power. He allows us to reflect up on the fact that transformational possibilities often emerge where we least expect them."

—Angela Y. Davis

"A rare and courageous voice speaking from a place we fear to know: Mumia Abu-Jamal's voice must be heard."
—Alice Walker

"A brilliant, lucid meditation on the moral obligation of political commitment by a deeply ethical—and deeply wronged—human being. Mumia should be freed, now."
—Henry Louis Gates, Jr.

"If Mumia Abu-Jamal has nothing important to say, why are so many powerful people trying to kill him and shut him up? Read him."
—John Edgar Wideman

"The first time I heard a tape of one of Mumia's radio broadcasts, it was the first time I fully understood why the government was so intent on putting him to death."
—Assata Shakur

"Refusing to be silenced by his incarceration . . . the flame of his keen intellect and irrepressible soul burns brightly, illuminating each mind that opens to his wise words."
—*ALA Booklist*

"Abu-Jamal's words flow like the very sap of trees, pulsing with energy and capturing the essence of life."
—*Library Journal*

"His writings are dangerous."
—The *Village Voice*

"Crucial reading for all opponents of the death penalty—and for those who support it, too."
—Katha Pollitt, *The Nation*

"Resonates with the moral force of Martin Luther King, Jr.'s 'Letter from Birmingham Jail.'"
—The *Boston Globe*

FREE THE PANTHERS

FREE ALL POLITICAL P

THE BLACK PANTHER

POLITICAL PRISON OF USA FASCISM

THE BLACK PANTHER

CAPITALISM PLUS RACISM

BREEDS

FASCISM

THE BLACK PANTHER

THE B

# WE
# WANT
# FREEDOM

# WE
# WANT
# FREEDOM

## A LIFE IN THE BLACK PANTHER PARTY

## MUMIA ABU-JAMAL

COMMON
NOTIONS

ISBN: 978-1-942173-04-5
LCCN: 2016952179

The Library of Congress has cataloged the original edition as follows:

Abu-Jamal, Mumia.
We want freedom : a life in the Black Panther Party / by Mumia
Abu-Jamal ; introduction by Kathleen Cleaver.
        p. cm.
Includes bibliographical references and index.
ISBN-10 0-89608-719-0 (alk. paper)—ISBN 0-89608-718-2(pbk. : alk. paper)
ISBN-13: 978-0-89608-718-7 (pbk. : alk. paper)
        1. Abu-Jamal, Mumia. 2. African American political activists—Biogra-
phy. 3. Political activists—United States—Biography. 4. Black Panther Party—Bi-
ography. 5. Black Panther Party—History. 6. Philadelphia (Pa.)—Race relations. 7.
Philadelphia (Pa.)—Biography. 8. African American prisoners—Biography. I. Title.
E185.97.A18 A3 2004
322.4'2'092--dc22
                                                            2003026777

Common Notions
131 8th St. #4
Brooklyn, NY 11215
www.commonnotions.org
info@commonnotions.org

Cover design by Josh MacPhee/Antumbra Design
Text design by Alexander Dwinell

Printed in the USA by the employee-owners of Thomson-Shore
www.thomsonshore.com

22  21  20  19  18  17  16                1  2  3  4  5  6  7  8  9

He who fights with monsters should be careful lest he thereby become a monster. And if thou gaze long into an abyss, the abyss will also gaze into thee.

—Friedrich Nietzsche, *Beyond Good and Evil*

# CONTENTS

# DEDICATION

TO THE ANCESTORS, the nameless ones who were dragged to living hells in shackles: "strangers in a strange land." To those young idealistic souls who wore the black and the blue. To those who sold papers in the dead of night, in smoky bars, and in the freezing grips of the wind (especially in the East). To those loving women and sensitive men who rose from their beds at five a.m. to prepare hot breakfasts for schoolchildren from coast to coast.

To Huey, and Eldridge, who are now with the ancestors. To Captain Reggie, to D.C. and B.C., to Pink, to "Stretch" Peterson, to Rene Johnson, to Jintz, to Gladys, to Billy O., to Bullwhip, to Sista Bernice (who became Safiya), to Zayd Malik Shakur, Afeni Shakur, Assata Shakur (the Shakur tribe); to Freddy Nolan, to Frank Jones, to Kathleen, to Geronimo and the Jagas; to the New York 3, to Kiilu Nyasha, to Rita, to Frannie, to Rosemari Mealy, and all the remarkable women who were the luminous glory of the Party. To my former boss, Judi Douglass. To Sista Love. To those known and unknown (like Delbert), who served the Party and their people under arms, and paid the highest price. For those dozens who survived, and remain languishing in the devil's dens still.

To Frances Goldin, who shopped around 'til she found a perfect fit for this work. To Noelle Hanrahan for sending valuable research materials. To those at South End Press, like Alexander Dwinell, Asha Tall, and the rest of the collective, who welcomed, shaped, and praised this project from its earliest incarnation. To my brave and insightful teachers and the thesis committee at California State University, Dominguez Hills; Drs. Myrna Donahoe, Joyce Johnson, and Frank Stricker, who approved an earlier version of this work for completion of an M.A.

To generations to come, who need to know that such a thing as the Black Panther Party was actually possible, and indeed vibrant.

I hereby dedicate this work.

Thank You.

*Mumia Abu-Jamal*

Mumia Abu-Jamal
Waynesburg, Pennsylvania

# Reflections
## INTRODUCTION TO A NEW, REVISED EDITION

**MANY YEARS AGO,** before I wrote my first book (*Live from Death Row*), I was in a lively discussion with a friend of mine. His name is Terry, Terry Bisson. He's a well-known writer of sci-fi, a genre that I love, and we were talking about something we both loved: books. He's actually quite a shy guy (amazingly, many writers are shy. I should know. I'm one of them!), but he confided in me, "This is my third book, and I'm quite proud of it."

"Which one are you proudest of, Terry?" I asked.

"That's hard, Mu. It's kinda like saying who's your favorite child. How can you do that?"

"I understand, but I wonder how it feels to write a book and let it go into the world. What if it bombs?"

"I look at my books the way a bird looks at her chicks: some soar, some stagger, and some fall to the ground. They're all yer babies! But you can do the best you can when you write 'em—then, you let go. They soar—or fall." From that conversation, I learned that every book has its own destiny.

That conversation arose out of the depths of consciousness when I learned that the book you're holding—*We Want Freedom*— was being republished. I felt the flush of joy that this work infused with boyish wonder and political toil and terror was being reborn; cast again, upon the winds of fate.

*We Want Freedom*'s republication comes at a time that can only be considered serendipitous: the era of mass Black (and multi-toned) outrage at the brutality of the State. Ferguson was smoldering. Then Cleveland. Staten Island. The Bronx. Chicago. Baton Rouge. Falcon Heights. I thought of sisters and brothers now gone from us; soldiers of the Black Revolution, like Zayd Malik Shakur; Safiya Bukhari; Geronimo ji-Jaga; Dr. Huey P. Newton; Fred Hampton... and the list goes on. How would they have interpreted—and responded to—this "new" age of protest to attacks on Black life? They would have perhaps started by pointing out how old this legacy of protest and resistance is.

I missed them all—my lost friends and comrades—yet felt uplifted by the young sisters (yes—mostly sisters) emerging as leaders of this new movement. Their cry—that Black Lives Matter has a historic resonance that anyone with ears and memory can't help but hear.

The drums. The drumbeats of protest; the calls to angry, seething masses to stand up against this profound indignity. It harkened back to the brief window of Occupy, reflected the Spanish *indignados*, yes. But it's boldness gave breath to that which so many in power hoped—wished—had become moribund—the Black Panther Party.

*We Want Freedom* argues, and hopefully demonstrates, that Black rebellion has deep roots in American soil; its seeds have sprouted across the centuries. As we will see the Black Panther Party emerged from this long history of struggle for Black liberation. History repeats itself in wild, wonderful, and unpredictable ways. Black Lives Matter also belongs to this tradition. We can see some parallels between the founding and message of both organizations. For the Black Panther Party the observation and filming of the police was an early tactic and the unjustified killing of a black man by police gave a focal point to the anger born of years of injustice. We Are Michael Brown and We Are Denzil Dowell. From the streets of Oakland the news of the police murder of a black man spread via the first issue of the

Black Panther newspaper—the social media of the day—and of course by people getting together and out in the streets. Both movements made the "controversial" statement—this murder is not acceptable and the insistence on the personhood of Black people was grounded in a movement for social change. Both movements were founded and led by young people and you better believe that the politics and strategies of both movements pissed people off … royally. The Black Panther Party located their message in a strong organization, a clear critique of the existing structure, and a demand for change. It is my hope that Black Lives Matter, which has the luxury of looking at the history of the Black Panther Party, will continue to develop their critique and program.

But history, properly understood, is often a cycle where social forces battle for supremacy positing contradiction against contradiction. Sometimes resistance surfaces where it is least expected and popular culture provides a window into a hidden social reality—causing shock, consternation, and delight!

Consider a recent phone call between me and a sista-friend.

"Did you see it? Did you see IT?" she squealed with excitement when picking up the phone.

"See what?" I replied startled.

"Did you see Beyoncé perform at the Super Bowl? She slayed it! She murdered it!?"

"Whachu talkin' 'bout, girl? What did she do?"

"You didn't see it?"

"I ain't see nuthin'— I ain't get my property yet."

"Oh My God, Mu— She did a halftime tribute to Malcolm X—and the Black Panthers!" she screamed.

"You shittin' me, girl!—Beyoncé did that?"

"Yuuuup— and they slayed it— it was for her new song, 'Formation.' She performed surrounded by somethin' like 30 sistas wearing black berets, leather, everything! It was amazing!"

I was speechless. I stuttered.

Her excitement was infectious, and as I saw it through her eyes, I saw something beautiful—and yes, "amazing."

"The cops are furious," she added with a chuckle. This triggered my own deep, belly laugh.

"Wow," I exclaimed. "I didn't see that coming. It sounds wonderful!" Something like this doesn't happen every day. It was a marker of how far the campaign against the police murder of Black people had come.

I thought back to the days of the late RnB and funk superstar James Brown. When he and his band released "Say It Loud—I'm Black and I'm Proud!," it went off like dynamite—cultural dynamite. It exploded—in ears, in minds, in hearts—across America and throughout the Black world.

Beyoncé's timing, coming as it did during the rise of the Black Lives Matter movement, means something. It may be a sign that the spark of emergent consciousness has started a fire.

The timing for the reemergence of *We Want Freedom* therefore, couldn't be better. Its republication both feeds and is fed by current struggles; it can add fuel to this new, bold, youth movement.

Movements—real social movements—always piss people off for they demand that which millions dread: change.

In the latter half of the nineteenth century abolitionists were shunned and denounced as crazy, as those who question the status quo always are. "How dare they call for the end of slavery!" people harrumphed. Before the war their demands seemed inconceivable to many—the enslavement of Black people was such a prominent feature of the US that even those without a direct property relationship could not imagine another world. But after the Civil War it seemed that abolitionists were everywhere—everybody was one.

Because we look at history from our own historical perspective, Lincoln, who spoke often and openly about his distaste for abolitionists, is today perceived as one!

Today, Black Lives Matter is raising quite the ruckus. If they prevail as a social movement they will become the reasonable ones. Reasonable as in, "of course Black lives matter!" who would even dare question such a thing? This is because social movements transform consciousness. They change minds. They change history.

In a white supremacist society the very notion that Black lives matter is a revolutionary idea; for America was constructed (by slave labor, I might add) based upon the idea that Black lives don't matter. That has been the official policy of the nation-state on this continent since the 1600s at least.

In this sense, Black Lives Matter is tearing up old things—notions, ideas, beliefs, and, yes, history, to resurrect the long, arduous and tortuous Black Freedom struggle.

They have read of the Black Panther Party (and the Black Liberation Army), and recognize themselves as part of a Black radical continuum. That is their strength.

Yet, as we have suggested, "history repeats itself," and this repetition takes both positive and negative forms.

The state is using COINTELPRO-type tactics to disrupt, misdirect, and ultimately destroy this latest incarnation of the will of the Ancestors. They will stop at nothing to prevail in retarding the Black freedom struggle. The words written in this text have documented these efforts with care and detail. It behooves Black Lives Matter activists to know what happened in the past, so as to see and sense what is happening today.

The state, said Marx and Engels, is but the executive committee of the ruling class. It exists to stabilize social relations and maintain positions of profound inequality. It is the task of social movements to transform such relations—to change them—to bring forth new ways of seeing, being, and living in islands of freedom. No one said it would be easy. But, surprisingly, it can be fun! Let this be one of *We Want Freedom*'s many lessons. To learn, to grow, to create new social relations can be exciting—and fun.

When James Brown and his band took to the airwaves singing "Say It Loud: I'm Black and I'm Proud!" children began singing it in the streets, it began being played in the bars and beauty shops, apartments blared it out of their windows into the summer streets. It pushed a new way of thinking into creation, and changed culture and music for millions. Just as James Brown continued to provide a soundtrack for the struggle, Beyoncé has continued to raise the issue of the murder of Black people through her videos and statements even as questions about whether she is supporting or appropriating the movement and queer and trans culture have been posed.

The reemergence of *We Went Freedom*, over a decade after its birth, is a sign of the hunger among the young to examine and learn lessons at risk of being lost through the dim window glass of history. It is, after all, their history; not mine. No Panther ever thought that the Party existed for us; it existed because the People demanded we come into existence and fight the fights that needed to be fought.

I have received many letters from readers of *We Went Freedom* over the years. One that sticks in my mind today was from Jon, a young man who read *WWF* in college. He wrote, "I feel cheated because this is the first time I have heard such stories. . . . Your words, your insights have made me and my colleagues question society and the state." Jon concluded by thanking me for my work and I'm happy to take this opportunity to thank him for reading *We Want Freedom*.

I also thank Common Notions for reaching out to me and bringing this book to the next generation. It thrills any writer to know that their work is appreciated and is still being read and I am no different in that regard.

I truly believe that there is much to be learned from the experiences lived by many in the Black Panther Party. I hope our struggles—past, present, and future—prove that the Party did not exist in vain, but made valuable, and sometimes noble contributions. I hope *We Want Freedom* has made, and will continue to make, a contribution to this process. For it was written precisely for times such as these.

May these pages become nourishing, enriching food for the revolution(s) to come.

Mumia Abu-Jamal
"Life Row"

Writing from the windy hills of northeastern Pennsylvania
SCI–Mahanoy, Frackville, PA
Summer 2016

# Introduction

## BY KATHLEEN CLEAVER

**WRITING FROM THE** barren confines of his death row cell, Mumia Abu-Jamal provides a remarkable testament in his latest book to the transformative impact of being part of the Black Panther Party. A high school student when he joined, reflection now polishes Mumia's extensively researched account that clarifies why, in his words, "the Party became the central focus of the lives of thousands of Panthers across the nation." Frank vignettes of unforgettable encounters he had—with fellow members, hostile opponents, larger-than-life Panther leaders, and brutal police are a sheer delight to read. His portrayal of the unquenchable enthusiasm for liberation that animated the Black Panther Party, most of whose members were, like Mumia, teenagers—and over 50 percent were young women—is refreshing. But personal experience comprises only one facet of *We Want Freedom: A Life in the Black Panther Party*.

Adapted from his master's degree thesis at California State University, Dominquez Hills, Mumia's book is accessible but not simple. He places the Black Panther Party in the context of the centuries-long resistance against domination and violence that Blacks have demonstrated during the unending fight to live as a free people. Some may find the way Mumia's analysis integrates the Black Panther Party into the history of radical challenges to slavery and racism eye opening, as that past is so rarely examined it remains generally unknown. Mumia applies the "house slave/field slave" dichotomy that Malcolm X popularized to draw a distinction between what he terms the venerated "civil rights model" of black history, arising from descendants of house slaves who identified their fortune with the well-being of their master, and that disfavored history generated by the descendants of brutalized field slaves, who reacted, as Malcolm described it, to the news master was sick by praying for his death. "Much African American history," Mumia writes, lies "rooted in this radical understanding that America is not the land of liberty, but a place of the absence of freedom, a realm of repression and insecurity." The Black Panther Party emerges from that disfavored history as the contemporary incarnation of that spirit of rebellion and resistance—subjected to modern techniques of sabotage, retaliation, and erasure from historical memory.

Before his 1982 railroading into prison for the murder of a Philadelphia policeman, Mumia Abu-Jamal was a working journalist. His perspective in *We Want Freedom* is not exclusively that of a Black Panther, although he does write movingly from that perspective about being among the founding members of the Philadelphia branch in May 1969. These young revolutionaries boldly affiliated with the Black Panthers at a time when the raids, bombings, shootings, arrests, imprisonment, and death at the hands of police forces and intelligence agencies were hallmarks of their campaign to destroy the organization. Inevitably, each member picked up some regional version of Panther lore, a heady combination of things they'd been told or read about, rumors they'd heard mixed with the surreptitious "disinformation" being circulated in the effort to disrupt the organization, all grasped in the midst of an intense experience which, for too many members, turned traumatic. I know countless Panthers have written about their experience in the Party, some circulating their manuscripts solely among family, others leaving them to languish unfinished in drawers, and the most imaginative producing screenplays or novels, but few ever get published. Each of us retains a unique playlist of mental recordings from our Black Panther Party days, with gaps remaining in what we knew then and time blurring the memories slipping away. We are still piecing together that experience when we encounter former Panthers, whether in films, or in books, or in person when we attend weddings, retreats, funerals, trials, cultural affairs, conferences, demonstrations, or family gatherings—still reinterpreting that indelible relationship. we had with each other in the Black Panther Party. Locked inside a Pennsylvania dungeon, Mumia is barred from going to such events, which testifies to his extraordinary talent, concentration, and spiritual strength in producing such a book.

I assure you, recreating Black Panther history is not a simple task—particularly in light of the sophisticated counter-insurgency operation we now know was being mounted against the organization, its leaders, supporters, members—and even specifically against Mumia, a high school recruit whom the Philadelphia Police Department and the FBI collaborated to destroy. Among the thousands of FBI documents released, one memorandum I've read sticks in my memory because of a chillingly brutal remark. The memo, dated March 9, 1968, was sent to the director of the FBI from a San Francisco–based special agent; it mentions on the second page that "the young Negro" wants something to feel proud of, but must learn that if he becomes a revolutionary, he will be a "dead revolutionary."

Recreating Black Panther history is not a simple task because some books and newspaper articles that one consults in order to understand significant events and establish their chronology have been corrupted by deliberately falsified, or at least suspect, information, such as the misleading book that former Black Panther Earl Anthony wrote in 1969, published by Dial Press in 1970, entitled *Picking Up the Gun*. Twenty years later Anthony revealed in a second book that he had been working undercover for the

FBI's COINTELPRO (the acronym for COunter INTELLigence PROgram) while he was in the Party. It is not a simple task because the Black Panther Party exploded across the country from a local Oakland formation into a national organization during 1968 and I saw that those of us involved had no time to record the process carefully. No one provided chapter and verse on how it happened and who did what, and too much was blurred by our deliberate glorification of imprisoned leader Huey Newton, then facing the gas chamber, as part of the all-absorbing international campaign waged for his freedom. The covert COINTELPRO operation that cracked the Black Panther Party into factions by 1971 depended upon meticulous techniques of generating distrust and paranoia, including the insidious portrayal of friends as each other's enemy and the insertion of undercover agents into sensitive positions to help convict or assassinate key leaders. A devastating consequence of that split has been the sense of abandonment and betrayal that barred former Panthers from communicating with anyone aligned with the demonized other faction for more than a generation. Legend, hearsay, and the lack of available factual records mar what has been passed on as "history."

Mumia confronts these obstacles admirably in *We Want Freedom,* drawing his own conclusions from the available scholarship, memoirs, and government documents, and supplying an intriguing narrative that arises from his personal observations. Even though Black Panther images and slogans have been rediscovered by popular culture, creating a climate in which the historical significance of the Black Panther Party can be recognized and debated remains a slow process. The slash and burn journalistic accounts and police-thriller style portrayals have hampered the development of substantive scholarship. The profound love that thousands of community folk and former members felt for their Black Panther Party, as well as the recent publication of several essay collections that acknowledged its political legitimacy, are encouraging a more serious approach to this history. Increasingly, young scholars choose to investigate the controversial era during which the Black Panther Party soared to international prominence then crashed back into obscurity, and more and more are devoting attention to specific aspects of the Black Panther Party. Mumia's book both complements and expands this new development; he contributes as a scholar as well as a participant, and someone whose participation changed the course of his life. His writing will make you laugh as you see what the daily existence of a young Panther was like, may puzzle you when you read something you didn't believe happened, help you make connections you had not thought of previously, and inspire you to learn more.

The chapter entitled "The Women's Party" was written with new material solicited by Mumia from women in the Party and made accessible through his supporters on the outside. Women who remember Mumia from his Panther days or have recently visited him in prison comment on his kindness, his innate spirituality, and his loving personality—which you will sense most clearly in this chapter on the nature of women's participation in the Black Panther Party. The chapter, much of which is in the women's own words, presents a nuanced and moving picture of women within a rapidly growing movement under siege, that was transforming itself and the understanding of what a woman's life could be. As Mumia writes, the woman's life in the party was, "Hard Work. Hard Study. Jailed Lovers. Survival. Striving. Times of promise. Times of terror. Resistance to male chauvinism. And hope." He concludes, "The Party may no longer exist, yet much of the spirit, the essence of collective resistance, of community service, of perseverance, continues in the lives of [women] who aspired to change the realities into which they and their people were born. They were, without question, the very best of the Black Panther Party."

Stack up what you read in *We Want Freedom* against the fact that the Philadelphia jury, uncertain of what motivated Mumia to allegedly kill police officer Daniel Faulkner in a murky case, was swayed to convict by learning of his membership in the Black

Panther Party. Inadequate material evidence, perjured eyewitness testimony, and an attorney with a drinking problem prevented even the shadow of fairness in Mumia's trial. This may help you comprehend the dimensions of the miscarriage of justice that led to the death sentence. This condemned man, this sensitive, thoughtful author has poured his energy into an amazing book that illuminates the truth of what his membership in the Black Panther Party was about, and reveals the extreme price extracted from him for having learned, and for now telling, that truth.

**KATHLEEN CLEAVER,** an activist scholar, currently teaches at Emory University School of Law. She quit college in 1966 to join the Civil Rights movement, then served as the Black Panther Party's Communications Secretary from 1967–1971. Cleaver co-edited the essay collection *Liberation, Imagination and the Black Panther Party*, edited a collection of writings by Eldridge Cleaver, *Target Zero: A Life in Writing*, and is at work on a forthcoming memoir *Memories of Love and War.*

CHAPTER ONE

# The Beginnings of the Black Panther Party and the History It Sprang From

I started with this idea in my head, "There's two things I've got a right to, death or liberty."

—Harriet Tubman, Black Freedom Fighter

**THE ORIGINS OF** the Black Panther Party seem surprisingly mundane, as we look from the other side of time's hourglass.

Two relatively poor college students, fresh from meager and uninspiring public schools, seek to join a junior college's Black student group to give voice to their emergent sense of activism.

They were, on the surface, unremarkable. Two Black men in their twenties, searching for meaning in a world that seemed content to ignore their existence. They were among doubtless thousands, if not tens of thousands, of young men and women who were among the first in their families—members of that first generation—to seek higher education. Their trek into such institutions was, in many ways, a voyage into a new and unfamiliar world. A trek that their earlier, unchallenging education left many youth woefully unprepared for.

What made these two emerge as remarkable men was not so much that they possessed remarkable qualities, as that this was a truly remarkable time.

It was the mid 1960s, movements were circling the globe like fresh winds blowing through stale, unopened, darkened rooms. Wafting on those winds were the seductive scents of rebellion, resistance, and world revolution!

In West Oakland, California, where Merritt College was then located, the biggest issue sparking discussion was the Cuban Missile Crisis of 1962. Although it seemed that the immediate problem of a nuclear war between the US and the USSR over Cuba had been averted, the terror of possible atomic war was as real as moonlight. The international tensions of the times caused the era's students to question the world they were growing into. And, if that were not enough, the rising Civil Rights movement in the US South brought domestic questions to the debate amongst the young.

A student named Bobby Seale walked the campus, observing and listening to those who possessed the power to engage in verbal combat and hold court. Speakers didn't just spout their opinions to silent observers, but engaged in debate, parrying a variety of rapid-fire questions from the massed throng. One speaker—a young guy named Huey—spoke with such militant conviction and knowledge that Bobby stood transfixed:

> I guess I had the idea that I was supposed to ask questions in college, so I walked over to Huey and asked the brother, weren't all these civil rights laws the NAACP was trying to get for us doing some good? And he shot me down too, just like he shot a whole lot of other people down. He said, it's all a waste of money, black people don't have anything in this country that is for them. He went on to say that the laws already on the books weren't even serving them in the first place, and what's the use of making more laws when what we needed was to enforce the present laws?[1]

This thriving, questioning atmosphere gave way to broader challenges. Huey had joined the school's Afro-American Association to try to formulate answers to the questions that hung in the air. Bobby was soon to follow:

> That's the kind of atmosphere I met Huey in. And all the conflicts of this meeting, all the blowing that was going on in the streets that day during the Cuban crisis, all of that was involved with his association with the Afro-American Association. A lot of arguments came down. A lot of people were discussing with

three or four cats in the Afro-American Association, which was developing the first black nationalist philosophy on the West Coast. They got me caught up. They made me feel that I had to help out, be a part and do something. One or two days later I went around looking for Huey at this school, and I went to the library. I found Huey in the library, and I asked him where the meetings were. He gave me an address card and told me there were book discussions.[2]

How does such a benign meeting presage the emergence of the Black Panther Party? What these recollections reveal are the various strands of thought that were circulating through the Black student and radical community at the time, and would later coalesce and congeal as the beginnings of ideology. The two men seemed to be searching for something—perhaps answers to why the world was as jumbled up as it seemed, perhaps for a way out of their daily grind, perhaps for that which Black Americans had searched for centuries—for freedom.

They were looking for an organization that would represent their collective voice. Even at this early stage, there existed positions that would later re-emerge espoused and reflected by the Black Panther Party: a questioning of the status quo; a sense of alienation not only from the US government, but, reflecting a class divide, also from the elite of the Civil Rights movement; and the germ of recognizing the importance of the international arena to the lives and destinies of Blacks in America.

Their first interaction also suggests the beginnings of the power relations that would last for the duration of the existence of the Black Panther Party. It is clear that, although younger, Huey P. Newton possessed a mind far more active, far more flexible, and far more wide-ranging than did Bobby Seale. Newton emerged as the teacher, though Seale too was pivotal.

Seale would introduce Newton to the Caribbean-born Algerian revolutionary Frantz Fanon through his masterpiece, *The Wretched of the Earth*. A notoriously slow reader, Newton would read the extraordinary book six times.[3] For Newton, and for many other Black Americans, Fanon's words were a revelation, not merely of African colonial conditions, but of the world's problems and why Black America was in such a wretched state:

> The mass of the people struggle against the same poverty, flounder about making the same gestures and with their shrunken bellies outline what has been called the geography of hunger. It is an under-developed world, a world inhuman in its poverty; but also it is a world without engineers and without administrators. Confronting this world, the European nations sprawl, ostentatiously opulent. This European opulence is literally scandalous, for it has been founded on slavery, it has been nourished with the blood of slaves and it comes directly from the soil and the subsoil of that under-developed world. The well-being and the progress of Europe have been built up with the sweat and the dead bodies of Negroes, Arabs, Indians and the yellow races.[4]

For one seeking to make sense of the vast, bleak panorama of poverty in the American ghetto, as contrasted with the projected stately order and opulence of white wealth, Fanon's brave and passionate prose held powerful illumination. Black folks in America saw themselves in the villages of resistance and saw their ghettos as little more than internal colonies similar to those discussed in Fanon's analysis.

Fanon's anticolonial and anti-imperialist perspective was not the only influence on the young Newton. The Black nationalist Malcolm X had a powerful impact upon him, one he termed "intangible" and "deeply spiritual."[5] Newton regularly visited Muslim mosques in the Bay Area and discussed the problems facing Black Americans with members of the Nation of Islam (NOI). He heard Malcolm X, accompanied by a young convert then named Cassius Clay, speak at Oakland's McClymond High School and found the intense young minister an impressive man "with his logic" and his "disciplined" mind.[6] He seriously considered joining the NOI, but growing up as a preacher's kid

> I could not deal with their religion. By this time, I had had enough of religion and could not bring myself to adopt an-

other one. I needed a more concrete understanding of social conditions. References to God or Allah did not satisfy my stubborn questioning.[7]

Fanon's analysis mixed well with Malcolm's militant anti-establishment oratory. Malcolm spoke often about the anticolonial liberation movements in Africa, Asia, and Latin America. He spoke also of the Bandung Conference (1955) in Indonesia where African and Asian nations pledged support to the anticolonial movement. Malcolm X and Fanon were deep influences on Newton and played a role in moving him to develop an anti-imperialist and radical perspective:

> From all of these things—the books, Malcolm's writings and spirit, our analysis of the local situation—the idea of an organization was forming. One day, quite suddenly, almost by chance, we found a name. I had read a pamphlet about voter registration in Mississippi, how the people in the Lowndes County Freedom Organization, had a black panther for its symbol. A few days later, while Bobby and I were rapping, I suggested that we use the panther as our symbol and call our political vehicle the Black Panther Party.... The image seemed appropriate, and Bobby agreed without discussion. At this point, we knew it was time to stop talking and begin organizing.[8]

Black and Third World freedom struggles, nationally and internationally, deeply influenced the two men that formed the Black Panther Party. Several books in addition to Fanon's were pivotal to this process.

While Robert Williams's 1962 *Negroes With Guns,* as well as the works of V.I. Lenin, W.E.B. Du Bois, James Baldwin, Dostoyevski, Camus, and Nietzsche fed the growing intellect of Newton, young people of that era were being fed soul food—cooked on the burning embers of Watts, the ghetto rebellion that raged the year before. The books of Black revolutionaries and other thinkers were deeply influential, but what to do?

In his twenty-fourth year of life, Newton would organize a group that would spread across the nation like wildfire. The Black Panther Party for Self-Defense (BPPFSD), founded on October 15,

1966, and later renamed the Black Panther Party (BPP), would gain adherents in over forty US cities, with subsidiary information centers (called National Fronts Against Fascism offices) across the nation.

The Black Panther Party was born.

## Southern Roots

If one examined the places of origin of leading members of the organization, despite its founding in northern California, one could not but be struck by the number of people who hailed from the South. The first two Panthers, Newton and Seale, were native to Louisiana and Texas, respectively. The BPP's Minister of Information, Eldridge Cleaver, was born in Arkansas and the Los Angeles chapter's Deputy Minister of Defense, Geronimo ji-Jaga (né Pratt), was also born in Louisiana. The Party's Chief of Staff, David Hilliard, and his brother, Roosevelt "June" Hilliard, were country boys from Rockville, Alabama. BPP Communications Secretary, and one of the first women to sit on the Central Committee, Kathleen Neal Cleaver, was born into an upwardly mobile Black family in Texas.[9] Elbert "Big Man" Howard, an editor of *The Black Panther* newspaper for a time, was a native of Chattanooga, Tennessee.

It seems the young folks who established and staffed the organization came from predominantly southern backgrounds and therefore had to have suffered a kind of dual alienation. First, the global, overarching feeling of apartness stemming from being Black in a predominantly white and hostile environment. Second, the distinction of being perceived as "country," or "southern," a connotation that has come to mean stupid, uncultured, and hickish in much of the northern mind.

They were born into families that brought up the rear of the Great Migration, that vast trek of Black folks fleeing the racial terrorism, lack of opportunity, and stringent mores of social apartheid of the US South. Although they arrived in California as youths and adolescents, they never truly felt at home there, looking to the bayous, deltas, fields, and farmlands of their birthplaces almost as ancestral homes. This was perhaps best voiced by David Hilliard:

> Yet Rockville remains a profound influence on my life.... "We're going back to the old country," my cousin Bojack used to say when we were growing up and preparing for a trip south. Rockville remains the closest I can get to my origins, to *being African*.[10]

For millions of African Americans living in the North, the same can be said. This almost rural mindset would have repercussions for the Party as it grew and expanded into northern cities with teeming Black ghettos.

## Roots of Black Radicalism

For decades, neither scholars nor historians bothered to address the existence of the Black Panther Party. If the BPP was a member of the family of Black struggle and resistance, it was an unwelcome member, sort of like a stepchild.

The accolades and bouquets of late twentieth-century Black struggle were awarded to veterans of the civil rights struggle epitomized by the martyred Rev. Dr. Martin Luther King, Jr. Elevated by white and Black elites to the heights of social acceptance, Dr. King's message of Christian forbearance and his turn-the-other-cheek doctrine were calming to the white psyche. To Americans bred for comfort, Dr. King was, above all, safe.

The Black Panther Party was the antithesis of Dr. King.

The Party was *not* a civil rights group. It did not believe in turning the other cheek. It was markedly secular. It did not preach nonviolence, but practiced the human right of self-defense. It was socialist in orientation and advocated the establishment (after a national plebiscite or vote) of a separate, revolutionary, socialistic, Black nation-state.

The Black Panther Party made (white) Americans feel many things, but safe wasn't one of them.

For late twentieth-century scholars and historians trained to study safe history, the Black Panthers represented a kind of anomaly, rather than a historical descendant of a long, impressive line of Black resistance fighters.

In fact, the history of Africans in the Americas is one of *deep resistance*—of various attempts at independent Black governance, of self-defense, of armed rebellion, and indeed, of pitched battles for freedom. It is a history of resistance to the unrelenting nightmare of America's *Herrenvolk* (master race) "democracy."

For generations, Blacks have dreamed of a social reality that can only be termed national independence (or Black nationalism). They gave their energies and their strength to find a place where life could be lived free.

The Black Panthers represented the living line of their radical antecedents. In the dichotomy popularized in a speech by Malcolm X, the Black Panthers represented the "field slaves" of the American plantation who did not disguise their anger at the oppressive institution of bondage; Dr. King's sweet embrace of all things American was typical of the "house slave" who—denounced by Malcolm—when the white slavemaster fell ill, asked, "Wassa matter, boss? We sick?"

"The field slaves," Malcolm preached bitingly, "prayed that he died."

The origins of that resistance may be dated (on the North American landscape) to 1526, when Spaniards maneuvered a boatload of captive, chained Africans up a river (in a land now called South Carolina) and nearly one hundred captives broke free, slew several of their captors, and fled into the dense, virgin forests to dwell among the aboriginal peoples there in a kind of freedom that their kindred would not know for the next 400 years.[11] Over that period of time, there would be several attempts to establish a separate Black polity away from the US mainland, situated in Africa, in Haiti, in Central America, or in Canada. With the exception of the struggling Republic of Liberia, established on Africa's West Coast in 1822 by US Black freedmen and -women under the aegis of the American colonization societies, none of the other projects offered a viable site for establishing a separate African American polity.

Even the Republic of Liberia had its critics. Indeed, Liberia was considered a mockery by nineteenth century Black nationalist Dr. Martin Delany. Traveling the world in search of an independent "Africo-American" nation-state, he left little doubt that Liberia was not the answer, calling it "a *burlesque* of a government—a pitiful dependency on the American Colonizationists, the Colonization Board at Washington city, in the District of Columbia, being the Executive and Government, and the principal man, called President, in Liberia, being the echo…"[12]

The inborn instinct for national Black independence found various forms of expression: For example, in 1807, in Bullock County, Alabama, Blacks organized their own "negro government" with a code of laws, a sheriff, and courts. Their leader, a former slave named George Shorter, was imprisoned by the US Army.[13] As early as 1787, a group of "free Africans" petitioned the Massachusetts legislature for leave to resettle in Africa, because of the "disagreeable and disadvantageous circumstances" under which "free Africans" lived in post-Revolutionary America.[14] The petitioning delegation was led by Black Masonic leader, Prince Hall, who exclaimed:

> This and other considerations which we need not here particularly mention induce us to return to Africa, our native country, which warm climate is more natural and agreeable to us, and for which the God of Nature has formed us, and where we shall live among our equals and be more comfortable and happy, than we can be in our present situation and at the same time, may have a prospect of usefulness to our brethren there.[15]

Here may be found one of the earliest manifestations of a back-to-Africa movement, expressed nearly 120 years before the heralded Black nationalist Marcus Garvey. It was a deep expression of alienation with American life, even in Massachusetts where Africans had perhaps the best and most free life in the colonies.

It would be disingenuous to suggest that only Blacks sought the establishment of a separate Black nation-state. Some of the deepest thinkers in American life expressed surprisingly similar thoughts to the Black Masonic leader.

Six years before Prince Hall's petition was submitted in Boston, one of the brightest minds of the Old Dominion was writing that there were "political," "physical," and "moral" objections to Blacks living in political equality with whites in the same polity. In the year he resigned from the office of Governor of Virginia, and several decades before he would occupy the office of president of the United States, Thomas Jefferson wrote:

> It will probably be asked, why not retain and incorporate the blacks into the state, and thus save the expense of supplying, by importation of white settlers, the vacancies they will leave? Deep-rooted prejudices entertained by the whites, ten thousand recollections by the blacks, of the injuries they have sustained, new provocations; the new distinctions which nature has made, and many other circumstances, will divide us into parties, and produce compulsions which will probably never end but in the extermination of one or the other race.[16]

What may surprise many is that another major American political thinker, Abraham Lincoln, while a sitting president, expressed quite similar views over three-quarters of a century later. In an 1862 address to a "Colored Deputation" in Washington, DC, the president expressed his thinking on Black colonization:

> Why should they leave this country? This is, perhaps, the first question for proper consideration. *You and we are different races.* We have between us a broader difference than exists between almost any two races. Whether it is right or wrong I need not discuss, but this physical difference is a great disadvantage to us both, as I think your race suffer very greatly, many of them by living among us, while ours suffer from your presence. In a word we suffer on each side. If this be admitted, it affords a reason at least why we should be separated.[17]

Lincoln proposed mass resettlement of US Blacks to lands in Central America.[18] What is remarkable is that Lincoln's vision, pronounced while the country was convulsed in the throes of civil war, shares so much with the Black separatism best typified by the former, formal position of the Nation of Islam. While the NOI's position is termed radical, racist, and hateful, Lincoln is lionized as the Great Emancipator. Not surprisingly, the "Colored Deputation" received the Lincoln resettlement proposal coldly.[19]

After the war ended with Union victory, a Republican Reconstruction-era governor of Tennessee, William G. Brownlow, would urge the US Congress to set aside a separate US territory for Black settlement. His 1865 proposal would establish a "nation of freedmen."[20] Historian Eric Foner has found in periods of heightened Black conflict with, and political disenfranchisement by, the white majority and its political elites, the hunger for African independence, or nationalism, is rekindled, and re-emerges in Black popular demands:

> One index of the narrowed possibilities for change was the revival of interest, all but moribund during Reconstruction, in emigration to Africa or the West. The spate of black public meetings and letters to the American Colonization Society favoring emigration in the immediate aftermath of Reconstruction reflected less an upsurge of nationalist consciousness than the collapse of hopes invested in Reconstruction and the arousal of deep fears for the future by the restoration of white supremacy. Henry Adams, the former soldier and Louisiana political organizer, claimed in 1877 to have enrolled the names of over 60,000 "hard laboring people" eager to leave the South. "This is a horrible part of the country," he wrote the Colonization Society from Shreveport, "And our race can not get money for our labor.... It is impossible for us to live with these slaveholders of the South and enjoy the right as they enjoy it."[21]

Nationalism, therefore, was a live option that had considerable support in both the Black and white communities, that waxed and waned according to the political, economic, and psychosocial context of life for Black folks in white America.

While periods of tension and strife gave rise to nationalist aspirations, for some the struggle for survival demanded that people take immediate, militant, and indeed violent action to protect their lives and their freedom. Nationalism may have been a considered aspiration; survival was sheer necessity. People thrown into an untenable situation had to find remarkable ways of getting out. Those qualities and impulses lie deep within the psyches and historical experiences of Black people in the Americas—people who have been far more radical than a tame, sweet, civil rights–oriented history might suggest.

## Black Roots of Resistance

When one speaks of African Americans, it is clear to many of whom we speak. What may be unclear, however, is how the very term itself masks deep ambiguities within Black and white consciousness. It is but the latest nominally socially accepted term for a people who long predate the United States.

Among all the myriad people who call themselves Americans, the sons and daughters of Africa—called variously Africans, Negroes (and various pejorative derivations therefrom), *gens de couleur,* Africo-Americans, Afro-Americans, colored people, Bilalians,[22] African Americans, and the recently revived people of color—view their nationality ambiguously, as if more a question than a self-evident certainty. That ambiguity is a natural result of the troubled history of Black people in the United States, who have tasted the bitter gall of betrayal by the nation of their birth, and, like the aboriginal peoples of the Americas, the so-called Indians (how long will we repeat the navigational errors of Columbus?), they have seen a long trail of broken promises.

Unlike most others who call themselves Americans, Africans did not immigrate here by choice, fleeing foreign princes in search of "freedom," but were brought here in sheer terror, shackled, chained, and against their deepest will. This is therefore a home, not by the choice of one's ancestors, but by a cruel kind of historical default.

The classic narrative of Olaudah Equiano, an eighteenth-century captive taken as a preteen boy from his Ibo clan in what would be modern-day Nigeria, reflects the terrors of millions of

West Africans who were forcibly brought to the West in the holds of slave ships. His first sight of such a vessel (he, a boy of eleven years, had never seen a river, much less a coastal sea), and the strange, pale beings, filled him with dread. He felt like prey before ravenous beasts:

> Their complexions too, differing so much from ours, their long hair, and the language they spoke, which was very different from any I had ever heard, united to confirm me in this belief. Indeed, such were the horrors of my views and fears at the moment, that if ten thousand worlds had been my own, I would have freely parted with them all to have exchanged my condition with the meanest slave in my own country. When I looked around the ship too, and saw a large furnace of copper boiling and a multitude of black people of every description, chained together, every one of their countenances expressing dejection and sorrow I no longer doubted of my fate; and quite overpowered with horror and anguish, I fell motionless on the deck, and fainted.[23]

Equiano thought these strange, red-faced beings were bad spirits who would surely kill and then eat him and the other sad-faced Black people. He used his wits and business acumen to survive a brutal bondage in Georgia, and, sold to a sea captain, lived on board slaving vessels, learned the craft of seamen, and traveled the world, eventually buying his freedom and settling in London.

His horrific memories of the torture, brutalities, and savageries of the slave trade stand like dark sentinels in the recesses of Black consciousness of what it means to be Black in America. Almost every African American knows that his or her ancestor entered the doorway to America through the stinking hold of a vessel such as that which transported Equiano.

These beginnings, so radically different from most other Americans, may be the psychic wellspring of so much that is radical in contemporary Black America. What white America perceived as radical may have been the norm in the very different context of Black life in the midst of a white supremacist, hostile, and patriarchal society. In a state where the violently enforced norm was white supremacy and Black devaluation, it should surprise no one that there was resistance, nor that this would stimulate a radical social response.

Much of African American history, then, is rooted in this radical understanding that America is not the land of liberty, but a place of the absence of freedom, a realm of repression and insecurity. Only such a people as this could create the haunting hymns of the spirituals, in which people sang so movingly of loss and yearning:

> Sometimes I feel like a motherless child,
> Sometimes I feel like a motherless child,
> Sometimes I feel like a motherless child,
> a loooong way from hooome,
> a long way from home!

Some Africans, early in the eighteenth century, resisted the status quo by seizing control of their slaveships and setting sail for freedom back in Africa. Ninety-six Africans aboard the *Little George* slipped their bonds and overpowered the crew. Some of the crew were not slain, but were locked in their cabins so that they could not interfere with the trek home. The Black naval rebels sailed for nine days and made landfall on the West African coast in 1730.

Two years later, the captain of the *William* was slain by its Black captives, its crew was set adrift in the waters of the Atlantic, and a new, rebel crew pointed the bow of the vessel homeward, to Africa.[24]

Nor were things quiet and sedate for Africans on land.

The period of the 1730s and 1740s has been seen by some historians as an era of incessant resistance. One contemporary observer described the period, almost as if he were referring to a prevalent disease, as "the contagion of rebellion" sweeping the colonies. Indeed, this spirit of rebellion flashed up and down the coasts of the British colonies and encircled the isles claimed by tribes of Europe in the West Indies, lighting fires of freedom in the dark night of bondage.

During the 1730s and early 1740s, the "Spirit of Liberty" erupted again and again, in almost all of the slave societies of the Americas, especially where Coramantee slaves were concentrated. Major conspiracies unfolded in Virginia, South Carolina, Bermuda, and Louisiana (New Orleans) in the year 1730 alone.[25]

Historians cite a remarkable man named Samba, who featured predominantly in the 1730 New Orleans revolt. He had previously led an unsuccessful rebellion against a French slave-trading fort back in Africa and had mutinied while aboard a slave vessel. The town fathers in New Orleans responded to his incessant quest for liberty by giving him a brutal, tortuous death. This state terror did not diminish the thirst for liberty surging in Black hearts in New Orleans. Captives there organized an uprising just two years after Samba's sacrifice.

Historians describe a coherent cycle of rebellion that threw the Atlantic into convulsions of resistance to the established colonial slavocracies:

> The following year witnessed rebellions in South Carolina, Jamaica, St. John (Danish Virgin Islands), and Dutch Guyana. In 1734 came plots and actions in the Bahama Islands, St. Kitts, South Carolina again, and New Jersey. The latter two inspired by the rising in St. John. In 1735–36 a vast slave conspiracy was uncovered in Antigua, and other rebellions soon followed on the smaller islands of St. Bartholomew, St. Martin's, Anguilla, and Guadeloupe. In 1737 and again in 1738, Charleston experienced new upheavals. In the spring of 1738, meanwhile, "several slaves broke out of a jail in Prince George's County, Maryland, united themselves with a group of outlying [or escaped] Negroes and proceeded to wage a small-scale guerrilla war." The following year, a considerable number of slaves plotted to raid a storehouse of arms and munitions in Annapolis, Maryland, to "destroy his Majesty's Subjects within this Province, and to possess themselves of the whole country." Failing that, they planned "to settle back in the Woods." Later in 1739, the Stono Rebellion convulsed South Carolina. Here the slaves burned houses as they fought their way toward freedom in Spanish Florida. Yet another rebellion broke out in Charleston

in June 1740, involving 150 to 200 slaves, fifty of whom were hanged for their daring.[26]

In a study of the radical underpinnings of Black thought it is not sufficient to provide a kind of caramel-colored, sepia-toned version of US history. Consider that these rebellions occurred but a few decades before the Declaration of Independence and the subsequent American Revolution. In those battles for liberty it is perhaps unremarkable to note that some 5,000 Blacks were eventually integrated into the Army of the Continental Congress, although General George Washington, a slaveholder from Virginia, initially opposed their enlistment. The First Rhode Island Regiment, an elite regiment of Black enlisted men and white officers, carried the day against the British at Yorktown, playing a pivotal role in forcing the surrender of Cornwallis.[27]

What is less well known is that well over ten times that number, some 65,000 Africans, joined the British cause. They joined not because of any craven loyalty to the Crown, nor any disloyalty to the colonies, but rather because of the age-old impetus of self-interest. Britain's Lord Dunmore offered freedom to all "negroes" who would fight for the Crown, and tens of thousands leapt at the opportunity. Dunmore organized a corps of Black former slaves into the Ethiopia Regiment, who wore the motto "Liberty to Slaves" on their tunics. This regiment helped the British capture and torch Norfolk, Virginia, on New Year's Day, 1776.

When the British were forced to withdraw in 1783, over 20,000 Africans fled the United States. Having fought for the losing side of the Revolution, they had no desire to remain in the slavocratic states. They may have lost the war, but they did not lose all. Many lived lives of freedom that their former countrymen would not experience for almost a century, settling in London, Nova Scotia, Ontario, and other British dominions.[28]

Seen from this perspective, did they really lose?

This is not to suggest that the British were, as a rule, liberators of African slaves. They were not.

Lord Dunmore was putting forth a war policy to the benefit of the Empire; if, in support of that objective, strategy dictated the freedom of a few thousand Africans, all to the good. The Irish-born British parliamentarian Edmund Burke, who promoted conciliation with the Americans, saw the Dunmore proposal as sheer hypocrisy. Burke asked whether Blacks should accept "an offer of freedom from that very nation which has sold them to their present masters?"[29]

Indeed, just over a decade before Dunmore's offer, Blacks living in the Spanish colony of Florida, and especially those hundreds of Maroons who lived in Fort Mosa, just north of St. Augustine, set sail for Cuba rather than live under the British Crown. Fort Mosa and the surrounding Black community it defended constituted one of the earliest Black settlements on the land that we now call the United States. Fort Mosa was the name that Black fugitives, Seminole Indians, and Floridian Spanish used. The English-speaking people of Georgia and South Carolina called the site Negro Fort and viewed it as a threat to the slave system. When the British took over Florida in 1763, the Maroons fled with the Spanish.[30]

For Africans, whether in Virginia or Spanish Florida, the central objective remained the same: which way freedom? If the price for freedom was to ally with the British against the slavery-addicted Americans, or to turn from Spain for liberty and dignity among aboriginal peoples like the Seminoles, so be it.

Freedom was ever the goal.

## Resistance After the "Revolution"

After what some historians have termed the Baron's Revolt of the *nouveau riche* Americans against the established, wealthy, and rapacious Crown of England for "freedom," there were millions of Blacks in the newly independent American states who knew that freedom was still not theirs. They were slaves before the "buckra war"[31] for freedom and independence and were still in bondage after it ended.[32]

The post-Revolutionary era brought the language of liberty out into the open, if not into reality. It also brought with it a methodology.

People must fight for their freedom.

On the Revolution's eve, whites of property, who cried loudest for "liberty" from British tyranny, strove mightily to tighten the shackles on the people they held in unremitting bondage. As radical historian Herbert Aptheker has noted:

> A letter written July 31, 1776, by Henry Wynkoop, a resident of Bucks County, Pennsylvania, to the local Committee of Safety requested the dispatching of ammunition in order to quiet "the people in my neighborhood [who] have been somewhat alarmed with fears about negroes and disaffected people injuring their families when they are in the service."[33]

The Revolution was scarcely a decade past when the following letter, posted some months earlier from Newbern, North Carolina, appeared in the *Boston Gazette* of September 3, 1792:

> The negroes in this town and neighborhood, have stirred a rumour of their having in contemplation to rise against their masters and to procure themselves their liberty; The inhabitants have been alarmed and keep a strict watch to prevent their procuring arms; should it become serious, which I don't think, the worst that could befal [sic] us, would be their setting the town on fire. It is very absurd of the blacks, to suppose they could accomplish their views, and from the precautions that were taken to guard against surprise, little danger is to be apprehended.[34]

Put quite another way, the southern correspondent suggests to the northern journal, in essence, "it is absurd for these negroes to think that the Revolution was about anything other than white liberty!"

It was, in fact, a Baron's Revolt, a revolution fought for the "liberty" of deciding who would hold Africans in bondage—Americans or the British? Who would reap the wealth from their forced labor? Who would receive the fruits of this stolen land that African labor produced?

Liberty, indeed!

It was during this post-Revolutionary era that the African people of the Americas launched massive armed rebellions that echo down the corridors of time for their sheer boldness in attempt and execution of their will to be once and forever free. Two centuries after their heroic bids for freedom, the leaders of these rebellions are still regarded with a strange American ambivalence that revolves around the crucible of race. To many whites they are seen as madmen; to some Blacks they are remembered as armed prophets of freedom. Gabriel Prosser (d. 1800), Charles Deslondes (d. 1811), Denmark Vesey (d. 1822), Nat Turner (d. 1831), and "Cinque" Singbeh Pi'eh (d.1839), of the mutiny aboard the Spanish schooner *La Amistad,* dwell in the hearts, minds, and souls of millions of contemporary African Americans, as people who fought against desperate odds, against a ruthless enemy, for a breath of freedom. Their names still live in millions of Black mouths, in stories told from generation to generation, almost two centuries after their passing.

Emblematic of this stellar and bloody period of armed Black resistance, one of that number who will exemplify how deeply this radical example has permeated Black spiritual consciousness, is Gabriel Prosser.

Deeply inspired by the biblical tale of Samson, Gabriel came to believe he had been appointed by the Lord to become the deliverer of his people. A young man of impressive physical and mental gifts, he shared his inner convictions with other captives. He interpreted the verses of the Bible with them, explaining that the tales told referred to the living present—summer 1800—and predicted the deliverance of the people from a hellish bondage. He preached this verse to his fellow captives:

> And when he came unto Lehi, the Philistines shouted against him; and the Spirit of the Lord came mightily upon him, and the cords that were upon his arms became as flax that were burnt with fire, and his bands loosed from off his hands. And he found a new jawbone of an ass, and slew a thousand men therewith.... And he judged Israel in the days of the Philistines for twenty years.[35]

The cords and bands of this passage mean the bondage of slavery, Gabriel explained. And the Philistines? They were the slavemasters, of course. Gabriel and his fellow captives were to steal or make weapons—the jawbones of an ass—and they would judge the Philistines and erect a Black kingdom—there, near Richmond—and live life in liberty.[36]

His inspiring manner and his masterful interpretation of the Bible drew people to join him in this great task. Before long, he was joined by his wife, Nanny, and his brothers, Martin and Solomon. As the movement spread, 1,000 rebels joined his force.

Gabriel conducted reconnaissance in Richmond to acquaint himself with armament stores and the lay of the land. As weapons and bullets were forged, the night to strike was selected. All was in readiness.

On the afternoon of the rising, two slaves, Tom and Pharoah, broke news of the plot to their master, who promptly informed the governor (and later president), James Monroe. Monroe quickly mobilized 650 men and placed state militia commanders on alert.[37]

The early evening march on Richmond by Gabriel's 1,000-strong force got mired, literally, as rains made the roads impassable. With travel so obstructed, they decided to disperse, not knowing that the rebellion had already been betrayed. An army of bondsmen and bondswomen, wielding farm implements, a few guns, and the inspiration of their "Black Samson," melted into the steamy August night, to await a new signal, having come within six miles of Richmond.

The second signal would never come. Over the next few days, a number of rebels, including their charismatic leader, Gabriel Prosser, were caught in the net. None could be compelled to confess or provide information on the plan. Monroe met Prosser, and the governor would later note: "From what he said to me, he seemed to have made up his mind to die, and to have resolved to say but little on the subject of the conspiracy."[38]

At least thirty-five rebels, including Gabriel, were hanged.

Like his compatriots in the Grand Conspiracy of Rebellion against bondage, Gabriel did not die to millions of his fellow captives. They still live on, in blessed memory, in spirituals, in legend, in tales in the night, and in the spirit of resistance of an oppressed people.

## Armed Self-Defense

We must add to the great and well-known names of revered historical figures the long and impressive history of hundreds, indeed thousands, of largely anonymous Africans who fought, sometimes armed, against the forces of white nationalism and white supremacist terrorism.

The 1763 flight of the Maroons and the abandonment of Fort Mosa did not end the use of the site. Half a century later hundreds of Africans fought a pitched battle against the Americans from the well-armed garrison, now known by all as Negro Fort. Blacks (and their "Indian" relatives) had good reason to live in an armed, well-defended fort along the banks of Florida's Apalachicola River, and it wasn't for the same reason that whites, who lived further to the west, would later live in or near forts.

The white fort-dwellers feared attacks from "Indians" who opposed encroachments upon their tribal lands.

The Black fort-dwellers feared attacks from whites (or Native Americans hired by them) who wanted to place them back in slavery.

Andrew Jackson as a Major General of the US Army, not yet president, left no doubt such a fear was justified by his communique to a Spanish governmental official in Pensacola, Florida, dated April 23, 1816:

> A Negro Fort erected during our late war with Britain ... [here, Jackson refers to the War of 1812, not the Revolution] has been strengthened since the period and is now occupied by upwards of two hundred and fifty Negroes, *many of whom have been enticed away from the service of their masters*—citizens of the United States: all of whom are well clothed and disciplined....[39]

Jackson, who would emerge in his military and political careers as the worst enemy the Native people ever encountered, threatened the Spanish commandant, telling him the fort would be "destroyed" if Spain failed to "control" its residents.[40]

Herbert Aptheker calculated Negro Fort's inhabitants at roughly 300 people (Black men, women, and children), with "some thirty Indian allies." He recounts a ten-day siege of the facility by US forces, which concluded when American cannon fire struck the fort's armory stores and exploded, killing some 270 of its inhabitants.[41]

Many Americans are generally familiar with the long history of US-"Indian" warfare, but how many know that the hardest fought battles were the three US-Seminole Wars? Or that these Black, white, and red wars were regarded as essentially wars fought for Black liberation? So many Africans fought on the side of the Seminoles that US General Thomas Jesup would write: "This, you may be assured, is a negro, not an Indian war."[42]

This war was fought to re-enslave Blacks who lived in "Indian" territories and because whites feared red-Black unity. It was also fueled by the ever-present white hunger for "Indian" lands.

White American contempt for Native land possession is evinced by their rapacious craving for it, wherever it existed, and their determination, by whatever means possible, to acquire it. As an attorney, John Quincy Adams, arguing in the US Supreme Court, put the case for white seizure of Native lands in stark terms:

> What is the Indian title? It is mere occupancy for the purpose
> of hunting. It is like our tenures; they have no idea of a title to
> the soil itself. It is overrun by them, rather than inhabited. It is
> not a true legal possession.[43]

In the Court's *Fletcher v. Peck* case, Adams's view was made into the law of the land, essentially legalizing seizure and land-theft, because Native Americans had a different cultural, legal, and spiritual relationship to the land. They didn't use paper and alphabetic formats to record their important events; they used skins or bark and pictographs to communicate ideas. They didn't inhabit land, they "overran" it.

Adams's argument of 1802 marked the legal justification for American *lebensraum* and expansion into "Indian" territories. What really incensed whites, however, was the spectacle of Africans living in their own villages as nominally free people, or Africans living in maroonage as part of the Seminole tribes. To Africans who escaped from a bitter bondage in neighboring Georgia, or North Carolina, life among the "Indians" in Seminole villages in Florida must have seemed a whole lot like freedom. For, even if bought or captured by a Seminole, a captive had standing that more resembled the institution of captivity in Africa than in the Americas. One's children were born free, regardless of the condition of the parent.

Moreover, many Africans lived in perfect freedom among the Seminoles, serving as interpreters and warriors. Some even became chiefs. It was this very issue, Black freedom, that led to the breakaway and formation of the Seminoles from the Creek nation. The 1796 Treaty of Colerain contained a pledge from headmen of the Creeks to return Black fugitives to owners in the United States. This pledge excluded the Lower Creeks who lived north of the Florida border and the Seminoles who lived south of it, who never felt themselves bound by the pact. This marked a permanent divide between them and their relatives to the north.[44]

Historians like J. Leitch Wright, Jr., utilize the term Muscogulges as a name for the people of this region, in part for the prominent usage of the Muskogee language. He notes that Creek is an English term applied to people living amidst the riparian regions of the Southeast. Similarly, the term Seminole is a Spanish appellation that has its roots in the term cimarron, an Americo-Spanish term for runaway.[45]

Wright reports that "Black Indians" played a pivotal role in establishing Muscogulge, or Seminole, territory as sites of resistance to white expansion and centers of Black freedom:

Blacks constituted an important component of the Muscogulges, especially of those living in Florida. For years [US soldiers and Generals] McIntosh and Jackson had persecuted them, destroying the Negro Fort, Miccosukee, and Bowlegs Town and sending off prisoners in strings to Georgia and Alabama. Even so, many had escaped and during the 1820s lived in swamps, hummocks, and islands in the vicinity of Tampa Bay. Seminole agent Gad Humphreys recaptured the fugitive Negro John, who belonged to a Saint Augustine widow, chained him first about the neck, and subsequently ordered the blacksmith to put on handcuffs and leg irons. But John escaped again ... and again ... and again, in each instance apparently aided by a black Seminole. Slave and free Negroes resided in Indian villages scattered throughout Florida, on Indian plantations on the Apalachicola River, and with whites in Saint Augustine and Pensacola, and they were variously known as Negroes, Negro-Indians, and Indians. A continuous and easy intercourse existed between black Muscogulges in Indian settlements and Negroes serving in Florida, Alabama, and Georgia on white plantations, as field hands or in Saint Augustine and other cities as domestics, artisans, and fishermen.[46]

Three wars and a number of smaller battles demonstrate a practice of armed resistance. The Seminole Wars were as much Black wars for freedom as they were Indian wars against white expansion into their lands and against their removal to reservations.

## John Brown's Army

No tale of a radical people would be complete absent mention of the raid on Harper's Ferry, West Virginia, by John Brown and his small yet intrepid cadre of Black and white freedom fighters. Although presented in traditional US history as the act of a madman, little noted is the fact that Brown had, among his property when captured, a newly written Constitution and Declaration of Independence.

The documents were drawn up by Brown and a group of freedmen at the Chatham Convention, in Chatham, Ontario. Composed of forty-eight articles, the new constitution shared much in tone with the US Constitution, but it spoke out boldly and uncompromisingly on the evil of slavery. Here was none of the sweet evasion of political compromise. Drawn up by men who knew both the indignity of slavery as well as the license of liberty, the document's preamble made overt their intention to abolish the "peculiar institution":

> Whereas slavery, throughout its entire existence in the United States, is none other than a most barbarous, unprovoked and unjustifiable war of one portion of its citizens upon another portion—the only conditions of which are perpetual imprisonment and hopeless servitude or absolute extermination—in utter disregard and violation of those eternal and self-evident truths set forth in our Declaration of Independence.[47]

The Declaration was a naked rebuke of the recent decision of the American Supreme Court in the infamous *Dred Scott v. Sandford* case of 1857, which upheld slavery even in "free" states and stated, in part:

> Therefore, we, citizens of the United States, and the oppressed people who, by a recent decision of the Supreme Court, are declared to have no rights which the white man is bound to respect, together with all other people degraded by the laws thereof, do, for the time being, ordain and establish ourselves the following provisional constitution and ordinance, the better to protect our persons, property, lives, and liberties, and to govern our actions.[48]

Brown and other sworn officers of the Chatham Convention did not fight for succession, but for a radical reformation of the American nation-state—one wholly and truly dedicated to freedom from human bondage.

During the 1859 siege of Harper's Ferry, Brown and his men seized the armory in an attempt to foment a mass slave revolt and to initiate an armed retreat to a redoubt in the nearby Allegheny Mountains. From there they hoped a sustained harassment campaign could be conducted against the slavery system.

While it is obvious that the raid failed in its intended objectives, it is also true that the raid, the losses sustained, and the execution of Brown came to be seen as symbols of the antislavery, abolitionist ideal and as the first shots fired of the Civil War.

Of the seventeen rebels who were slain at Harper's Ferry, nine were Black, several of whom had joined the action on the spot. One of the Blacks who survived the action and lived to tell the tale was Osbourne Anderson. While critical of his errors, Anderson lauded "Captain Brown" for his nobility, noting, "even the noble old man's mistakes were productive of great good":[49]

> John Brown did not only capture and hold Harper's Ferry for twenty hours, but he held the whole South. He captured President Buchanan and his Cabinet, convulsed the whole country…and dug the mine and laid the train that will eventually dissolve the union between Freedom and Slavery. The rebound reveals the truth. So let it be![50]

Many a Union soldier would sing of John Brown's body two years after his hanging, as they marched through the charred ruins of a Confederate stronghold during a bitter, wrenching war. Nearly 200,000 of the soldiers for the Union were Black men, some former slaves. Over 37,000 would die in the conflagration.

## From Then 'til Now

At first blush, it appears that this discussion of radical, rebellious resistance to the American way of bondage takes place in the remote, distant past.

Nothing could be further from the truth.

The writer William Faulkner wrote, "The past is never dead. It's not even the past."[51] Faulkner spoke of the durability of the myth of the (white) Lost Cause, an ennobled vision of the role of the South. It saw the Confederacy as principled defenders of state sovereignty and upholders of national honor against the northern invaders, carpetbaggers, and assorted scalawags.

If the past is not past to contemporary generations of white southerners, how can one presume that it is past for generations of African Americans, almost all of whom find their families little more than two generations removed from a bitter peonage in the southlands of American apartheid? For Black Americans, the unforgotten past is not a four-year war that is reflected in the ubiquitous monuments or the frequent flying of the Confederate battle flag (said to honor one's heritage).

To Blacks cognizant of history, what remains unforgotten is the unending war that has lasted for five centuries, a war against Black life by the merchant princes of Europe. Unforgotten is the man-theft, the wrenching torture, the unremitting bondage— bondage that occurred for centuries to ensure that the Americans could sell cotton to the British, or that the British could sweeten their tea, or that the French could sweeten their cocoa, or that the Dutch could add great sums to their bank accounts.

This "past" is written in the many-hued faces in the average Black family, which may easily range from darkest ebony, to toffee, to café au lait, each a reflection of white rape of African women or of the tradition of concubinage exemplified by the New Orleans *les gens de couleur libres*. For many Blacks, the past is as present as one's mirror.

It is in this sense that history lives in the minds of Black folk. In people who draw their inspiration from the rebellious, resistant, liberational examples of people like Nat Turner, Gabriel Prosser, "Cinque," Harriet Tubman, Charles Deslondes, Denmark Vesey, and Sojourner Truth.

Contrary to what is generally supposed or socially projected in an era when the civil rights model holds sway, Blacks are far more militant, and far more angry, than their "leaders" suggest.

This was realized by Donald H. Matthews, an assistant minister of the African-American Methodist Church when he began to teach Bible classes in Oakland's Taylor Memorial in the 1960s. As a Black clergyman, he attended a traditional seminary, where he studied the classic texts of contemporary Protestant thought, such as those set forth by Karl Barth (1886–1968) or Paul J. Tillich (1886–1965). Let us suppose that he diversified his scholarship with the relatively re-cent works of the late Dr. Martin Luther King, Jr. (1929–1968).

One so educated would be woefully unprepared to meaning-fully address the myriad depths and scope of the social, spiritual, and psychological problems facing average African Americans. Matthews writes of the revelations that emerged when parish-ioners brought bitter memories and equally bitter experiences to bear as they shared their collective pain with the preacher:

> I frankly never had realized the excruciating price that my elders had paid in carving out a place of dignity and humanity.
>
> The women told their stories of having to wear dresses of ex-traordinarily modest length to deflect the "attentions" of white men. This solution, however, seldom was satisfactory, and girls often found themselves on northern-bound trains and buses to protect their sexual choice and bodily integrity.
>
> The men spoke of resisting the efforts of land-owners who "suggested" that their wives should work alongside them in the backbreaking work of sharecropping with poor tools on poorer land. These acts of courage also tended to result in midnight train rides north, often just ahead of a lynch mob....
>
> *I was startled to realize their political sensibilities were closer to Malcolm X than to Martin King* and that they had Christian beliefs not to be found in Tillich's or Barth's systematic theologies. It was this combination of deep feeling, resistance, and African-based religious concepts that I could not find in my black theological texts, either. So I was left with their powerful and profound sto-ries without a method of interpretation that did them justice.[52]

These women of Oakland, California, were poor, church-go-ing, internal immigrants from the south. The last rivulets of the torrents that produced the great, black river that came to be called the Great Migration brought with them a searing rage that the soothing balm of Christian love and redemption could not quench. Matthews notes that his Wednesday night Bible class hailed mostly from Arkansas and Texas, with others from the Deep South, and so possessed the same history as the founders of the BPP.[53]

They spoke the deep, hidden truths of millions of women and men of their generation, of the loss of homeland that all who emigrate experience, of the anger attendant with such loss, and, undoubtedly, of the loss of hope when one learns that the new land, with its own brand of harassments, fears, insecurities, and transnational negrophobia, is not the heralded Promised Land.

That riotous, unresolved, roiling energy fed into the entity we came to call the Black Panther Party.

Armed resistance to slavery, repression, and the racist delusion of white supremacy runs deep in African American experience and history. When it emerged in the mid 1960s from the Black Panther Party and other nationalist or revolutionary organizations, it was perceived and popularly projected as aberrant. This could only be professed by those who know little about the long and protracted history of armed resistance by Africans and their truest allies. The Black Panther Party emerged from the deepest traditions of Africans in America—resistance to negative, negrophobic, dangerous threats to Black life, by any means necessary.

CHAPTER TWO

# The Deep Roots of the Struggle for Black Liberation

> For you are prisoners of war, in an enemy's country—of a war, too, that is unrivaled for its injustice, cruelty, meanness....
> —Frederick Douglass (in an article urging Black captives to revolt against the slave system)[1]

THE ROOTS OF armed resistance run deep in African American history. Only those who ignore this fact see the Black Panther Party as somehow foreign to our common historical inheritance.

Many forces converged to bring about the organization bearing the name of the Black Panther Party. One of them, of course, was the powerful psychological and social force of history. In the 60s, many books began to emerge on the theme of Black history. Long-forgotten or little-mentioned figures began to come to life to a generation that, having not grown up in segregated educational environments, was less familiar with the historical currents underlying Black life.

The smoldering embers of Watts, a ghetto area in Los Angeles that burned just one year before the Black Panther Party's formation, were also bright in the minds of Huey and Bobby.

For six days in August 1965, Watts erupted in a rebellion that saw some $200 million worth of property go up in smoke. By week's end some thirty-five people were dead, most the result of police gunfire. In Watts, as elsewhere during that decade, conflict between Black urbanites and the predominantly white police was the trigger for this explosion.

For the Reverend Dr. Martin Luther King, Jr., Watts was a profound eye-opener. The middle-class, somewhat genteel preacher seemed stunned by the sheer scope and rancor revealed by the Watts Rebellion. Watts appeared to mark a major turning point in his vision of what America was and what it could become.[2]

Post-Watts, Dr. King would speak of the Black ghetto as a "system of internal colonialism." In one speech before the Chicago Freedom Festival, he would exclaim, "The purpose of the slum is to confine those who have no power and perpetuate their powerlessness...." He would further declare, "The slum is little more than a domestic colony which leaves its inhabitants dominated politically, exploited economically, segregated and humiliated at every turn."[3]

In a word, Watts radicalized King.

If Watts had that effect on a man of decidedly middle-class orientation, what of people who came from, and saw life from, the bottom of the social pecking order? For them, Watts wasn't a shock or a surprise. It was an affirmation of the same inchoate rage that boiled in their very veins.

That radical, rebellious spirit constituted a powerful social force that would attract tens of thousands of alienated ghetto folks to either join or support the Black Panther Party. Yet that radical spirit did not begin in Watts, but came from much older, much deeper roots.

The devastation and resistance of Watts sent a powerful signal to Huey and Bobby, two men in their twenties, that Black folks were ready and willing to fight and, if need be, to die for their freedom. Huey would later write in his personal and political autobiography, *Revolutionary Suicide:*

> One must relate to the history of one's community and its future. Everything we had seen convinced us that our time had come.

> Out of this need sprang the Black Panther Party. Bobby and I finally had no choice but to form an organization that would involve the lower-class brothers.[4]

Watts raises the question of the social role of mass violence in the shaping and formation of public policy.[5]

It is, too, a measure of the power of the corporate, white supremacist media that the term riot almost invariably evokes imagery of Black folks tearing through the streets in a frenzied orgy of destruction. But in fact, most riots were the instruments of whites, who used mass violence to terrorize Blacks and deny them citizenship.

Joe R. Feagin, a past president of the American Sociological Association, has written of the white riots of the early twentieth century:

> Whites sometimes used violence to enforce informal patterns of discrimination. During one white-generated riot in 1900 in New York, a mostly Irish police force encouraged whites to attack black men, women, and children. One of the most serious riots occurred in 1917 in East St. Louis. There white workers, viewing black immigrants from the South as a job threat, violently attacked a black community. Thirty-nine black residents and nine white attackers were killed. This was followed in 1919 by a string of white riots from Chicago to Charleston.[6]

This racist mass violence was an important factor in the enlistment of millions of white men (not to mention at least half a million white women!) to support the Ku Klux Klan (KKK) between 1910 and 1930. In that period, Klan affiliation was a ticket to political success, as Warren G. Harding and Hugo Black both knew well. The Klan and like-minded groups waged open war against entire Black communities, and the dead cannot now be calculated.

In Black historical literature, notably in the writings of Du Bois, 1919 is known and remembered as Red Summer, for the explosions of violence against Black life throughout the US. A similar recollection does not seem to disturb the slumber of white historians. There were twenty-six white riots in 1919 alone, with major ones in Chicago, Illinois; Knoxville, Tennessee; Longview, Texas; Omaha, Nebraska; Phillips County, Arkansas; and Washington, DC.[7] Even before this bloody period, white riots against Blacks were far from rare. In 1863, the so-called Draft Riots of New York City left at least one hundred people dead (the majority of them Black). That event, sparked by Irish who opposed both the aims and the necessity of the Civil War, marked the deadliest riot in US history.

White workers were attacking Blacks to sustain their social dominance, an assertion (and grim celebration) of their new-found status in the Americas as *whites* (as opposed to Irish—a subordinate group under British domination in their homeland).

The violence of these whites may be termed reactionary violence, as their actions served to consolidate repressive social arrangements. The violence of Watts, coming as a reaction to the violence of State actors—beating, harassing, or berating Black citizens—is not of the same order. It may be termed radical violence, or violence in response to the violence of, or on behalf of, the State.

## Christiana Resistance

With this historical perspective on riots, we will look at an event when Blacks engaged in radical liberational violence, not to hurt whites, but to preserve their own freedom. This event also demonstrates how a term like riot can prove misleading by masking the objectives of acts of mass violence.

In most history texts, if this conflict is noted, it is usually done under the name of the Christiana Riot. Black historian Ella Forbes, who examines the conflict from an Afrocentric perspective, calls it the Resistance, to more accurately reflect the context and nature of the action and the explosive social and political impact of the armed Black resistance.

In early September 1851, Edward Gorsuch, a Maryland slave owner, backed by his family, friends, and a US deputy marshal, descended on the little hamlet of Christiana, in southeastern Pennsylvania, to seize several escaped captives and to return them to slavery. Unfortunately for them, their human prey was staying in an organized, armed community, which had no intention of allowing their people's return to bondage.

William and Eliza Parker were intrepid freedom fighters who emerged as leading members of a Black self-defense group formed to defend the growing fugitive farm community of Christiana. Their resolution and determination would be tested with the coming of the Gorsuch posse.

It is unclear why the Gorsuch posse, consisting of Edward Gorsuch, his son Dickinson, his nephew, his cousin, two neighbors, a newly appointed US deputy marshal, Henry Kline, and two other paid officers,[8] knew to target the Parker home. Perhaps he had intelligence gleaned from the omnipresent snitches in the area that steered him to the dwelling.

William Parker, through his own contacts in Philadelphia, was forewarned of the coming slave-nappers. When Gorsuch and his group arrived at the house in the predawn hours of September 11, 1851, they initially entered but were forced to retreat. William Parker's account gives us some inkling of the tone and tenor of the time:

> I met them at the landing, and asked, "Who are you?" The leader, Kline, replied, "I am the United States Marshal." I then told him to take another step, and I would break his neck. He again said, "I am the United States Marshal." I told him I did not care for him nor the United States. At that he turned and went down stairs.[9]

Gorsuch, William Parker, and others present engaged in an extended discussion of the Bible, quoting passages from memory as if their recitations would dissuade either man from his deeply entrenched position. At length, they tired of the games and the true object of the meeting became plain:

> "You had better give up," said old Mr. Gorsuch, after another while, "and come down, for I have come a long way this morning, and want my breakfast; for my property I will have or I'll breakfast in hell. I will go up and get it."[10]

What the old slave owner didn't know was that inside the entrance were a number of well-armed men. His son, however, standing at a point of elevation, saw into the upstairs room, sprang down, and caught his father before he went further, yelling, "O father, do come down! Do come down! They have guns, swords, and all kinds of weapons! They'll kill you! Do come down!"[11]

The nine armed whites had not reckoned on five armed Blacks who were determined to be free.

When Dickinson argued with his father to leave and hire one hundred men to return to take them by force, William Parker was unmoved, telling them to bring 500 men. "It will take all the men in Lancaster to change our purpose or take us alive," he answered.

Eliza Parker then signaled to nearby members of the community Black defense group by blowing her horn. This garnered an immediate response from the US marshal, who fired a shot at Eliza. He missed her, and she continued to sound the alarm.

Her alarm brought out some forty-five Black men and women and some neighboring white, Quaker farmers.

Eliza's horn had signaled not only the neighboring Black self-defense organization, but the next phase of the resistance. Indeed, her role, according to William, did not end with the clarion call to the community. For when some inside the house began to weaken in the face of the threats from the slave-nappers, it was she, Eliza, who scuttled the idea of surrender.

William Parker would later write that she "seized a corn-cutter [similar to a machete] and declared she would cut off the head of the first one who should attempt to give up."[12] Parker later wrote in detail of his face-to-face struggle with the stubborn Gorsuch, who, by not leaving, apparently opted for his "breakfast in hell":

> I...struck him a heavy blow on the arm. It fell as if broken. I doubled my fists to knock him down....Bricks, stones, and sticks fell in showers. We fought across the road and back again, and I thought our brains would be knocked out.
>
> I caught him by the throat....Then the rest beat him....If we had not been interrupted, death would have been his fate.
>
> We were then near enough to have killed them, concealed as we were by the darkness.

I told him we would not surrender on any conditions. I intend to fight.... I intend to try your strength. I told him, if he attempted it, I should be compelled to blow out his brains.

Before he could bring the weapon to bear, I seized a pair of heavy tongs, and struck him a violent blow across the face and neck, which knocked him down. He lay for a few moments senseless.[13]

This was a battle, one fought with fists, corn-cutters, and swords. Most battles are fought for land, for wealth, or for the whim of kings. This was a battle for freedom, and though little known, as significant as any in American history.

For those who tasted freedom, who worked their own plots of land so that their families could survive and prosper, who knew what life was worth, freedom was not to be surrendered easily.

It would be wrong to paint the Parkers as people who fought for the freedom of others who were unwilling to fight. They all fought. They had to fight.

The Christiana Resistance was waged a year after the government's ignoble passage of the Fugitive Slave Act (FSA) of 1850, which threatened the lives and liberty of all Black people whether slave or "free." As the contemporary Black nationalist Martin Delany explained:

By the provisions of this bill, the colored people of the United States are positively degraded beneath the level of whites—are liable at any time, in any place, and under all circumstances, to be arrested—and upon the claim of any white person, without the privilege, even of making a defence, sent into endless bondage. Let no visionary nonsense about *habeas corpus,* or a fair *trial,* deceive us; there are no such rights granted in this bill, and except where the commissioner is too ignorant to understand when reading it, or too stupid to enforce it when he does understand, there is no earthly chance—no hope under heaven for the colored person who is brought before one of these officers of the law....[14]

Under such provisions as these, Africans had slim and grim choices: resistance or a return to bondage.

Thousands chose resistance.

From Pittsburgh, Pennsylvania, hundreds fled to Canada to escape the reach of the FSA. According to the *Liberator* of October 4, 1850, "nearly all the waiters in the hotels" left for the border. "They went in large bodies, armed with pistols and bowie knives, determined to die rather than be captured," the radical journal recorded. An entry referring to Blacks crossing the border from Utica, New York, was similar.

The revered Harriet Tubman, called "Gen'ral Moses" by her admirers for her courageous role in bringing freedom and hope to thousands of people in bondage, spoke for many when she said she could "trust Uncle Sam with my people no longer." The Fugitive Slave Act and its repressive provisions forced her to carry her charges "clear off to Canada."[15]

The Gorsuches were shot (Dickinson, although badly wounded, survived), their other relatives were beaten and driven from the homestead, and the US deputy marshal, Kline, beat a full and hasty retreat. The women, full of fury at men who would steal their people to return them to the hated slavery system, rushed from the house at the fallen Gorsuch armed with corn-cutters and scythe blades, and in Parker's words, "put an end to him."[16]

With the slave-catching posse dead, wounded, beaten, and dispersed, the Christiana rebels had to flee the area. William Parker and two of his men who began the resistance (believed to have been Samuel Thompson and a man named Pinckney) used the well-known routes of the Underground Railroad to make their way northward. They stopped briefly in Rochester, New York, at the home of the most famous Black abolitionist of the age, Frederick Douglass, himself an escaped captive from Maryland and a defender of freedom by any necessary means. Douglass conducted the harried and hunted party to their final depot: freedom in Canada. As thanks, Parker presented Douglass with Gorsuch's pistol. Although it was bent and unable to fire, the abolitionist prized the souvenir. Later, Eliza would join William, and they would raise their family there on a farm, in freedom.

Meanwhile, the armed rebellion of Christiana ignited a firestorm of controversy in the US, north and south. The *Philadelphia Bulletin* used the event to launch a broadside at what it perceived as the greatest evil, abolition:

> The melancholy tragedy of Christiana, in this State, by which two citizens of Maryland lost their lives, has established, in letters of blood, the dangerous character of the modern abolitionists.... We have, on more than one occasion, predicted this result from the doctrines of the abolitionists—*Men who advocate an armed resistance to the law, especially in a republic, are enemies of order.*[17]

Order, to the editors of the Philadelphia daily, meant legal support for slavery; any who would resist that evil, even ex-slaves themselves, were branded "enemies of order."

To Douglass, ever the radical abolitionist, the lawfulness of the Fugitive Slave Act must yield to the rightness of resistance to it. The radical journalist and editor of the antislavery journal *The North Star* cared little what the press said. He lauded the events of Christiana as dealing a fatal blow to an evil law:

> But the thing which more than all else destroyed the fugitive slave law was the resistance made to it by the fugitives themselves. A decided check was given to the execution of the law at Christiana, Penn.... This affair ... inflicted fatal wounds on the fugitive slave bill.[18]

Indeed, Douglass argued, the Christiana Resistance came close to making the hated fugitive slave bill "a dead letter."[19] Historian Philip Foner called Christiana "one of the major harbingers" of the coming Civil War. Just over a century (and fifteen years) after the so-called Christiana Riot, another so-called riot, Watts, would spark militant movements across the nation. As Christiana signaled the coming of the Civil War, so Watts signaled a rising militance of Blacks, one expression of which was the Black Panther Party.

Beneath the fact of Watts, beyond the existence of the Black Panther Party, was a seething anger, a bubbling cauldron of Black rage, that Martin Luther King's somewhat sweet, ethereal speech at the Lincoln Memorial in Washington, DC, several years before, could hardly assuage.

More to Black urban appetites was the cutting, insightful, militant speech of Malcolm X, whose critique of the heralded March on Washington was widely read, and heard over Black radio:

> The Negroes were out there in the streets. They were talking about how they were going to march on Washington.... That they were going to march on Washington, march on the Senate, march on the White House, march on the Congress, and tie it up, bring it to a halt, not let the government proceed. They even said they were going out to the airport and lay down on the runway and not let any airplanes land. I'm telling you what they said. That was revolution. That was revolution. That was the black revolution.

> It was the grass roots out there in the street. It scared the white man to death, scared the white power structure in Washington, D.C. to death; I was there. When they found out this black steamroller was going to come down on the capital, they called in ... these national Negro leaders that you respect and told them, "Call it off." Kennedy said, "Look you all are letting this thing go too far." And Old Tom said, "Boss, I can't stop it because I didn't start it." I'm telling you what they said. They said, "I'm not even in it, much less at the head of it." They said, "These Negroes are doing things on their own. They're running ahead of us." And that old shrewd fox, he said, "If you all aren't in it, I'll put you in it. I'll put you at the head of it. I'll endorse it. I'll welcome it. I'll help it. I'll join it."

> This is what they did at the march on Washington. They joined it ... became part of it, took it over. And as they took it over, it lost its militancy. It ceased to be angry, it ceased to be hot, it ceased to be uncompromising. Why, it even ceased to be a march. It became a picnic, a circus. Nothing but a circus, with clowns and all....

> No, it was a sellout. It was a takeover.... They controlled it so tight, they told those Negroes what time to hit town, where to

stop, what signs to carry, what song to sing, what speech they could make, and what speech they couldn't make, and then told them to get out of town by sundown....[20]

Martin's "dream" is better known to most Americans, but to Black people, especially those teeming millions barred within US ghettos, Malcolm's words were closer to the mark, closer to the heart.

When Watts erupted, it did not erupt in a vacuum. In 1964 and 1965, violent outbreaks were occurring in every part of the country. In Florida, the killing of a Black woman and the threat to bomb a Black high school caused an uproar; when a white minister who sat in front of a bulldozer to protest housing discrimination was killed, Cleveland erupted; the fatal shooting of a fifteen-year-old Black boy by an off-duty cop set it off in New York City. Similarly, mass violence (called "riots") rocked Rochester, Jersey City, Chicago, and Philadelphia.[21]

And then there was Watts. What became the most violent urban outbreak since World War II began with something that had been commonplace in African American communities—violent police behavior.

A Black motorist was forcibly arrested, a bystander was clubbed, and a young Black woman was seized and falsely accused of spitting on a cop. Watts exploded. The uprising raged from August 11 to 16, 1965; fires swept through the neighborhoods. Some 4,000 people were arrested during the rebellion.

The summer of 1966 showed that Watts was not the end of conflict and suggested it may have been a kind of beginning. Cities burned and armed conflicts raged, some between members of Black self-defense groups and the National Guard. Firebombs were hurled in Chicago; Cleveland saw several Blacks shot by white cops and white civilians.

By 1967, rebellions were raging all across America—123 major and minor uprisings or "outbreaks," according to the National Advisory Committee on Urban Disorders. Some eighty-three people died of gunfire, mostly in the mass violence that occurred in Newark and Detroit. As the committee noted, "The overwhelming majority of the persons killed or injured in all the disorders were Negro civilians."[22]

It was into this social context of mass disorder and urban chaos that the Black Panther Party emerged—as a response to the massive violence perpetrated against Blacks and as a way to focus and organize the resultant mass anger into a cohesive political movement.

Riots, by their very nature, are disorganized and incoherent. The Black Panther Party wanted to signal an end to this disorganization and introduce the revolutionary alternative: organization, discipline, purpose, self-defense.

## Beginnings

The Black Panther Party for Self-Defense began with books. Huey Newton had done extensive reading about revolutionary organizing and revolutionaries. He scored several hundred copies of the Red Book (*Quotations from Chairman Mao Tse-Tung*) from several radical Asian friends and began hawking them on the campus of the nearby University of California, Berkeley. Bobby Seale would later write that Huey came up with that idea because he suspected the very idea of "Negroes with Red Books" would spark the curiosity of Berkeley's white radicals and thereby move them to support the fledgling effort.[23]

That, however, was a tactic, not an objective. Selling the Red Book made money; and money would be used to buy what revolutionaries the world over found indispensable: guns. While the predominant civil rights groups of the era pitched their raps to the press, or the white liberal community, or the Negro bourgeoisie, Huey knew that mere words would not break through the thick shell that ghetto Blacks had to have to survive in racist America. Huey knew that guns, openly and freely displayed, would reach them.

To reach them, he had to attract their attention.

Attention would not be long in coming. The Black Panther Party started as an Oakland phenomenon, with perhaps a dozen members who could be relied upon to make meetings. Nearby Richmond was also showing a small degree of interest.

Newton had studied the California penal codes (he suggests, in *Revolutionary Suicide,* that such knowledge made him a better thief) and learned that weapons possession was protected by state statute, and guns could be carried in public as long as they were not concealed. The Party therefore developed the nation's first armed police monitoring patrols. Party members would be armed, with loaded weapons, cameras, tape recorders, and law books. When approaching a traffic stop, they would loudly announce state law allowed citizens to observe police stops and arrests. Huey's legal research would ensure that the proper legal distance would be kept. People would see members of the Party standing in their defense against the hated representatives of the white power structure. The Panthers would advise suspects of their legal rights. Such actions proved a powerful organizing tool in the first year of activity.

In April 1967, a twenty-two-year-old Black man named Denzil Dowell was shot and killed by a white deputy sheriff in Richmond. Some of Dowell's family members contacted the Party when local authorities ruled the killing was justifiable homicide, and the Party launched its own investigation. More importantly, for organizing purposes, the Party sent "twenty Panthers out there armed with guns, disciplined, standing thirty or forty feet apart on every corner of the intersection" where the Black man was murdered.[24]

The Panthers announced the results of their preliminary investigation, which cast considerable doubt on the police version of the killing, and rallied in the streets against the slaying. They denounced the brutality of the cops, "in full view of the local police."[25] As Seale would later write, "[W]e were educating the people that we would die for them. This was the position we always took with brother Huey P. Newton."[26] The rally was a brilliant organizing success because "just about everybody out there joined the Party that day."[27]

The Dowell case provided a further opportunity for the growing group. On April 25, 1967, the first issue of *The Black Panther Community News Service* came off the press, in the form of a mimeographed, four-page newsletter, edited by Eldridge Cleaver. *The Black Panther's* maiden edition was full of fire:

> [T]he white cop is the instrument sent into our community by the Power structure to keep Black people quiet and under control...it is time that Black People start moving in a direction that will free our communities from this form of outright brutal oppression. The BLACK PANTHER PARTY FOR SELF-DEFENSE has worked out a program that is carefully designed to cope with this situation.

Eldridge, paroled after an extended stint in California prisons, brought a bite and a wit to *The Black Panther* that ensured that Black folks who dared read it would be moved as by nothing they had read before. Cleaver's articulate phrasing, married with the clever artistic depictions of Emory Douglas, would make *The Black Panther* a reading experience that few would forget.

The Richmond demonstration, the newsletter (soon to be reborn as a full-fledged newspaper), and the armed community police patrols would prove irresistible to ghetto youth who had simmered under the glare of overtly racist cops. They longed to join the swelling Civil Rights movement, but had not because they could not bear to join any group which would meekly submit to racist violence, as demanded by some civil rights organizations. The 1967 revolts marked a rise in Black militancy, a psychic change of pace that the middle-class leaders of the southern-based Civil Rights movement could not address, and word spread about the actions of the Black Panther Party. The Black journalist William Gardner-Smith remarked, "The '67 revolts marked the entry of the tough ghetto youths into the race battle, and the existing organizations, led by intellectuals or the middle-class, could not cope with them—the Panthers had to be born."[28]

Just over six months into the Party's existence another event would push the organization into the minds and consciousness of millions around the nation. On May 2, 1967, armed members and supporters of the Party "invaded" the California State Assembly in Sacramento. The state assembly had probably never seen armed (not to mention, Black) "lobbyists" on its debate floor before, and the incident resulted in tremendous visibility for the Party.

Huey Newton, on parole for a past offense, wisely opted to sit out the event. Despite being arrested along with twenty-five other Panthers, Bobby Seale, following Newton's instructions to the letter, read the entirety of Newton's boldly penned Executive Mandate denouncing the pending Mulford Bill. The bill was a direct legislative attempt to change California gun laws in response to BPP armed police patrols. Newton wrote:

> Black people have begged, prayed, petitioned and demonstrated, among other things, to get the racist power structure of America to right the wrongs which have historically been perpetrated against Black people. All of these efforts have been answered by more repression, deceit, and hypocrisy. As the aggression of the racist American Government escalates in Vietnam, the police agencies of America escalate the repression of Black people throughout the ghettos of America. Vicious police dogs, cattle prods, and increased patrols have become familiar sights in Black communities. City Hall turns a deaf ear to the pleas of Black people for relief from this increasing terror.
>
> The Black Panther Party for Self-Defense believes that the time has come for Black people to arm themselves against this terror before it is too late. The pending Mulford Act brings the hour of doom one step nearer. A people who have suffered so much for so long at the hands of a racist society must draw the line somewhere. We believe that the Black communities of America must rise up as one man to halt the progression of a trend that leads inevitably to their total destruction.[29]

While the Party's armed Black presence probably contributed to ensuring the passage of the bill, the Party's message was clearly stated in the startling photos of leather-clad Black men marching through the state's capitol buildings with arms at parade rest.

The Sacramento demonstration launched the Party into a national orbit, perhaps long before it was ready. The Party was swarmed with applications from young men and women around the nation who wanted to open branches of the new organization in their local communities.

The Party, not yet a year old, was growing at a rapid pace.

Over the next three years, the Party expanded almost exponentially. It first spread to Richmond, then over the bay to San Francisco, and then southward to Los Angeles.

It sprang out from California to every possible region where a Black community welcomed its youth and energy; north to Seattle; east to Kansas City; to the Black Mecca of Chicago; to Boston; New York's Harlem, Bronx, and Brooklyn boroughs; Winston-Salem, North Carolina; Baltimore; Nashville, Tennessee; and New Orleans.

By 1969 over forty chapters and branches existed, with several thousand people sworn to membership in the Party.

In Philadelphia, the nation's former capital, a handful of young men would form the core of the Black Panther Party in that city. I was among them—in the spring of 1969, beginning my fifteenth year of life:

*It is difficult to pinpoint the exact moment the Black Panther Party was formed in Philadelphia, because, in fact, there were several such formations: one in South Philadelphia, one in Germantown, and one in North Philadelphia. The North and South Philadelphia formations would merge, and the Germantown group, a mysterious gathering that apparently only sold papers, would wither.*

*As in any such political organization, there was intense jockeying for power, divided between younger and older and between north and south sections of the city. The men met each other, quietly, in a Center City bookstore, where* The Black Panther *and various books were sold. Some days later they met in a tiny ghetto apartment in South Philly, at 14th and Kater Streets, right over a bar. The men were to argue and debate who would lead and who would follow. An aggressive, tall, fast-talking young man named Bill Crawford seemed to have the edge, with his fiery tongue and dark shades covering his strange, amber-colored eyes. His only real adversary was an older, slow-talking, darker-hued man, Terry McCarter, whose clever, patient, southern-cadenced manner had appeal.*

*It was decided that a phone call would be made to Black Panther National Headquarters to solve the dispute, but the answer related to us was that Oakland would choose no one. According to one caller, either David or June Hilliard, the BPP Chief of Staff or his assistant, when asked about formally recognizing the Philadelphia branch, replied, "You don't hafta be a Black Panther to make revolution."*

*His statement, while objectively true, did not discourage those of us who were determined to join the organization that seemed closest to our dreams. The meetings continued, as we pondered National's seeming indifference. Did they get calls like that all the time? Were they being cautious of folks they didn't know? Were they seriously trying to limit expansion? Was this a test, to see if we were serious about opening a branch?*

*These questions were never sufficiently answered. Or perhaps they were answered by our actions, as we stubbornly resolved to just do the work. Officers were chosen, and daily tasks were assigned. When the oldhead, Terry, was chosen for captain, the young buck, Bill, raged out of the apartment, vowing to catch the next thing smoking to Oakland to resolve this problem. He clearly felt he was the superior candidate and hinted that Oakland would change our choice. In fact, we never heard back from him.*

*I was chosen Lieutenant of Information, a heady role for a manchild who had barely reached his fifteenth summer, and assigned to develop propaganda for the Party—even though no office had yet been opened. Leaflets were prepared, drawing largely from the BPP newspaper for style and tone, announcing the existence of a local branch.*

*How does one provide contact data on a leaflet in the absence of an office? Not to worry. I simply attached my home number to the bottom of the leaflet, which would not have been remarkable were it not for the fact that "home" was where I lived with my mother. This led to some interesting, if somewhat passionate, exchanges between us. It also led to some remarkable telephone calls.*

*Caller: Yello—Is zis uh, Moo-my-uh, of the Black Gorilla Party?*

*Answerer: This is Mumia of the Black Panther Party—who the hell is this?*

*Caller: Yeah—This is Roy Frankhouser of the United Klan of America, headquartered up 'ere in Reading, P.A. We're havin' a burn-a-nigger festival this weekend, and we wanna invite cha to come. You interested?*

*Answerer: I doubt I'll be able to make it, but you can bring yho ass down to Philly—we got somethin' real nice for ya.*

*Caller: Well, uh—can I ask ya a question there, Moomyah?*

*Answerer: What's that?*

*Caller: Do niggers eat shit?*

*Answerer: Do you?*

*Caller: Nah, uh—really! I'm curious! Isn't that where yer brown color comes from?*

*Answerer: I can't believe you that silly, man. Ain't you got nothin' better to do?*

*Caller: Well, we got the kill-a-nigger festival I told ja about....*

*Answerer: Man, I can't believe a grown man your age ain't got nothin' betta to do than play ona damn phone! Are you retarded, man?*

*Caller: Naw, I'm curious.*

*[The phone is hung up.]*

The call probably wasn't formally reported to my captain although I'm fairly certain that we discussed it, more like—"Man, you ain't gonna believe the nutty shit that I'm getting on my phone...." What is memorable, however, is the distinct accent of the caller. His high-in-the-throat, almost nasal pronunciation sounded more at home in the ethnic enclaves of South or Northeast Philadelphia (pronounced "Fluffia" by them) than distant, rural Reading. Was it really the Klan; were they really so stupid, so childish, that a teenager could so quickly dismiss them as juvenile?

It may have been, but to the youth on the receiving end of the call, it sounded like a typical Philadelphia cop.

*Terry, because of his low-key, laid-back approach, was incurring more criticism than acceptance in his role of captain. It did not help matters that he seemed more drunk than sober these days. Inevitably, another power struggle developed, and Captain Terry was quietly retired in favor of a younger, more aggressive (and sober!) North Philadelphian—Reggie Schell. Captain Reg would corral the necessary resources to open the first office of the Black Panther Party in Philadelphia in late spring 1969. The site he selected at 1928 West Columbia Avenue was in the very heart of North Philly, the site of a police-sparked revolt (the city's press would say "riot") several months before. The office would become a magnet, attracting radical and revolutionary Black youth (and others) from all corners of the city.*

*The New York chapter, which had regional jurisdiction over the East Coast, sent its Deputy Field Marshal, Henry Mitchell, to check out the branch. With acerbic, earthy speech and arrogant, proud authority, New York gave Philadelphia its intense scrutiny.*

*Mitchell, his face seemingly etched with a permanent scowl, was barking like a drill instructor as he issued orders to the novice troops and the newly minted captain. But by day's end, the city was given a passing mark. We were told to strengthen and fortify office and housing, ordered to report regularly, and abruptly left alone.*[30]

Thus was the Philadelphia branch of the Black Panther Party born.

## CHAPTER THREE

# A Panther Walks in Philly

> There is not perhaps anywhere to be found a city in which prejudice against color is more rampant than in Philadelphia. Hence all the incidents of caste are to be seen there in perfection. It has its white schools and its colored schools, its white churches and its colored churches, its white Christianity and its colored Christianity, its white concerts and its colored concerts, its white literary institutions and its colored institutions.
>
> —Frederick Douglass (ca. 1862)[1]

**WHEN FREDERICK DOUGLASS** made this comment, he had spent over two decades living in freedom. He was personally familiar with Rochester, New York, the coastal regions of Maryland, Boston, and England, where he secured the funds to legally purchase his freedom. As an editor, writer, and abolitionist speaker of some renown, he undoubtedly traveled further than many, perhaps most men, white or Black, of his time. Here was a man who was a deep thinker, a sharp speaker, and an astute observer of life, with a broad range of experience. One wonders, why would Philadelphia bring so foul a taste to his distinguished palette?

In Philadelphia one finds the perfect example of American ambivalence on race. It is formally a northern city, but as it virtually straddles the mythical Mason-Dixon line, it is, in many ways, a southern city as well. It boasts the historical distinction of being the nation's first capital, the site of the signing of both the Declaration of Independence and the Constitution, but also of sustained racial and ethnic rivalry, conflict, and repression.

Known worldwide as an almost mythical birthplace of liberty, the hope of freedom acted as a kind of psychic magnet, drawing the poor and oppressed from the class-bound aristocracies of Europe in rivers of emigration, as well as Black captives escaping from southern bondage and Black freedmen and -women fleeing a humiliating and soul-sapping southern apartheid. The Philadelphia that the stalwart Frederick Douglass beheld with snarled contempt would more than double in size in half a century, rising from 650,000 people in 1860 to 1.5 million by 1914.[2]

It was a city of extremes, with pronounced differences in wealth, power, and influence. For although millions of Europeans came to the English colonies with visions of a land where streets were paved with gold, they found cities awash in staggering poverty, with wealth concentrated in the hands of a few. The cities of the colonial era had almshouses or poorhouses, but these were hardly sufficient. "It is remarkable," one citizen of Philadelphia said in 1748, "what an increase of the number of beggars there is about this town this winter."[3]

A century later, although the white working class could find work in cities, their standard of living was miserable. In Philadelphia, they lived fifty-five to a tenement, one room per family. There were no toilets and no garbage collection, and fresh water or even fresh air was virtually nonexistent.[4] Many whites fought against their Black contemporaries' efforts to find work and tried to ensure they would not. Edward Abdy, a British visitor to Philadelphia in 1833, described the efforts of local Irish to remove Blacks from gainful employment. "Irish laborers were actively employed in this vile conspiracy against a people of whom they were jealous, because they were more industrious, orderly and obliging than themselves."[5] While Abdy's report may be influenced by the longstanding and deep-rooted antipathy between the British and the Irish, his remarks present evidence of what seemed to be deep anti-Black feeling among the Irish both in Philadelphia and New York:

Forty years ago a colored man appeared, for the first time, as a carman in Philadelphia. Great jealousy was excited among that class of men; and every expedient was tried to get rid of a competitor whose success would draw others into the business. Threats and insults were followed by a report that he had been detected in stealing. The Quakers came forward to support him. They inquired into the grounds of the charge, and published its refutation. Their patronage maintained him in his situation, and encouraged others to follow his example. There are now plenty of them employed. At New York, a license cannot be obtained for them, and a black carman in that city is as rare as a black swan.[6]

George Lippard is now forgotten, but before the work of Harriet Beecher Stowe stole the scene, he was the best-selling novelist in America. His 1844 novel *The Quaker City* told of a Philadelphia that was hideously violent, racist, and proud in its ignorance. He drew characters from the streets and headlines of the penny press, and one of his most memorable was an Irish rioter called Pump-Handle, who, in Irish-accented English, explained how he got his name:

Why you see, a party of us one Sunday afternoon, had nothin' to do, so we got up a nigger riot. We have them things in Phil'delphy. Once or twice a year, you know? I helped to burn a nigger church, two orphans asylums and a school-house. And happenin' to have a handle in my hand, I aksedentally hit an old nigger on the head. Konsekance was he died. That's why they call me Pump-Handle.[7]

Lippard, although a novelist, used his skills as a radical journalist to draw accurate portrayals of the city where he lived and worked.

What were not fictional, but strictly factual, were the scores of racist riots against Black achievement, abolitionism, and Black freedmen and -women who lived in the city. Seven major mob attacks occurred between 1834 and 1838; among the most reported was the "Flying Horse Riot" of 1834. Radical and race historian Noel Ignatiev has written in his *How the Irish Became White:*

On a lot near Seventh and South Streets in Philadelphia, an entrepreneur had for some time been operating a merry-go-round called, "Flying Horses." It was popular among both black people and whites, and served both "indiscriminately." Quarrels (not necessarily racial) over seating preference and so forth were frequent. On Tuesday evening, August 12, a mob of several hundred young White men, thought to be principally from outside the area, appeared at the scene, began fighting with the black people there, and in a very short time tore the merry-go-round to pieces. The mob then marched down South Street, to the adjacent township of Moyamensing, attacked a home occupied by a black family, and continued its violence on the small side streets where the black people mainly lived. On Wednesday evening a crowd wrecked the African Presbyterian Church on Seventh Street and a place several blocks away called the "Diving Bell," operated by "a white man, and used as a grog shop and lodging house for all colors, at the rate of three cents a head." After reducing these targets to ruins, the rioters began smashing windows, breaking down doors, and destroying furniture in private homes of Negroes, driving the inmates naked into the streets and beating any they caught. One correspondent reported that the mob threw a corpse out of a coffin, and cast a dead infant on the floor, "barbarously" mistreating its mother. "Some arrangement, it appears, existed between the mob and the white inhabitants, as the dwelling houses of the latter, contiguous to the residences of blacks, were illuminated, and left undisturbed, while the huts of the negroes were signaled out with unerring certainty."[8]

By midweek, when the fury had ebbed, several Blacks had been killed and two churches and at least twenty homes were destroyed. Hundreds of Blacks fled that part of town for other neighborhoods or sought refuge across the Delaware in New Jersey. This brutal violence, perpetrated by Irish gangs (many of them organized into the neighborhood fire companies), usually went unpunished. On the off chance that someone was arrested, Philadelphia juries duly acquitted them, especially when the victims were Black.[9] The bloody and bitter feuds between the largely immigrant Catholics and the so-called nativists (other non-Catholic whites) often retreated when the target of local ire was a Black person or institution (such as a church). Then the nativist-Catholic divide would dissipate into whiteness against Blackness.[10]

Three years after the terrorist violence of the Flying Horse Riot and the destruction of the Diving Bell, Pennsylvania Hall (built with Black and abolitionist money in Center City, Philadelphia) was burned to the ground by several thousand whites who disapproved of Blacks and whites coming together to meet and discuss the heated issue of the day—slavery. The nativist commander of the Philadelphia militia, Col. August James Pleasonton, who witnessed Pennsylvania Hall being consumed by the flames, would later note:

> There are serious apprehensions that the injudicious, to say the least, but as many think highly exciting and inflammatory proceedings of abolitionists, which have recently taken place here, and the disgusting intercourse between the whites and the blacks, as repugnant to all the prejudices of our education, which they not only have recommended, but are in the habit of practising in this very Abolition Hall, will result in some terrible outbreak of popular indignation, not only against the Abolitionists, but also, against the colored people.[11]

Pleasonton's view, aside from its elegant phrasing, could hardly be distinguished from that of the most uncouth Fenian of the period.

As for the cops or firemen of the day, little help could be expected from that quarter. Both, to the extent they existed at all, were little more than the accretion of local, ethnic street gangs who used their positions to scam and threaten people for money. These street gangs, for whom the fire company or the police were but an instrument, had names like the Rats, the Bleeders, the Blood Tubs, the Deathfetchers, and the Hyenas.[12] It was for good reason that the American wit Mark Twain once quipped that people insured their homes, not against fire, but against the firemen. Failure to pay them might result in arson, a riot, or both!

This was the Philadelphia that Douglass loathed and perhaps feared.

It would be unfair and inaccurate to suggest that the anti-Black feeling in Philadelphia, or in other northern cities, for that matter, was the exclusive province of the white lower or working classes. At the highest levels of state and federal government, as well as in circles of wealth and influence, there was ample evidence of a pronounced antipathy for Blacks and of the fact that the popular rhetoric about "Philadelphia liberty" did not extend to them.

In 1837, a Pennsylvania constitutional convention overtly prevented Blacks from voting in the state.

At the time of the sensational Christiana Resistance in nearby Lancaster County, Pennsylvania, the *Philadelphia Bulletin* published an editorial that left no question as to whose side it defended in the conflict:

> Who is to prevail, the many or the few? The Old Saxon blood, which at vast sacrifice, founded these republics; or these African fugitives, whom we Pennsylvanians neither wish, nor will have?... Where the interests of two races come into collision, the weaker must yield, not merely as a matter of might, but, according to our republican doctrines of right also. Among ourselves, we whites understand this, and act upon this....[13]

Nor did the official voice of the state of Pennsylvania differ, in essence, from that of the bigotry of the *Bulletin* on the issue of liberty for those "African fugitives," in flight from bondage, who made their way to the "free" state. Margaret Morgan escaped from the slave system and fled to Pennsylvania in search of liberty. She found instead a state that spoke about freedom, but not for those who would seem to have needed it most—the enslaved.

When her capture by a Maryland slave-catcher was held to violate Pennsylvania's "personal liberty" laws, Maryland's attorney general argued, that the Constitution did not apply to Blacks. For they, as slaves, he argued, were not a party to the national pact and thus were not contained under the Preamble "We, the People." Pennsylvania agreed with her sister state, admitting their adversary's claims. Lawyers for Pennsylvania took what one legal scholar called a feeble position:

> Pennsylvania says: Instead of preventing you from taking your slaves, *we are anxious that you should have them; they are a population*

*we do not covet;* and all our legislation tends toward giving you every facility to get them; but we do claim the right of legislating upon this subject so as to bring you under legal restraint, which will prevent you from taking a freeman.[14]

As might be expected of a court composed predominantly of slave owners, the Supreme Court held for Edward Prigg, agent of the slave owner, and overturned Pennsylvania's "personal liberty" law as unconstitutional. For Margaret Morgan and her children—including her youngest, born into a "free" state—the Court's majority opinion meant a return to bondage.

The majority opinion in *Prigg v. Pennsylvania* (1842), penned by Justice Joseph Story of Massachusetts, made it clear that the state's claim to "personal liberty" applied to everyone, except slaves:

> The rights of the owners of fugitive slaves are in no just sense interfered with, or regulated by such a course.... But such regulations can never be permitted to interfere with or to obstruct the just rights of the owner to reclaim his slave, derived from the Constitution of the United States; or with the remedies prescribed by Congress to aid and enforce the same.

> Upon these grounds, we are of opinion that the act of Pennsylvania upon which this indictment is founded, is unconstitutional and void. It purports to punish as a public offence against the state, the very act of seizing and removing a slave by his master, which the Constitution of the United States was designed to justify and uphold.[15]

The *Prigg* case would prove a harbinger of the judicial insults to come, among them, *Dred Scott v. Sanford*, decided nearly a decade later. The *Prigg* case was also a precursor of the infamous Fugitive Slave Law of 1850. Pennsylvania's lawyers betrayed Margaret Morgan, her five children, and thousands like her throughout the northern state. Instead of defending liberty, they defended comity between sister states and, by extension, the legality of slavery. Once again, the courts favored the illusion of human beings as property, as chattel, rather than the reality of humans yearning for liberty from base tyranny.

## Philadelphia Modernity

The Philadelphia of the mid-twentieth century remained a conflicted, class-conscious, racially stratified city.

Black Philadelphia's population burgeoned, fueled in large part by the Great Migration which sent wave upon wave of a Black rural flood into urban centers like Pittsburgh, New York, Chicago, Boston, San Francisco, Seattle, and Oakland. In these centers were established de facto Black Quarters, areas of containment and isolation, policed by law and social custom to minimize and restrict Black movement, mobility, and dispersal.

Ghettos are not natural growths, like bunions; they are legal constructs that are the fruit of the long-held beliefs and practices of segregation, and they survived its alleged death through restrictive covenants that forbade the selling of millions of units of housing to African Americans. This legal restriction had its equally effective corollary in social and customary practices of pricing property at rates that were prohibitive to the vast majority of the ghetto population.

Over the generations, central North Philadelphia, West Philadelphia, Southwest Philadelphia, and, to a lesser extent, small pockets of South Philadelphia became shorthand for Black Philadelphia. This did not mean these were the only places one found Black inhabitants, but it meant these areas were ones where Blacks dwelt in predominance.

Conversely, there were areas of the city, notably Northeast Philadelphia, East Oak Lane, Kensington, and South Philadelphia, where Black folks walked, drove, or strove to live and work at their peril. To see Black homes marred by racist graffiti or firebombed by whites dwelling in neighboring homes was not an odd occurrence in the city with a name meaning Brotherly Love. Nor was it a rare occurrence for a Black pedestrian to be put to the chase for daring to walk in a "white" neighborhood.

These private, communal acts were echoed by official ones, done in the name of the city, by the police. Black Philadelphians came of age with the deeply felt knowledge that they could be beaten, wounded, or killed by cops with virtual impunity. The predominantly white police seemed like foreigners in a dark village who treated their alleged fellow citizens with the vehemence one reserves for an enemy. For ghetto youth, this took the form of the police using the maddened self-hatred and regional antipathy between youth of various gangs to foment yet more hatred and violent reprisal. One favorite tactic they routinely utilized was to pick up a few youngsters from one gang, place them in a patrol car, drive them to enemy gang turf, let them out of the vehicle, and scream curses and insults against the enemy gang. To the young men left standing as the cop car raced off at breakneck speed, their choices were few and unenviable: stand and fight against the swarm of sworn enemies or run like the devil, hoping to get to safe territory before they got badly beaten, shot, or worse.

It is into this milieu that the Black Panther Party came into being in Philadelphia. Once the chapter was formed, other questions remained.

What would this new organization do?

How would we let folks know we existed?

What would be our focus?

These were but some of the challenges facing the group and met by the late spring of 1969:

*With the renting, repair, cleaning, and painting of the storefront at 1928 West Columbia Avenue, the local party would have its first formal presence (odd apartments and private homes had sufficed previously), a reliable place where people could contact us. The time could not have been more perfect for our arrival, for the clear air, the bright sky blue, the very essence of the season of new life was upon us. As soon as we had finished painting the walls (Panther powder blue, with black glaze adorning the moldings), affixed a few posters to the walls (Malcolm X, Che Guevara, Huey and Bobby, armed), and used pressure-sensitive letters to inscribe the inside of the fronting glass with the black, capital, gold-edged letters:* ꓬꓕꓤAꟼ ꓤƎHꓕИAꟼ ꓘƆAꓶꓭ *people began appearing at our door. What drew them was the bold letters blaring from the window:* BLACK PANTHER PARTY.

*That seemingly simple message drew in the young, the old, and those in the middle, from the cautious to the curious. Students came in, eager to sell the paper.*

*Even the established, like the real estate owner who rented the property to the Party and who owned properties all around the neighborhood took pains to demonstrate his nationalist credentials. He confided to us that he went to the historically Black college, Lincoln University, with the revered Kwame Nkrumah, the first President of the independent West African nation of Ghana.*

*But to have an office was not enough. The fledgling organization had to do something. After much thought, and a request from the national office, the captain ordered us to assemble at the State Building, at Broad and Spring Garden Streets, near the center of the city, to demonstrate for the freedom of the imprisoned BPP Minister of Defense, Huey P. Newton, who was facing murder charges stemming from a car stop and shoot-out in Oakland. The objective was to snag some publicity for the Party, and thus to inform the city's huge Black population of our presence.*

*The date is May 1, 1969, and between fifteen and twenty of us are in the full uniform of black berets, black jackets of smooth leather, and black trousers. As we assemble, a rousing chant of "Free Huey!" is raised. Leaflets are distributed to passersby, and we are able to inform some people of our presence and how to contact us.*

*Several of Huey's articles are read over the megaphone, and, before long, we have a somewhat rousing rally on our hands. Some of the excited kids from the nearby Ben Franklin High School cut their classes to attend the rally, and several papers are sold. Captain Reggie reads from Huey's "In Defense of Self-Defense," which noted, in part:*

> The heirs of Malcolm now stand millions strong on their corner of the triangle, facing the racist dog oppressor and the soulless endorsed spokesmen. The heirs of Malcolm have picked up the gun and taking first things first are moving to expose the en-

dorsed spokesmen so the Black masses can see them for what they are and have always been. The choice offered by the heirs of Malcolm to the endorsed spokesmen is to repudiate the oppressor and crawl back to their own people and earn a speedy reprieve or face a merciless, speedy, and most timely execution for treason and being "too wrong for too long."[16]

*Cameras went off like popcorn, but we had no real idea who the mostly white photographers were. We assumed they were the press, but some had the unmistakable air of cops about them. It never dawned on us that some were FBI agents building a file on us. Mostly, it was because, in an age of global revolution, it didn't seem too extraordinary to be a revolutionary. Didn't America come into being by way of the American Revolution?*

*Here we were, reading the hard, uncompromising words of the Minister of Defense of the Black Panther Party at the State Building in the heart of the fourth largest city in America, while red-faced, nervous, armed cops stood around on the periphery of our rally … what did we think would happen? We thought, in the amorphous realm of hope, youth, and boundless optimism, that revolution was virtually a heartbeat away. It was four years since Malcolm's assassination and just over a year since the assassination of the Rev. Martin Luther King, Jr. The Vietnam War was flaring up under Nixon's Vietnamization program, and the rising columns of smoke from Black rebellions in Watts, Detroit, Newark, and North Philly could still be sensed—their ashen smoldering still tasted in the air.*

*Huey was our leader, and we felt, with utter certainty, that he spoke for the vast majority of Black folks. He certainly spoke for us. We loved and revered him and wondered why everybody else didn't feel the same way. Our job was to make all see this obvious truth. His work moved us all deeply, and we believed we could in turn move the world. This feeling motivated us to sell* The Black Panther *newspaper with passion and spirit, for Huey himself had written that "a newspaper is the voice of the party, the voice of the Panther must be heard throughout the land."[17]*

*We struggled daily to make it so. We got up early and didn't go to sleep until late. For most of us, Party work was all that we did, all day, into the night.*

*Our little branch blossomed into the biggest, most productive chapter in the state and one of the most vigorous in the nation.*

*A year after our rally, our branch sold 10,000 Party newspapers a week and had functioning Party offices in West Philadelphia and Germantown. The Party nationally sold nearly 150,000 papers through direct street sales and paid subscriptions per week. The Party was literally growing by leaps and bounds, both locally and nationally. From our original fifteen-odd members in the spring of 1969, a year later virtually ten times that number would call themselves members of the Black Panther Party of Philadelphia.*

*We spoke at antiwar rallies. We attended school meetings. We met with high school students. We met in churches. We worked with gangs and provided transportation to area prisons. Everywhere we went, we brought along the Ten-Point Program and Platform of the Black Panther Party, as a guideline for our organizing efforts.*

*By any measure, we made an impressive beginning.*

It was May 1969.

A young man named O.J. Simpson had just been named the number one NFL draft pick by Buffalo, a year after winning the Heisman for his performance as running back for University of Southern California.

The album *Blood, Sweat and Tears* (by the group Blood, Sweat and Tears) would win the best album Grammy.

The Oscar for Best Picture would be awarded to *Midnight Cowboy*.

The great Muhammad Ali had been stripped of his heavy-weight boxing crown two years previous, and the championship was vacant.

The number one first-round draft pick for the NBA was a lanky, Afro-coifed youth named Lew Alcindor of UCLA, who went to Milwaukee.

In April, the US military had mobilized its biggest troop deployment of 543,400 soldiers.

In just three months, half a million young folks would gather in a remote corner of New York called Woodstock.

Shortly thereafter, a quarter million people would march in front of the White House demanding an end to the Vietnam War.

Before the month of May ended, a police raid in New Haven, Connecticut, would threaten the very stability of the Party.

Chairman Bobby Seale and Ericka Huggins would face murder charges. In all, eight Panthers would be arrested, and at least one would agree to turn state's evidence. If convicted, Seale would face the electric chair.

## CHAPTER FOUR

# The Black Panther Party

> We had seen Martin Luther King come to Watts in an effort
> to calm the people and we had seen his philosophy of non-
> violence rejected. Black people had been taught nonviolence;
> it was deep in us. What good, however, was nonviolence when
> the police were determined to rule by force?
> —Huey P. Newton, *Revolutionary Suicide*[1]

**THE FIRES OF** the Watts Rebellion did far more than destroy; like flame in the kiln of a potter, the reddish-orange, hungry tongues of combustion are capable of creation.

As suggested earlier, the fires of Watts differed in significant ways from the many "riots" that had ravaged American cities for the better part of a century before. Those previous riots were often mass upheavals of whites attacking Black life or Black property. They therefore served the needs of white nationalism.

Watts was different in that it reflected Black urban anger at the white power structure and was a rebellion against a racist status quo. Eldridge Cleaver wrote in his first book, *Soul on Ice,* that before the revolts, young men in prison regarded Watts as a place of shame, or worse, an epithet. After the rebellion, Cleaver noticed a marked difference among "all the Blacks in Folsom [prison]." They were going around proclaiming, "I'm from Watts, baby...and proud of it."[2]

Watts took on a meaning to Black Americans that symbolized a kind of resistance that was anathema to the likes of Dr. King or his co-integrationists of the National Association for the Advancement of Colored People (NAACP).

The Black Panther Party came into existence, not to support or supplement the major civil rights organizations, but to supplant them.

The major civil rights groups were shocked and stymied by the outrage revealed by Watts. Those who would organize the Black Panther Party looked to Watts as inspiration and an ashy harbinger of things to come.

That is because, at its deepest levels, overtly and covertly, the Black Panther Party believed in revolution—the deep, thoroughgoing transformation of society from the ground up. It did not believe that the country would, or ever could, embrace the claims of its Constitution.

Although it has rarely been observed in these ideological terms, the Black Panther Party was a Malcolmist party far more than it was a Marxist one. Though all Panthers owned and were required to study Mao's Red Book, and the Party claimed to adhere to the principles of Marxism-Leninism, few Panthers actually pored through turgid, laborious translations of key Marxist texts. These were not required reading, although some advanced cadre chose to do so.

But few Panthers had failed to read (or, if illiterate, failed to hear) the speeches of Malcolm X. For Huey and Bobby, the admiration and almost quiet reverence for Malcolm is abundantly clear:

> We read also the works of the freedom fighters who had done so much for Black communities in the United States. Bobby had collected all of Malcolm X's speeches and ideas from papers like *The Militant* and *Muhammad Speaks*. These we studied carefully. Although Malcolm's program for the Organization of Afro-American Unity was never put into operation, he had made it clear that Blacks ought to arm. Malcolm's influence was ever-present. We continue to believe that the Black Panther Party exists in the spirit of Malcolm. Often it is difficult to say

exactly how an action or a program has been determined or influenced in a spiritual way. Such intangibles are hard to describe, although they can be more significant than any precise influence. Therefore, the words on this page cannot convey the effect that Malcolm has had on the Black Panther Party although, as far as I am concerned, the Party is a living testament to his life work. I do not claim that the Party has done what Malcolm would have done. We do not say this; but Malcolm's spirit is in us.[3]

Malcolm was a hard-core Black nationalist, and the early BPP was a hard-core Black nationalist organization. But Malcolm also represented more; his extraordinary life demonstrated the power of growth, of development, of personal transformation, and, indeed, service to one's community. His personal voyage from criminal, from thief to militant minister had tremendous appeal to many Panthers. It especially resonated with those whose earlier careers took them through the State's penal institutions, and those who would be sentenced there for Party work.

## Community Service

From the Party's earliest days, the organization took community service seriously. It was seen as a way to demonstrate to Black folks that the Party was serious about defending the Black community, even against the cops, the most hated and feared figures imposed upon the community. It is fitting that one of the Party's first programs was the Police-alert Patrols, where members trailed cop cars in the Black neighborhood, armed with guns, tape recorders, cameras, and law books. Newton knew that this program had very serious risks, given the nature of the police. These risks were outweighed by gaining the trust of the people of the Black community, who had been betrayed by virtually every previous political incarnation:

> With weapons in our hands, we were no longer their subjects, but their equals.

Out on patrol, we stopped whenever we saw the police questioning a brother or a sister. We would walk over with our weapons and observe them from a "safe" distance so that the police could not say we were interfering with the performance of their duty. We would ask the community members if they were being abused. Most of the time, when a policeman saw us coming, he slipped his book back into his pocket, got into his car and left in a hurry. The citizens who had been stopped were as amazed as the police at our sudden appearance.[4]

For Huey, the patrols were meant for the people, to give them a real, live demonstration of what the Party was about—and also for the police, who were used to harassing and brutalizing Black citizens with impunity. While the weapons and the patrols were perfectly legal under California law, he knew that many of the Oakland police, who, like many of Oakland's Black community, were natives of southern states, would be livid because they no longer possessed a monopoly on violence.

"A law book, a tape recorder, and a gun" were all that were needed, Huey explained. "It would let those brutalizing racist bastards know that we mean business."[5] In accordance with Huey's study of the law, BPP patrollers agreed to accept arrests nonviolently—to a limit. Newton and Seale promised to "do battle only at the point when a fool policeman drew his gun unjustly."[6]

[W]e had hit on something unique. By standing up to the police as equals, even holding them off, and yet remaining within the law, we had demonstrated Black pride to the community in a concrete way. Everywhere we went we caused traffic jams. People constantly stopped us to say how much they respected our courage. The idea of armed self-defense as a community policy was still new and a little intimidating to them; but it also made them think. More important, it created a feeling of solidarity. When we saw how Black citizens reacted to our movement, we were greatly encouraged. Despite the ever-present danger of retaliation, the risks were more than worth it. At that time, however, our activities were confined to a small area, and we wanted Black people throughout the country to know the Oakland story.[7]

The Police-alert Patrols were a hit with Black Oaklanders and undoubtedly led to increased membership in the Party. Yet this was just one program out of many that the organization established.

By 1968 the Seattle chapter had instituted its Free Breakfast for Children Program, where Panthers gathered food (often from supportive neighborhood merchants), assembled the necessary personnel, and cooked breakfasts for neighborhood kids. The average breakfast, though nothing fancy, filled the belly and was far more than most could find at home. It consisted of fried eggs, toast, a few slips of bacon, and grits. Oftentimes, community members would volunteer to help with these efforts. Due to its popularity in the community and strong support by the Party, demonstrated by an order issued by Chairman Seale, every chapter or branch had a breakfast program by 1969.

The Free Breakfast for Children Program was, by far, the most popular of all the Party programs. It also served as a unique opportunity for the secular BPP and the Black church to establish a working relationship since most breakfast programs were situated within neighborhood churches and staffed by Panther men and women. Father Earl Neil, a Black priest assigned to Oakland's St. Augustine Episcopal Church, was an early and vocal supporter of the Black Panther Party and made some interesting comparisons between the Party and the traditional church:

> Black preachers have got to stop preaching about a kingdom in the hereafter which is a "land flowing with milk and honey" ... we must deal with concrete conditions and survival in this life! The Black Panther Party ... has merely put into operation the survival program that the Church should have been doing anyway. The efforts of the Black Panther Party are consistent with what God wants ...[8]

The Breakfast Programs had other less obvious yet equally beneficial effects. Getting up early to serve neighborhood kids and spending some time with them before they were bundled up for school gave many Panthers a real example of what we were working for—our people's future. Most Panthers, fresh out of high school, didn't have children and thought of them, if at all, abstractly. The program, filled five days a week with smiling, sniffling young boys and girls, lifted our hearts at the beginning of the day, steeling us to hit the streets to sell *The Black Panther* or enabling us to go to other community programs with a bounce in our steps. One may not spend time around children and not be lightened by the experience.

As the Breakfast program succeeded so did the Party, and its popularity fueled our growth across the country. Along with the growth of the Party came an increase in the number of community programs undertaken by the Party. By 1971, the Party had embarked on ten distinctive community programs, described by Newton as survival programs. What did he mean by this term?

> We called them survival programs pending revolution. They were designed to help the people survive until their consciousness is raised, which is only the first step in the revolution to produce a new America.... During a flood the raft is a life-saving device, but it is only a means of getting to higher ground. So, too, with survival programs, which are emergency services. In themselves they do not change social conditions, but they are life-saving vehicles until conditions change.[9]

Among these programs were the Intercommunal News Service (1967); the Petition Drive for Community Control of Cops (1968); Liberation Schools, later called Intercommunal Youth Institutes, (1969); People's Free Medical Research Health Clinic (1969); Free Clothing Program (1970); Free Busing to Prisons Program (1970); Seniors Against Fearful Environment (SAFE) Program (1971); Sickle Cell Anemia Research Foundation (1971); and Free Housing Cooperative Program (1971).

In later years, the Party would initiate other programs including Free Shoe Programs, Free Ambulance Services, Free Food Programs, and Home Maintenance Programs.

While clearly every branch of the Party didn't offer all of these programs, most did operate the basics: a free breakfast program, a clinic, and a free clothing program. The bigger chapters, such as New York, Chicago, and Los Angeles, tended to provide the widest range of community services, while smaller branches tended to concentrate on the most popular programs.

While these programs were definitely political, they were conceived of as instruments to promote the political development and radicalization of the people, Newton understood that they had practical applications as well: serving human needs. As one who grew up in the ghetto, Newton understood the very real poverty and subsistence issues affecting many in the community:

> The masses of Black people have always been deeply entrenched and involved in the basic necessities of life. They have not had time to abstract their situation. Abstractions come only with leisure. The people have not had the luxury of leisure. Therefore, the people have been very aware of the true definition of politics: politics are merely the desire of individuals and groups to satisfy first, their basic needs—food, shelter and clothing, and security for themselves and their loved ones.[10]

In Kansas City, Missouri, the Black Panther Party opened its Free Community Clinic and named it for the slain Bobby Hutton, the Party's first martyr, killed by Oakland cops as he surrendered with Eldridge Cleaver on April 6, 1968. BPP affiliates in Brooklyn, Harlem, Boston, Cleveland, Philadelphia, Seattle, Chicago, and Rockford, Illinois, followed suit. Members of the Health Ministries received rudimentary health care and first aid training in order to staff the clinics, but professional help was necessary also. In many cities, community-minded physicians were found who opened up their offices in our clinics, donating time and services to the most depressed communities. Dr. Tolbert Small, for example, contributed his time and efforts to the Oakland clinic.[11] In Philadelphia, a kind, thoughtful, and gentle man named Dr. Vaslavek staffed the clinic.

For most Panthers, our lives in the Party were dedicated to community service. That meant long, sustained work to keep our community programs running, but it also meant battling the State when it came at us with paramilitary attacks, unjust arrests, and, perhaps most often, legal battles in which the State attempted to utilize its judiciary machinery to destroy or disrupt Party organizing efforts.

Sometimes, however, community service meant trying to push the revolutionary struggle further, to create beachheads of focused communal resistance, to create a climate conducive to change. One of those attempts was the Revolutionary People's Constitutional Convention.

## An Attempt at Freedom in Philadelphia

In the American myth of nation-building, Philadelphia looms large as the birthplace, or cradle, of liberty. The icons of the Liberty Bell, the Constitution, and various places of residence of prominent American revolutionary figures provide a lucrative tourism industry and also serve as a touchstone for many Americans when they think of American colonial history.

When leading Party members began organizing and agitating for the Revolutionary People's Constitutional Convention (RPCC) to be held in Philadelphia, it was, in a sense, a very real, conscious attempt to subvert the history of the colonials, by creating a new historical icon: a constitution in which all ignored segments of the American polity could be heard, and be represented. A way of developing a revolutionary superstructure that would be the groundwork of a new society.

It was not envisioned as a BPP project, per se, but as an effort of people from various movements on the so-called left, who would meet and contribute to the building of this infrastructure, to help bring both a constitution and a resistant entity into existence. Contacts were made to the various student groups, the socialist organizations, women's groups, Native groups, and gay and lesbian groups to come together to contribute to this framework. The Party wanted to initiate a process to draft "a constitution that serves the people, not the ruling class."[12]

The convention was set for September 1970, but initial approval from Temple University to host it was rescinded after Philadelphia's police pressured them. Finally, a tall, slim-faced, bespectacled priest whose diocese covered North Philadelphia would agree to the convention and allow his manorial buildings to be used for the event.

I met with Rev. Paul Washington, and he could not have been more gracious, nor more supportive. He calmly explained that his buildings had been used by the Black Power Conference back in 1966, when radicals and nationalists from throughout the country had gathered to hash out movement objectives. He didn't see how this could be much different.

Not content with forcing a scramble for a new venue, the police, as armed agents of the ruling class, went out of their way to sabotage the event by raiding three local Panther offices less than a week before the convention was to begin. This was classic Frank Rizzo. But the bombastic Philadelphia police commissioner, an acolyte of the sinister J. Edgar Hoover, had badly miscalculated. His troops raided local offices and busted top-level and rank-and-file Panthers all around the city, blaming them for the shooting of a cop several nights before. Within hours, not only were all of them out of jail, but the arrests, done in traditional Rizzo overkill with cops stripping people, only served to fire up people and make them more, not less, supportive of the Party.

On September 4, 1970, the convention went off without a hitch, with at least six thousand participants (far more than in 1787!) from all across the country. As Rev. Washington recalled:

> On September 4, registration for the convention began at the Church of the Advocate. Everyone who lined up to register was frisked by members of the Black Panthers—a strange experience for some, who had never before been searched for weapons on their way into a church building. The search did have the effect of establishing who was responsible for law and order at this event—the Panthers, not the police. The weekend was not only peaceful, but extraordinarily so. The streets of North

Philadelphia seemed for once to belong to the people of North Philadelphia. It was Huey Newton's and not Frank Rizzo's time to be center stage.[13]

It was, truth be told, a remarkable time to be a Panther, for the outpouring from the dozens of communities who attended and supported the convention seemed to suggest that the hour of revolutionary unity and promise had come. While thousands attended these plenary (or planning) sessions at the church, and the various meetings held elsewhere on planning and policy in furtherance of the new Constitution, thousands of other well-wishers gathered outside, on the streets, Black, white, Latinx,[14] some merely gawkers, but most overtly supportive.

While various workshops hammered out the language and platform planks, the high point would be the appearance of Huey P. Newton, the revered Minister of Defense, newly freed from prison after the May 1970 reversal of his manslaughter conviction. While most Panthers would never admit it, many of us were nervous. The ever-present threat of cops attacking or even the underlying threat of being in Rizzo's Philly wasn't the source of the nervousness.

The source was Huey.

While many of us had never met him and certainly had never sat down and talked with him, all of us had seen the grainy, black-and-white films produced by Newsreel, a radical youth film collective. We were singularly surprised to actually hear the voice of the Minister of Defense—high, nasal, twangy with a twist of California-country.

Huey, whom we all would have died for in a heartbeat, was not a good public speaker. If you loved him, or revered his courage and sacrifice, it didn't matter. But this was not a Black Panther convention; it was peopled by folks from across the country, from all walks of life.

The time came for Huey to take the platform; a phalanx of Panthers swooped to the stage, in protective position up front.

Huey, short, muscular, his Afro picked to perfection, wearing a resplendent soft black leather jacket, strolled to the lectern, and a swell of applause hit the room, a vast auditorium that the Party had successfully negotiated from Temple. There was great applause, ovations, huzzahs, and hosannas … and then Huey spoke:

> Friends and comrades throughout the United States and throughout the world, we gather here in peace and friendship to claim our inalienable rights, to claim the rights bestowed us by an unbroken train of abuses and usurpations, and to perform the duty which is thus required of us. Our sufferance has been long and patient, our prudence has stayed this final hour, but our human dignity and strength require that we still the voice of prudence with the cries of our sufferance. Thus we gather in the spirit of revolutionary love and friendship for all oppressed people of the world, regardless of their race or of the race and doctrine of their oppressors.
>
> The United States of America was born at a time when the nation covered relatively little land, a narrow strip of political divisions of the Eastern seaboard. The United States of America was born at a time when the population was small and fairly homogenous both racially and culturally. Thus, the people called Americans were a different people in a different place. Furthermore, they had a different economic system….
>
> The sacredness of man and of the human spirit require that human dignity and integrity ought to be always respected by every other man. We will settle for nothing less, for at this point in history anything less is but a living death. *We will be free,* and we are here to ordain a new constitution, which will ensure our freedom by enshrining the dignity of the human spirit.[15]

There was applause, sometimes spirited applause, but it was applause for the *presence* of Huey P. Newton, not his ideas. Huey was not fooled by the subtle difference:

> As I talked, it seemed to me that the people were not really listening, or even interested in what I had to say.
>
> Almost every sentence was greeted by loud applause, but the audience was more concerned with phrasemongering than with ideological development. I am not a good public speaker—I tend to lecture and teach in a rather dull fashion—but

the people were not responding to my ideas, only to my image, and although I was very excited by all the energy and enthusiasm I saw there, I was also disturbed by the lack of serious analytical thought.[16]

Huey, unfortunately, wasn't the only one "disturbed."

Captain Reggie was perhaps a bit more laconic, but his observation was apt. Huey, he reasoned, "just lost people."[17]

Huey, brilliant, brave, and bold as he was, didn't understand that politics is often "phrasemongering" and that those who can successfully master that skill can also successfully mobilize powerful social forces.

He did not.

He could not … and a powerful moment was lost.

David Hilliard and many other Party members from the period remember the Revolutionary People's Constitutional Convention as an abject failure. The RPCC, for all intents and purposes, dissolved, and a secondary, working session, planned for Washington several months later, never really took off. They also look to Huey's poor performance at the Philadelphia plenary session as a nadir of the Party's attempt to institutionalize a truly revolutionary movement in the US.

Time may mellow that assessment somewhat.

The Party did indeed attempt something massive and, perhaps with the exception of John Brown's Chatham Convention in Canada, something almost unprecedented. It tried to erect a revolutionary institution that would formalize a truly multicultural, multiclass, multigendered revolution against the repressive status quo. While the Party dared greatly, it was not, in truth, a failure of the Party so much as it was a failure of the movement entire.

Were millions of white youth, no matter what they claimed their political or ideological persuasions, really ready to embark on a revolution, one that did not prize whiteness?

Were millions of feminists ready to join in working coalition with men and women of color, to destroy white supremacy as a binding stitch for the White Nationalist (*Herrenvolk*) Republic?

Were millions of mostly white gays and lesbians willing to join a political entity where, though represented, they were not in the ascendancy?

It is indeed possible that the Black Panther Party, which saw itself as profoundly nonracist, could not appreciate the deep levels of white supremacy that lay subsumed within much of the white left. They opposed the war in Vietnam—yes; they opposed the excesses of the Nixon/Mitchell regime—yes; they may have felt an ideological affinity with the Civil Rights movement—yes; but *were they ready to do all that was necessary to break asunder from their Mother Country—White America?*

While Huey's speech was lackluster, dry, academic even, he and other Panthers did articulate a new constitutional arrangement that transformed power relations in a new nation. They did that.

Moreover, if the will was present in the hearts and souls of those thousands assembled to truly support the vision, then it would not have been abandoned to the dust of history. It would not be hidden, as was the Chatham Convention, to the realm of patient scholarship, instead of the realm of our dreams.

What was not lacking in that small, sweaty room in Philadelphia in 1787, where men gathered to draft the US constitution, windows barred from the angry throng outside, was will.

Again in Philadelphia, nearly 200 years later, with thousands inside, thousands outside, with throngs praising their presence and their mission, a new constitution did not emerge. It is not logical to solely blame those who brought them together. Nor is it fair.

It may be argued that the Black Panther Party, to the extent that it was possible, performed in the role of a shadow state—with its Ministries, its uniformed personnel, its soldiers, and its persistently independent voice that spoke in sharp opposition to that of the US government.[18] Professor Nikhil P. Singh has argued that the Party's actions, indeed, its very existence, posited an alternative that called into question the very existence, or authority, of the US nation-state. In Singh's analysis:

> The Panthers, then, were a threat to the state not simply because they were violent but because they abused the state's own reality principle, including its monopoly on the legitimate use of violence. Patrolling the police armed with guns and law books was in this sense a form of mimicry in which the Panthers undermined the very notion of policing itself by performing, and in effect deforming, it themselves. Here, we must grasp the fact that the police themselves are among the most important of the state's "actors." The continued, repeated performance of the police function is crucial to the institution of the everyday fantasy of being subject to a national, social state. By misrecognizing the status of policing as it operated within Black communities, the Panthers effectively nullified this fantasy and substituted a radical alternative. By policing the police, in other words, the Panthers signaled something far more dangerous than is generally acknowledged: the eruption of a nonstate identity into the everyday life of the state. That such a small and relatively poorly equipped band of urban Black youth could demand so much attention from federal and local police only attests to the tenuousness of the state itself and the degree to which it depends upon controlling and even silencing those who would take its name in vain.[19]

If actions that marked the Party's daily life in forty-four communities across the nation presented such a challenge, what of the proposed Revolutionary People's Constitutional Convention, which by its very existence, pointed to the defective nature of the original convention of 1787, with its coterie of racists, slave owners, misogynists, and wealthy landowners?

Which constitutional convention was, indeed, far more representative of the masses of people in America? Which was more racially mixed? Which more culturally mixed? Which more reflected the average guy or gal in the cities or towns across America?

Researcher Jerry Fresia, in his remarkable *Toward an American Revolution,* paints a picture of the Constitutional Convention of 1787 as something far removed from the people. This was an assembly of opulence, of means, and of men who, in fact, deeply trembled at the thought of the mob—the many, unhappy poor who populated the colonies. It was not for naught that Gouverneur Morris, a coauthor of the Constitution and Pennsylvania delegate, noted, "I see and see with fear and trembling, that if the disputes with Britain continue, *we shall be under the domination of a riotous mob*. It is in the interest of all men therefore, to seek reunion with the parent state."[20] Fresia's notes on the convention are indeed telling:

> The series of meetings that led to the convention were engineered by men who did not like the Articles. They were part of an elite consensus that was forming in reaction to the many rebellions (black and white) and democratic tendencies among excluded people and it was their private meetings that led to the initiative for the Constitutional Convention. At every turn, the popular voice was absent, and elites were increasingly empowered. *No special popular elections were held to select delegates.* Instead, delegates to the Convention were selected by the state legislatures, who were already once removed from the limited electorate. Moreover, the Constitutional Convention had been called to *amend the Articles only and any proposed changes had to be approved by all the states before they were adopted.* But the Framers defied these legal stipulations, abandoned their authorization to amend the Articles only, designed an entirely new centralized national government, and inserted in the Constitution that it should go into effect when ratified by *only nine states.* J. W. Burgess has stated that what the Framers "actually did, stripped of all fiction and verbiage, was to assume constitutional powers, ordain a constitution of government and liberty and demand a *plebiscite* thereon over the heads of all existing legally organized powers. Had Julius or Napoleon committed these acts, they would have been pronounced *coup d'etat.*"[21]

In historical retrospect, which convention was more representative of the people of the nation?

The Black Panther Party, at this "Convention from the Bottom," had hundreds of committed activists, from a variety of movements, sitting down and convening workshops, where a wealth of ideas was discussed. Various workshops developed reports. According to the Party:

Taken as a whole, these reports provided the basis for one of the most progressive Constitutions in the history of human-kind. All the people would control the means of production and social institutions. Black and third world people were guaranteed proportional representation in the administration of these institutions, as were women. The right of national self-determination was guaranteed to all oppressed minorities. Sexual self-determination for women and homosexuals was affirmed. A standing army is to be replaced by a people's militia, and the Constitution is to include an international bill of rights prohibiting U.S. aggression and interference in the internal affairs of other nations.... The present racist legal system would be replaced by a system of people's courts where one would be tried by a jury of one's peers. Jails would be replaced by community rehabilitation programs.... Adequate housing, health care, and day care would be considered Constitutional Rights, not priviliges."[22]

This was the fruit of the Party's call for a convention of the many, not the few.

It reflected the Party's understanding (perhaps influenced by the perceptions of its California founders, who lived in small Black communities, relative to their eastern, or southern kin) that we all live together in this vast land, and, as such, none of us could do all that was necessary alone.

The Revolutionary People's Constitutional Convention manifested a distinct tendency within the BPP that distinguished it from its contemporaries, and left it, especially within nationalist circles, subject to some criticism. The very framework of the RPCC conflicted with the norm of the more insular nationalist groups of the era. This meant that although the Black Panther Party did not have non-Blacks in its ranks, it did think about and act upon the idea that coalitions across lines of race and ethnicity could prove effective in reaching broader segments of the US and global polity.

## Internationalism = "Intercommunalism"

In the beginning, the Black Panther Party for Self-Defense was, for want of a better term, a Malcolmist party. As early as 1967, under seven months into the Party's existence, Newton would speak of the BPP as "the heirs of Malcolm."[23] The influence of Malcolm X permeated early BPP thought, rhetoric, and self-perception. In this formative period, the BPP used language and themes that did not significantly differentiate it from other Black nationalist groups of the period, such as the Revolutionary Action Movement and the Black Liberators (of St. Louis, Missouri). Such groups drew their inspiration from Malcolm X, and his speeches, tapes, and articles were sources of ideological positions and purity.

This meant, in practical terms, that whites were anathema to any organizational or political work. In his earliest incarnation, Malcolm, as a young NOI minister, referred to whites as devils, and many nationalists held similar views, even if they did not embrace his pre-*hajj* Muslim ideas.

Because Newton read widely in the years prior to the development of the Party, he did not limit himself to Malcolm as an inspiration, or as source material, for either his or the Party's ideology. He was a perceptive reader. He was original in his thinking. He read, not to consume the quantity of words as they rushed across the page, but to gather, question, challenge, and deconstruct ideas. He read, and was influenced by, writings on the Algerian, Kenyan, Russian, Chinese, and Cuban revolutions. These studies influenced him, as did spiritual and philosophical texts, like works on Buddhism and by the German philosopher Friedrich Nietzsche. Newton's intellectual development, and as a direct correlate, the Party's intellectual ideas came from a range of sources, and the Party was therefore open to a variety of influences.

Because Huey was a preacher's kid, he developed early on a skepticism toward religious dogma, and, as he quite easily questioned the existence of a god, he could not abide the existence of a devil. Whites were not gods, nor were they devils, he reasoned. They were but human beings who, because of the mind-bending toxin of racism, often behaved badly when it came to people of color. Therefore, the enemy is racism, the toxin, not whites, who were in*toxic*ated.

It is largely under Newton's influence that the Party emerged as an antiracist group and opened the door to interactions with those whites who would not try to undermine the Party's platform. From this, a working alliance with the largely California-based Peace and Freedom Party (P&F Party) emerged. This coalition would launch the Black Panther Party deeply into the consciousness of many Californians, through the posters and campaigns of the P&F Party, which ran various Black Panther Party members for state and regional offices. Perhaps the most renowned was the candidacy of Eldridge Cleaver for president of the United States in 1968 (he polled some 36,000 votes in perhaps half a dozen states). Cleaver, a brilliant orator, could rock a crowd with his quick wit and colorful language. One of his albums, *Soul on Wax,* was a big seller in Panther offices, and his speeches would play (or blare through neighborhood loudspeakers) for hours throughout the day. On the record, he moved a group of nuns to chant "Fuck Reagan."

Yet for the BPP internationalism didn't just mean Black/white interactions; it meant working with Chicanxs, Puerto Ricans, Native Americans, Asian Americans, and others. If the revolution were to be successful, it needed the participation of all in the creation of a new society.

This was the essence of Newton's idea of intercommunalism. He reasoned that interactions across communities were the primary connections for building a new society and that, in an age of empire, nations could no longer exist and, therefore, neither could true internationalism. He coined the term intercommunalism to describe this new relationship.[24] As Newton explained it:

> We found that because everything is in a constant state of transformation, because of the development of technology, because of the development of the mass media, because of the firepower of imperialism, *because of the fact that the United States is*

*no longer a nation, but an empire,* nations could not exist, for they did not have the criteria for nationhood.[25]

Nations, thought Newton, were far more than flags, embassies, or even standing armies. If the imperialists could penetrate a given nation-state's economy, culture, airwaves, and, indeed, consciousness with relative impunity and impose its will, that imposition is imperial. The recipient, while certainly a geographical, ethnic, linguistic, and perhaps cultural community, is not a nation in the classical sense. It is the shell of a nation, at best.

Thus, the Black Panther Party inaugurated the Black revolutionary political practice of working closely with disparate and diverse ethnic and racial groupings, and it influenced the development of similar political formations in other non-Black communities.

For Black Americans, however, Newton diverged from his colleagues in the nationalist community further when he split from their almost iconic fascination with ancient Africa. Again, using an intercommunal analysis, Newton would explain:

> The economic power of the U.S. rulers is so great that there is no denying its effect upon the rest of the world. This economic power is manifested in the concentration of production capabilities and raw materials in the hands of American forces. What the United States cannot obtain and develop, it can synthesize in its technological laboratories.

> Looking further at the situation, let us consider black Americans. Tied only historically to Africa, they can lay no real claim to territory in the U.S. or Africa. Black Americans have only the cultural and social customs that have evolved from centuries of oppression. In other words, U.S. blacks form not a subjugated colony but an oppressed community inside the larger boundaries. What, then, do the words "black nationalism" concretely mean to the U.S. black? Not forming anything resembling a nation presently, shall U.S. blacks somehow seize (or possibly be "given") U.S. land and expect to claim sovereignty as a nation? In the face of the existent power of the United States over the entire world, such a nation could only be a fantasy that could lead to the extinction of a race.

What does "Pan-Africanism" mean to the black African who did not live Nkrumah's dream, but lives in the real nightmare of U.S. economic/military might? For what does a national flag actually mean when Gulf Oil is in control? Or if Gulf Oil is expelled, what happens to the "nation" that cannot supply for its own needs?

The oppressed people of the world face a serious dilemma: the Chinese people are threatened by the American Empire, just as blacks globally and people in South America are similarly threatened. Even Europe bends to the weight of the United States, yielding theoretical, national sovereignty.[26]

Huey and the Party founded by him were iconoclastic. Both tried to demolish old ideas and notions that dwelt deep in consciousness. To say that both were controversial is an understatement. They were both projected as so far from the so-called mainstream as to be aberrant. Newton, who loved the struggle for ideas, would perhaps relish the claim, but would equally challenge the definition of mainstream as a creation of upper class, bourgeois culture.

To Newton what was perhaps an aberration was the set of social relations handed down to us, for they were based not on rationality or humanity, but on violent repression and malevolent conditioning, like racism, classism, and chauvinism.

Yet ideas do not change simply because some social actors come up with better, or even more logical, ways of looking at the world. It can scarcely be argued that freedom was not better than bondage, yet abolitionists had to fight for over a century, and a war divided the nation, before this idea prevailed.

Similarly, it can be said that the notion of women's equality seems so obvious to us now. However, it took 200 years and tortuous, dangerous, much-damned organizing for that idea to prevail in the nation's political psyche. These ideas prevailed because people fought for them, and did so against terrible odds.

In short, it took deeply committed people, organized into movements, to force these changes.

The same could be said about some of the ideas promoted by the Black Panther Party decades ago. While practiced in that time and place, these ideas have not found purchase in the American political economy. Moreover, a changing political environment has made many of those ideas, such as socialism and the working alliances of people across race, ethnicity, and gender, not as popular today. We live in an era when reactionary nationalism seems to prevail, when the very notion of white (or other) Americans interacting in Black affairs seems like anathema. The relatively new, New Black Panther Party, formed by people raised in the Nation of Islam, seems to reflect this shift.

There are other reasons why this is so; principally among them is a history that breeds deep distrust between African Americans and European Americans.

## Downside of "Intercommunalism"

The Black Panther Party, as perhaps the most influential exemplar of the Black revolutionary ethic of the latter twentieth century, had serious barriers to its expansion and the continued development of its ideas. It could analyze ideas and promote the seemingly correct ideological solutions to social conflicts and crises. Yet it had to contend with the deep and, perhaps, at the time, unarticulated white nationalism that pervaded consciousness during the period.

Some social scientists contend that this tendency is deep within American consciousness and colors all it perceives. One scholar has likened America's addiction to whiteness as a way of thinking closely akin to that of South African apartheid (which in turn drew many formative lessons from the US). Scholar George Fredrickson has described both the United States and South Africa as *Herrenvolk* states:

> More than the other multi-racial societies resulting from the "expansion of Europe" that took place between the sixteenth century and the twentieth, South Africa and the United States (most obviously the southern United States during the era of slavery and segregation) have manifested over long periods of time a tendency to push the principle of differentiation by race

to its logical outcome—a kind of *Herrenvolk* society in which people of color, however numerous or acculturated they may be, are treated as permanent aliens or outsiders.[27]

Fredrickson drives the historical analogies further to reveal the roots of both societies in racial conflict and bitter, often archviolence:

> The basis for our first comparison, therefore, is the common fact of a long and often violent struggle for territorial supremacy between white invaders and indigenous peoples. Starting from the small coastal settlements of the seventeenth century, the whites penetrated into the interior of North America and southern Africa; by the end of the nineteenth century they had successfully expropriated most of the land for their own use by extinguishing the communal title into private property within a capitalistic economy. The indigenes were left with a collective ownership of only a small fraction of their former domain in the form of special reserves. Divesting the original inhabitants of their land was essential to the material success of these settler societies.[28]

What Fredrickson argues is that the very notion of American nationhood is interlaced with the notion of whiteness, as it is in South Africa. It will take generations of discrete experiences to disabuse these notions. (Indeed, in the American historical experience, not even a ruinous civil war, where some 600,000 people perished, successfully transformed the American mind, as the post-Reconstruction-era pogroms and lynchings of Blacks proved.)

The upshot of this *Herrenvolk* history is that white radicals of the 1960s were ill equipped to respond to the challenges of a Black revolutionary formation that claimed primacy of the revolutionary movement. In essence, they could not truly follow Black leaders.

Newton later recognized another reason for the failure of Black Panther efforts of the period; the radicals led no one:

> Our hook-up with White radicals did not give us access to the White community because they did not guide the White community. The Black community did not relate to them, so we were left in a twilight zone where we could not enter the Black

community with any real political education programs; yet we were not doing anything to mobilize Whites.[29]

These are concrete reasons why racial politics remain atomized in the dawn of the twenty-first century. People live, think, struggle, and die in different worlds, where their experiences, not to mention consciousness, rarely, if ever, mingle.

We live in a world that Huey saw decades ago, when he advanced his notion of "intercommunalism" amid the ridicule and derision of his contemporaries. He foresaw an era of "reactionary intercommunalism" when the US Empire strode the world largely unhindered.

The key to this US imperial expansion, Newton wrote in 1972, the year of Nixon's remarkable Beijing visit, would be the capitulation of the Soviet Union, an event that would have far-reaching impact:

> Russia's first mistake came in the form of an incorrect analysis: that socialism could co-exist peacefully with capitalist nations. It was a blow to the communities of the whole world that led directly to the crippling of the people's ability to oppose capitalist/imperialist aggression and aggression's character. Remember, the capitalists claim that as soon as you agree to accept their trade and fall under their economic ideology, then they will agree to have peaceful co-existence.

> The Russians allowed this to happen through naiveté or treachery. Regardless of how this came about, they damaged the ability of the Third World to resist. They could have given the Third World every technique available to them long ago. With the high quality of Soviet development at a time when the United States was less advanced than it is today, the Russians could have built up the necessary force to oppose imperialism. Now, all … they can do is whimper like whipped dogs and talk about peaceful co-existence so that they will not be destroyed. This presents the world with the hard fact that the United States is the only state power in the world. Russia has become, like all other nations, no more than a satellite of the United States. American rulers do not care about how much Russians say they are the Soviets, as long as Ford can build its motor company in their territory.[30]

According to Newton's analysis, both Vietnam and Russia amounted to "the overexpansion of capitalism, which turned into imperialism and then into an empire with its reactionary intercommunalism."[31] In essence, he concluded, it meant "Americans themselves enjoying a higher quality of life than everybody else, at the expense of everybody else."[32]

The world that he foresaw is now upon us.

## Panther Loose on the Coast

For white Americans, Philadelphia represents liberty's cradle; for Panthers, it was Oakland.

It was the homeland, the birthplace of the Black Panther Party. For a fifteen-year-old from Philly, it was almost like going to heaven:

*Although National Headquarters was in the tony town of Berkeley, the gritty port city of Oakland was the real shebang. That was where Huey grew up, it was where the Party came into being, and where most of the dirtiest fighting took place in the formative experiences of the organization.*

*I longed to go there and, one day, was sent there to sell some papers. I was thrilled.*

*When I got to West Oakland, I was struck by several things: first, the ordinariness of it; second, I was again amazed at what folks considered ghetto, and how that term is often relative. Their houses, semi-detached and surrounded by green carpets of grass, closely resembled the houses in Philadelphia's West Oak Lane neighborhoods, which were seen by the ghetto residents of Philly as good living. Compared to the fine homes in the nearby hills, they were, of course, of lesser quality. Third, I was struck by the quiet level of hostility I sensed when I tried to sell the newspaper around the community. I had sold papers in Philadelphia, in the Bronx, in Queens, and in Harlem, yet this was the first time I sensed such resistance. Nobody verbalized anything, but it was written on too many street faces to ignore. Why? I never learned why, but in retrospect, one wonders, was this an early reaction to an emergent "black ops" phase of the Party underground? No one spoke about it, but there was something there, quiet, yet discernible.*

*However unremarkable it seemed to me, it reminded me that, relatively speaking, ghettos still possess a certain sameness about them; there is an unmistakable psychic aura of funk about them.*

*It was indeed in Oakland that I received my introduction to the local constabulary; but it was not in the green ghetto of West Oakland.*

*As the next week's issue of* The Black Panther *had been laid out and was en route to the printers, a Panther sister named Sheila and I were sent out to hawk papers. We opted to hit downtown Oakland. She took one side and I took another. When I crossed the street, I did so in the middle of the block instead of at the crosswalk, where a lonely light stood. I didn't hesitate to scoot across the street, as I had all my life in Philly if the traffic were light.*

*No sooner had I crossed when a cop car rolled up. Two dark-uniformed cops exited the sedan and explained that I had violated an Alameda County ordinance against jaywalking.*

*Jaywalking?! I was dumbfounded. I was under arrest for jaywalking. Moments later so was Sheila because she had crossed after the cops pulled up to see what was going on.*

*I had yearned to see Oakland, I thought, now I'm gonna meet the most vicious, racist pigs in America. I expected to get whipped unconscious by these creeps in black uniforms.*

*The cops handcuffed me and Sheila, as I braced for a pummeling or a rain of racist insults. The cops spoke with such politeness that I was indeed shocked. "Sir," this; "Sir," that; "Ma'am," this; "Ma'am," that; I had never heard cops talk this way, either in Philadelphia, or in the Bronx. "Watch your head, sir," as I was placed in the vehicle, cuffed.*

*I looked at Sheila, and I just knew that when we got to the station, or precinct, or whatever they called it out here, the blackjacks, the kicks, the punches would rain like water.*

*To my utter surprise, they never came.*

*Our newspapers were seized, and, as we were juveniles, we were taken to the Alameda County Juvenile Hall.*

*It was then that the real meaning of what had happened dawned on me. What does it matter how polite the cops are when they lock you up and put you in jail—for jaywalking!?*

*If we were not selling copies of* The Black Panther, *would this have happened?*

*I don't think so. They were beating us, softly.*

*We were placed in small rooms; while not classic, barred cells, they were clearly rooms constructed for restraint. We signaled to each other that we would agitate for a phone call, and when we were able, she called her mother who lived in Berkeley and could come to pick her up.*

*Sheila's mom appeared shortly thereafter, a small, bespectacled white lady (it was a day of shocks!), who nervously hustled her baby out of the clink. Sheila looked guilty as she left, as if she didn't want to leave her Panther brother behind. But there was little choice. She bravely curled her fingers into a Black Power salute and raised it to her comrade.*

*I smiled and returned it.*

*I would miss her, but I was glad to see her escape the pig's clutches.*

*Sheila went home.*

*I went to jail.*

*It was a juvenile jail (as I was under twenty-one), but it was a jail nonetheless.*

*I was remanded to the juvenile authority, because, unlike Sheila, I was some 3,000 miles away from home. There was no way my mom would, or even could, come pick me up.*

*For starters, she hadn't the slightest idea where I was.*

*While I called home occasionally, and even came by the house as often as I could, I lived with the Party and was cautious about breaking security by letting her know my every move. It would only worry her, which I didn't want to do unnecessarily.*

*I loved her like crazy.*

*But I also loved life in the Party.*

*As Sheila left, and I went through the processing stage, I was placed in a single-cell-like enclosure.*

*I thought about all the other Panthers in cells all across the nation, Bobby Seale and Ericka Huggins, facing death in New Haven; the Panther 21 facing centuries in New York's gulags; the Panthers who were recently busted in a southern California shoot-out at the LA chapter; brothers and sisters like me; and thoughts of them warmed me like a campfire near the soul.*

*They were facing real drama! Here I was, for jaywalking! I had nothin' to holler about. I stretched out on the cool, plastic-covered mattress and slept.*

*I had just lain down and shut my eyes, it seemed, when I heard the sounds of the door being opened. I forced myself awake and stood up, feeling that an attack could come at any moment.*

*A big dude appeared at the door and began barking orders at me. I looked at him like he was speaking Korean. The only word I understood was "strip," and I certainly wasn't going to do that. I had heard about prison rape.*

*"Strip," he said again, to which I again replied, "No!"*

*He returned five minutes later and seemed genuinely surprised that I hadn't removed a single stitch of clothing. "Boy, didn't I tell you to strip?" he thundered.*

*"Man, I ain't doin' a damn thing! We gon' fight!" I answered.*

*"Well, you ain't gettin' no shower then!" he announced angrily and slammed the door shut.*

*Shower? What was this dude talkin' about? It never dawned on me that he worked there. He wore regular clothes. I just thought he was a guy.*

*Several days later, I was taken to the counselor's office at the center, and a man began asking questions about who I was, why wasn't I in school, and so forth. I explained to him that I was working for the Black Panther Party.*

*At one point he said, "Young man, don't you know that we can keep you here until you're twenty-one years old?"*

*I looked him in the eye and said, "So what? When I get out, there'll still be a Black Panther Party!"*

*He shook his head.*

*Moments later, he was dialing the phone to my mother's house in Philadelphia, asked to verify her name, and passed the phone over to me.*

*"Mama?"*

*"Wes—Is that you?"*

*"Yes, Mama—"*

*"Boy—What did I hear this man sayin'—? Where are you?"*

*"I'm in Alameda County, Califor—"*

*"Cali—what? Boy, what are you doin'—? You better carry yho narrow behind—Boy! What in the Sam Hill—Cali-What?!?!?!"*

*"Mama—mama—I'm workin' out here ona paper, for the Party— you know—"*

*"Boy—How long you been out California?"*

*"Yeah, Mom—I'm OK—"*

*"OK?—Didn't I just hear this man say you was callin' from some kinda jail—?"*

*"Mama—Mama—I'm in here for jaywalkin'—jaywalkin'! Out here they real strict about traffic laws ... I just crossed the street, and—"*

*"'Crossed the street?'—Boy, you done crossed the whole country!—Wes——mph! Boy, if you don't get yho bony behind back here—"*

*"Mama—Mama! I can't, Mom—I can't—I'm doin' important work, Mom."*

*"Like gettin' yhoself locked up, boy? How important is that?"*

*"Mama—It's gonna be alright—we got lawyers out here that are real good—This ain't nothin' but harassment—when the last time you heard about somebody gettin' busted for jaywalkin', huh, Mom?"*

*"Boy—umph, umph, umph! Boy you somethin' else, boy—I'm tellin, you, Califor—!—umph, umph, umph! Boy, you are crazy, you know that, donchu?"*

*Her maternal fear was melting to pride that her boy was so aggressively doing something for our people. She was afraid. She was angry. But she was pleased as well. I could hear it in her voice, her high country laugh. She knew that I felt deeply about what I was doing.*

*As I listened to her pride and love override her fear, I thought about the many mothers like her; like Sheila's mother, probably good, church-going (or temple-going) folks who were probably simpatico with the sweet teachings of Rev. Dr. Martin Luther King, Jr., but who, deep down, were proud of the moxie shown by the Panthers. They might not help with the Breakfast Program. But when they read of us, or thought of us, in the private chambers of the heart, the mind, the soul, they admired us. Once I heard that tone in her voice, her deep sense of humor, I knew I was alright. Unlike perhaps thousands of youth throughout this vast state, I wasn't here for robbery or rape, I wasn't here for hurting my people; I wasn't here for "crime." I was here for defending my people. I was here because I was a member of the Black Panther Party.*

*Within a few weeks, I was back out, no worse for wear.*

*I was out of jail and back in the swing of things. I was working on the paper, selling them and editing stuff coming in from all the branches and chapters across the country.*

*My boss, editor Judi Douglass, seemed pleased with my work, and that pleased me. We worked hard to make the paper the best it could be.*

*This young Panther was home.*[33]

The days were long.

The risks were substantial.

The rewards were few.

Yet the freedom was hypnotic. We could think freely, write freely, and act freely in the world.

We knew that we were working for our people's freedom, and we loved it.

It was the one place in the world that it seemed right to be.

## CHAPTER FIVE

# "Huey's Party" Grows

The main function of the party is to awaken the people and to teach them the strategic method of resisting the power structure.
—Huey P. Newton[1]

**UPON REFLECTION, IT** would appear somewhat unlikely that Huey P. Newton would be the prime mover in the formation, development, and construction of a revolutionary group like the Black Panther Party.

An intense, shy, small-framed man, preacher's son, small-time thief, street tough, pretty boy, illiterate, and, years later, Ph.D., and, still later, drug addict, Newton was a man of endless complexity whose character oscillated between the brilliant and the nihilistic.

As a youth, Huey hated to leave his house, because older boys would pick on him and call him names. In a revealing discussion with his former partner and one-time head of the BPP, Elaine Brown, the private Huey emerges as a man consumed with fear:

"A lot of what I am has to do with fear," he said to me out of nowhere one of those first nights I came to see him in Oakland. "And what I understand about fear. I wasn't afraid only in the Soul Breaker. Like you, I've been afraid much of my life."

"You know, niggers on the street don't like 'pretty niggers,'" he continued, making me wonder whether he was speaking about him or me.

"They called me 'pretty' and 'high yellow nigger' and other motherfuckers. The problem with niggers on the street, of course, is that they don't know what to hate for their oppression."[2]

To conquer his profound fear of the streets, Huey sought the counsel of his older brother, Walter, who schooled him with valuable insights into both street and life realities. Walter explained that the guy who seemed like the biggest bully was often the guy with the biggest fear. "He was probably more afraid than you," Walter reasoned.

The older Newton taught the younger how to walk, how to talk, and how to fight. In essence, he taught him to confront and to overcome his fear.

It worked, to a degree, but Huey would confide to Elaine, "I was still scared every day."[3]

He countered that fear by becoming the aggressor:

Every blood on the street was a potential threat, unless I knew he was a friend. After my first fights, though, I recognized that they bled like me. ... By the time I became a teenager, I was challenging the first fool that looked at me wrong, and walking around with an ice pick in a paper bag.[4]

Youngsters on the street were forced to look at the skinny pretty boy differently—as "Crazy Huey."[5]

Those preteen rites of passage sank deep roots in the man, who learned important lessons about how the world worked. These terrifying yet transformative years and core experiences may have taught Huey that things are not always what they seem: bullies are often cowards, fear must be confronted, force yields to force, and if one isn't a friend, fight him.

While Newton graciously credits his friend Bobby Seale with the cofounding and development of the Black Panther Party, it seems self-evident that the intense, driven, acutely brilliant, self-conscious, and mercurial Newton was the motivating force. Seale seems more peripheral in the endeavor.

To state the case quite another way, Huey was the active principle in their partnership. Huey was fire; Bobby was smoke.

It seemed that while Bobby encouraged Huey, Huey inspired Bobby. Bobby may have acted as stable foundation for the fiery youth known as Crazy Huey. But if Huey had not existed, it seems unlikely that the Black Panther Party would have become the revolutionary, hard-edged, aggressive entity that it became, or perhaps even come into existence at all.

One of the first things done was to set forth a program, a statement of objectives for the group. With little variation, the set of objectives would remain in the form written by Newton in the first two weeks of October 1966. There is no question as to who wrote the lion's share of the text, for as Seale relates:

> From the first of October to the fifteenth of October, in the poverty center in North Oakland, Huey and I began to write out a ten-point platform and program of the Black Panther Party. *Huey himself articulated it word for word. All I made were suggestions.*[6]

This short set of ideas would be memorized, recited, and taught by tens of thousands of Party members, across the nation and around the world, for over a decade.

## The Ten-Point Program

The list of ten major objectives was split into two sections, in a form that brought to mind the long printed section of the Nation of Islam's newsweekly, *Muhammad Speaks,* entitled "What We Want—What We Believe." In it we see the thought process and concerns of the twenty-four-year-old Newton, as well as his hoped-for objectives:

October 1966

Black Panther Party
Platform and Program

What We Want

What We Believe

**1. We want freedom. We want power to determine the destiny of our Black Community.**

We believe that black people will not be free until we are able to determine our destiny.

**2. We want full employment for our people.**

We believe that the federal government is responsible and obligated to give every man employment or a guaranteed income. We believe that if the white American businessmen will not give full employment, then the means of production should be taken from the businessmen and placed in the community so that the whole of the community can organize and employ all of its people and give a high standard of living.

**3. We want an end to the robbery by the capitalist\* of our Black Community.** [\*in the original text, the term "white man" was used; it was changed shortly thereafter to "capitalist"]

We believe that the racist government has robbed us and now we are demanding the overdue debt of forty acres and two mules. Forty acres and two mules was promised 100 years ago as restitution for slave labor and mass murder of black people. We will accept the payment in currency which will be distributed to our many communities. The Germans are now aiding the Jews in Israel for the genocide of the Jewish people. The Germans murdered six million Jews. The American racist has taken part in the slaughter of over fifty million black people; therefore, we feel this is a modest demand that we make.

**4. We want decent housing, fit for shelter of human beings.**

We believe that if the white landlords will not give decent housing to our black community, then the housing and the land should be made into cooperatives so that our community, with government aid, can build and make decent housing for its people.

**5. We want education for our people that exposes the true nature of this decadent American society. We want education that teaches us our true history and our role in the present-day society.**

We believe in an educational system that will give to our people a knowledge of self. If a man does not have knowledge of himself and his position in society and the world, then he has little chance to relate to anything else.

**6. We want all black men to be exempt from military service.**

We believe that Black people should not be forced to fight in the military service to defend a racist government that does not protect us. We will not fight and kill other people of color in the world who, like black people, are being victimized by the white racist government of America. We will protect ourselves from the force and violence of the racist police and the racist military, by whatever means necessary.

**7. We want an immediate end to POLICE BRUTALITY and MURDER of black people.**

We believe we can end police brutality in our black community by organizing black self-defense groups that are dedicated to defending our black community from racist police oppression and brutality. The Second Amendment to the Constitution of the United States gives a right to bear arms. We therefore believe that all black people should arm themselves for self-defense.

**8. We want freedom for all black men held in federal, state, county and city prisons and jails.**

We believe that all black people should be released from the many jails and prisons because they have not received a fair and impartial trial.

**9. We want all black people when brought to trial to be tried in court by a jury of their peer group or people from their black communities, as defined by the Constitution of the United States.**

We believe that the courts should follow the United States Constitution so that black people will receive fair trials. The 14th Amendment of the U.S. Constitution gives a man a right to be tried by his peer group. A peer is a person from a similar economic, social, religious, geographical, environmental, historical and racial background. To do this the court will be forced to select a jury from the black community from which the black defendant came. We have been, and are being tried by all-white juries that have no understanding of the "average reasoning man" of the black community.

**10. We want land, bread, housing, education, clothing, justice and peace. And as our major political objective, a United Nations-supervised plebiscite to be held throughout the black colony in which only black colonial subjects will be allowed to participate for the purpose of determining the will of black people as to their national destiny.**

When in the course of human events, it becomes necessary for one people to dissolve the political bands which have connected them with another, and to assume, among the powers of the earth, the separate and equal station to which the laws of nature and nature's God entitle them, a decent respect to the opinions of mankind requires that they should declare the causes which impel them to the separation.

We hold these truths to be self-evident, that all men are created equal; that they are endowed by their Creator with certain unalienable rights; that among these are life, liberty, and the pursuit of happiness. *That, to secure these rights, governments are instituted among men, deriving their just powers from the consent of the governed; that, whenever any form of government becomes destructive of these ends, it is the right of the people to alter or to abolish it, and to institute a new government, laying its foundation on such principles, and organizing its powers in such form, as to them shall seem most likely to effect their safety and happiness.* Prudence, indeed, will dictate that governments long established should not be changed for light and transient causes; and accordingly, all experience hath shown, that mankind are more disposed to suffer, while evils are sufferable, than to right themselves by abolishing the forms to which they are accustomed. *But, when a long train of abuses and usurpations, pursuing invariably the same object, evinces a design to reduce them under absolute despotism, it is their right, it is their duty, to throw off such government, and to provide new guards for their future security.*

This simple list of objectives gave Panthers in whatever part of the country they found themselves, the basis for organizing and working with a broad cross-section of the community—for students, the platform's point five would apply; for prisoners, point eight; and so on.

The full platform and program, usually accompanied by a photo of Newton bearing a shotgun, would be reprinted in every issue of *The Black Panther* newspaper and would be foremost in the minds of every person who joined the Party.

## Beyond Program

The Ten-Point Program, required to be memorized by people joining the Party, reflects the nationalist origins of the Party and the positions articulated by Malcolm X before his assassination. Many of the points also reflect Huey's intense study of and fascination with the law, as evidenced by his citations of the US Constitution, a verbatim excerpt of the Declaration of Independence, and his call for a UN-supervised plebiscite.

But the program, while central to the Party, was not the ideology of the Party; it was more of an organizing tool. It was a way of getting folks to think about change, and it proposed solutions to problems faced by Black folks across the nation.

What was the ideology of the Black Panther Party?

It depends on which period of its existence, for the Party was always in a process of development and change.

While the Party, as we have seen, began as a staunchly nationalist formation, following in the footsteps of Malcolm, other external influences forced a reevaluation of those earlier positions.

## Cultural Opponents

In the Party's earliest days, the opponents of the Newton-led Black Panther Party for Self-Defense came from the Black Panther Party—of Northern California! This formation was a nationalist one, but opposed the BPPFSD's stance on weapons on the grounds that the Oakland group was prematurely paramilitary. It proposed a more political, as in electoral, orientation. The Oakland group replied with Mao's dictum, "Political power grows out of the barrel of the gun."[7] Oakland confronted the San Francisco–based group, and by the end of 1967, the Frisco group dissolved. Some joined their former rivals. Others simply ceased their activities.[8] Another San Francisco–based group, Black House, cofounded by the well-known, newly sprung Eldridge Cleaver, was more attracted to cultural affairs than political affairs. Among its most prominent supporters were Black playwrights Amiri Baraka and Ed Bullins. Another playwright, Earl Anthony (who later admitted he was a snitch!), noted that the Black House was "most critical" of the Black Panther Party for Self-Defense and opposed their politics.[9]

The Black Panther Party confronted their opposition with its usual audacity. Armed Panthers entered the Black House headquarters and ordered its members evicted. They left the premises, and the BPPFSD "occupied" the site.[10]

The Party's early conquests made it ill equipped for the conflicts with the United Slaves (US) organization, headed by the Black scholar Maulana "Ron" Karenga. While the Party had easily absorbed or neutralized opposition in the Bay Area, it had trouble when it tried to expand into Los Angeles. The US organization had grown in the wake of the Watts Rebellion and had assembled a group of young men trained in self-defense techniques, called *Simba Wachuka* (Young Lions in KiSwahili, an Eastern and Central African language). The young men were fiercely loyal to Karenga and even dressed in imitation of their leader, with bald heads and distinctive Fu Manchu-style mustaches. Earl Anthony, who had joined the Party in Oakland, was invested with the rank of captain and sent to Los Angeles to organize a BPP chapter. Unknown to the Party however, Anthony was a paid informant for the FBI. In fact, in furtherance of the Bureau's mission, he worked feverishly to sabotage and worsen relations between the newly emergent Los Angeles Panthers and the US organization. While posing as a loyal captain of the Black Panther Party, Anthony was reporting to his FBI handlers every conversation of consequence and providing valuable intelligence about the inner workings and weaknesses of both the BPP and the US organization. The FBI wanted conflict between the two groups, and Anthony slavishly complied.

Despite Anthony's duplicity and due in a large part to the work of Alprentice "Bunchy" Carter, a native of Los Angeles and the Deputy Minister of Defense of the city's chapter, who relied upon his old ties with the notorious Slauson street gang, the Panthers were soon able to organize a strong chapter.

What began as a territorial conflict quickly developed into an ideological one.

The US organization had developed a significant power base in both the Black Congress (a gathering of black groups in LA) and at the University of California at Los Angeles, where a struggle was brewing over who would be named director of the new Black Studies Program. Carter and his Panther ally, Deputy Minister of Information Jon Huggins, were both students of UCLA's High Potential Program, and both were angling to have influence on the choice of director of the Black Studies Program. The director could become a powerful source of political and ideological influence in the Black intellectual community. Karenga, however, was equally determined to have a say in the outcome.

Despite the Party's relative novelty in the city, and perhaps because of it, the Panther delegates were gaining influence and support both on campus and in the greater community. When meetings offered no solution that the two groups could agree on, two US members opted for the final solution to the persistent Panther problem. They shot Bunchy and Jon to death on January 17, 1969.

M. Wesley Swearingen, an FBI agent who worked in the Los Angeles racial squad, was told that the FBI used two of its informants, George and Larry Stiner, who were members of the US organization, to kill Bunchy and Jon. Swearingen has written about the informant who made this data public:

> Darthard Perry, a self-admitted and publicly acclaimed informant for the FBI, filed an affidavit in a Black Panther Party lawsuit against the government charging that he knew that the United Slaves members who were responsible for the murders of the Panthers were FBI informers. Perry claims that the mur-

ders committed by the Stiner brothers, who were convicted and sent to jail in 1969, and their subsequent escape in the 1974 prison break from San Quentin, were engineered by the FBI. I then discovered the unthinkable, that FBI informants had actually been instructed by FBI agents to assassinate several other Black Panther members.

As of 1992, the Stiner brothers were still listed as fugitives. Either the FBI has disposed of the Stiners or they are in the FBI's Witness Protection Program. I know that Darthard Perry was an FBI informant and that he is telling the truth about the FBI.[11]

The slaying of Bunchy and Jon left the field open for the US organization to control the UCLA post. It left it also with considerable political problems, as both slain Panthers were seen popularly as martyrs who gave their young lives in defense of the Revolution and the Party. The US organization won the battle, so to speak, but lost the larger war, as the Party grew in the hearts of people, both in Los Angeles and across the nation.

The assassinations of Bunchy and Jon condemned the very notion of cultural nationalism for the Party; it became anathema. The Party tried to purge old ideas that seemed similar to it. In the newspaper, adherents were derided as "pork chop nationalists." The Party suspected members of the US organization were paid agents of the State, and opposed both their ideological positions and their political stances. Huey would be critical of the tendency, calling it:

> [R]eaction [to] instead of responding to political oppression. The cultural nationalists are concerned with returning to the old African culture and thereby regaining their identity and freedom. In other words, they feel that the African culture will automatically bring political freedom. Many times cultural nationalists fall into line as reactionary nationalists.[12]

What the conflict also did was serve as a catalyst for further thinking and ideological development. The US organization conflict was a spur for the Party to look at alternatives to the empty Africanisms that were expressed by the cultural nationalists' wearing of African dress, the adoption of African names, and the acquisition of a smattering of KiSwahili. While the idea of revolutionary nationalism held sway for a time, it had to give way to a kind of revolutionary internationalism. This was only logical, given the persuasive international and ideological influences that the Party leadership was exposed to.

## Revolutionary Internationalism

The Party, and its top leaders, influenced as they were by the West Indian psychiatrist Dr. Frantz Fanon; modern China's revolutionary founding father, Mao Tse-Tung; Latin America's martyred "Che" Guevara; Ghana's Kwame Nkrumah; and others, saw internationalism as a natural, logical development from the increasingly co-opted nationalism of the period. This co-optation could perhaps be best seen in Richard Nixon bizarrely proclaiming "Black Power!" as he endorsed his notion of Black capitalism.[13]

The Party looked to liberation struggles and revolutions around the world as inspiration and guidance for the Revolution that would one day emerge in the heart of the United States. All around the world, people were fighting for their freedom from foreign, usually colonial, domination. Africa, Asia, and Latin America were ablaze with the fiery light of rebellion. They seemed like external counterpoints to Watts and Newark. In the so-called First World, students, veterans, women, and Blacks were loudly and openly challenging the repressive and well-oiled machinery of the status quo.

As campuses became places of challenge and as the antiwar movement began to swell in the streets with the well-to-do and white working class, the Black Panther Party heard echoes of anti-imperialist resistance from almost every quarter.

The Revolution seemed as inevitable as tomorrow's newspaper headlines.

As a direct result of its increasing internationalism and the heightening conflicts with State forces, many of the Party's leading members sought refuge abroad. Eldridge Cleaver, facing attempted-murder charges stemming from the April 1968 shoot-out in Oakland in which Party treasurer Bobby Hutton was killed and fearing certain assassination in prison, clandestinely made his way to Cuba. Captain Bill Brent, an associate from Cleaver's prison days, would hijack a plane to Cuba where he remains to this day. National Field Marshal Don Cox would arrive at the Party's international headquarters in Algiers in March 1970. Shortly thereafter, his pregnant wife would join him there. New York Panthers Sekou Odinga and Larry Mack, escaping the mass arrests crippling New York's leadership through the infamous *Panther 21* case, would hijack a plane to Guinea and then make their way to Africa's northern coastal city of Algiers by June 1970. Odinga would later welcome his bride and twin sons to the offices there. Former *Panther 21*–accused Michael "Cetawayo" Tabor, and his wife, Newton's personal secretary, Connie Matthews, went to live in Algiers in spring 1971.

By the fall of 1974, even Huey Newton himself would begin his life in exile, as he fled the threat of several outstanding felony charges by making a new home in Cuba's countryside. The founder of the Black Panther Party would not return to the US for three years.

For many Panthers, revolutionary internationalism meant the option of refuge from the repressive apparatus of the State.

But revolutionary internationalism was more than securing a safe haven. This ideological stance meant supporting liberation movements in their struggle against the US imperialists. For the Party's information chief, this meant communicating, as directly as possible, with those fighting for the Empire, and trying to convince them to battle against US imperialism.

The Party's paper ran a provocative letter penned by Eldridge Cleaver entitled, "Letter to My Black Brothers in Vietnam." In it the Minister of Information appealed to Black soldiers directly, explaining that they shouldn't fight against the Vietnamese, who weren't the enemies of Black folks. Rather, Black soldiers sent to Vietnam should "start killing the racist pigs who are over there giving you orders."[14]

This internationalist stance perhaps saw its most extreme expression in the controversial "Pilots for Panthers" program, when the Party offered to trade imprisoned Panthers for captive US Army soldiers and officers in the custody of the National Liberation Front of Vietnam (NLF). A famous photo was published in *The Black Panther* featuring a well-tanned BPP Minister of Information, Eldridge Cleaver, accompanied by four members of the NLF above the caption: "In Solidarity Against A Common Enemy—the NLF of South Vietnam and the Black Panther Party FF [Freedom Front] Babylon."[15] It was classic Eldridge.

Yet their revolutionary internationalism wasn't always on the receiving end. Newton did more than offer a POW exchange with the Vietnamese. He offered an undetermined number of Black Panther troops to aid the Vietnamese in their struggle against the US Empire. Indeed, the Deputy Commander of the South Vietnamese People's Liberation Army, Nguyen Thi Dinh, accepted the offer and, in a letter to BPP leadership, wrote: "With profound gratitude, we take notice for your enthusiastic proposal; when necessary, we shall call for your volunteers to assist us."[16]

This revolutionary internationalist position was echoed in other work done by Cleaver, who announced BPP support for the Palestinian struggle, and, in response to a query about the Party's position on Al Fatah, declared, "We support them. Absolutely! And revolutionaries all over the world. We see our battle as one and the same—a fight against imperialism and capitalism—and that fight can't be divided."[17]

Weeks later, Cleaver would appear publicly with Al Fatah's head, Yasser Arafat, at a support conference.[18]

While Al Fatah and BPP officials took advantage of this powerful propaganda opportunity, it was but another *expression* of revolutionary internationalism. In an interview with CBS news reporter Richard C. Hottelet, Fatah's Algerian representative, Abu Bassem, announced that Al Fatah's high command accepted his recommendation to train Black Panthers in urban guerrilla tactics and sabotage. According to Hottelet, Bassem said, "When the time comes, the Panthers will carry out quick and deep strikes in the United States, assassinations of men responsible for the policy of discrimination from high levels to low, and sabotage to factories and capitalist institutions."[19]

Although it is doubtful that this training ever occurred, in this era of revolutionary internationalism such rhetoric didn't seem extraordinary.

This revolutionary internationalism was more than merely skin deep, as may be seen in the educational materials that every Party member was expected to study. Panthers were expected to read these materials so that they could intelligently discuss issues at weekly Political Education (PE) classes and also to simply learn the science of revolution from those people who had lived it. Thus, almost every Panther had a personal copy of the *Quotations from Chairman Mao Tse-Tung,* known colloquially as the Red Book for its bright red plastic slipcover, and its Marxist-Leninist-Maoist (that is, red) orientation. The Red Book, featuring brief excerpts from the lengthy writings of Mao, was translated from Mandarin Chinese into clear, accessible English and thus had an enormous impact on the political development and ideological perspective of those Panthers with little formal schooling. A more challenging and perhaps even more significant text was Frantz Fanon's *The Wretched of the Earth.*

While Mao was influential, Fanon was inspirational, for we knew he was, above all things, a Black man, from the Americas, who was an integral part of a real-life revolution. Fanon, this son of Africa, was a Black man waging a war against imperialists in North Africa, with his mind and his hands. His words had a deep and abiding resonance for us. The importance of Fanon to Party members can be seen in the observations of a leading

Central Committee member, Kathleen Neal Cleaver, who served in the Party's International Section in Algiers for several years. She termed his influence "profound":

> The crucible of civil war forged the writings of Frantz Fanon, the Black psychiatrist from Martinique who fought alongside Algerian revolutionaries for independence from France. His books became available in English just as waves of civil violence engulfed the ghettos of America, reaching the level of insurrection in the wake of the assassination of Dr. Martin Luther King, Jr. in 1968. Fanon died in 1961, a year before Algeria obtained the independence he had given his life to win, but his brilliant, posthumously published work *The Wretched of the Earth* became essential reading for Black revolutionaries in America and profoundly influenced their thinking. Fanon's analysis seemed to explain and to justify the spontaneous violence ravaging Black ghettos across the country, and linked the incipient insurrections to the rise of a revolutionary movement.[20]

In explaining the power of Fanon's analysis, Cleaver illustrates why the Black Panther Party was not a civil rights organization, but a liberation organization, dedicated to revolutionary transformation rather than reformist window-dressing (otherwise known as the installation of "black faces in high places"):

> The opening sentence of *The Wretched of the Earth* said, "National liberation, national renaissance, the restoration of nationhood to a people ... whatever may be the headings used or the new formulas introduced, decolonization is always a violent phenomenon." Fanon's penetrating dissection of the intertwining of racism and violence in the colonial scheme of domination was compelling to Blacks fighting in America; it provided a clearly reasoned antidote to the constant admonition to seek changes peacefully. Fanon explained how violence was intrinsic to the imposition of White colonial domination, and portrayed the oppressed who violently retaliate as engaged in restoring human dignity they were stripped of by the process of colonization. His analysis of the tortured mentality of the colonized person and the therapeutic nature of fighting to destroy colonial domination provided radical Blacks in America with deep insights—into both their own relationship to a world-wide revolution underway and to the profound kinship

between their status in America and that of colonized people outside America.[21]

## Caged Panthers

As Panthers were inspired by revolutionaries abroad, the very existence of the Black Panther Party inspired people in prisons. Prisoners formed organizations based on the Party's audacious example and some even formally affiliated with the Party. George Jackson is perhaps the most renown of the imprisoned Panthers. Jackson, who under a public defender's advice had pleaded guilty to a $70 gas station robbery, was imprisoned for more than a decade under California's infamous indeterminate sentences. This injustice aroused his fury at the state that caged him. His prison writings, especially *Soledad Brother* which sold over 400,000 copies, gave eloquent voice to that fury. His passion was echoed by tens of thousands, both within and without prison.

While in prison, Jackson undertook a considerable study of history, Marxism, and sociology in an attempt to learn why life was so hard for Black people. He became a militant prisoner organizer, and drew over 40 misconducts for assaulting prison guards. He organized the brothers around him, telling them they were no longer criminals but Black revolutionaries. To that end he organized a clandestine cadre at San Quentin known as the *People's Army*. His revolutionary organizing prowess earned him a moniker rarely attributed to a prisoner—and one earned by the legendary Black freedom fighter Harriet Tubman—the General. He later joined the Black Panther Party and cofounded a San Quentin chapter. When a white prison guard was killed at Soledad Prison in 1970 Jackson, along with Fleeta Drumgo and John Clutchette, (collectively known as the Soledad Brothers) were charged in his death based purely on their political activity and faced the death penalty.

George Jackson's younger brother Jonathan, not trusting that the courts would deliver justice, tried to secure the Soledad Brothers' freedom. On August 7, 1970, in the midst of a trial in San

Rafael, California an armed Jonathan Jackson, at 17 years old, entered the Marin County Courthouse and calmly declared, "Gentlemen, I'm taking over." He, along with three Black revolutionary prisoners, took the judge hostage. While in the parking lot trying to negotiate for the release of the Soledad Brothers, Marin County sheriffs would open fire, killing four men—Jonathan, William Christmas, James McClain, and the judge—in the hail of bullets that perforated the escape van. One prisoner, Ruchell Magee, would survive the carnage. The Marin County shootout would give rise to the manhunt for Dr. Angela Davis, who was charged with conspiracy in the courthouse killings, for allegedly providing the weapons to Jackson. She was acquitted on June 4, 1972.

Jonathan's action drew nation-wide media attention to the case of the Soledad Brothers and their trial. On August 21, 1971, days before George Jackson's trial was to begin he was shot and killed by prison guards during an alleged prison escape attempt. George Jackson, invested with the high rank of Field Marshal of the Black Panther Party by the Minister of Defense (making Jackson the only prisoner-member of the Party's Central Committee), received a hero's funeral in Oakland, with Huey P. Newton delivering a heartfelt eulogy.[22] Half a year later, the two surviving Soledad Brothers, Drumgo and Clutchette, would be acquitted by an all-white jury of murder charges.

George Jackson was hardly alone in his prison membership. In 1971, the same year of Jackson's informal state execution, three young men, Herman "Hooks" Wallace, Robert Hillary King, and Albert Woodfox, formed a chapter of the Party in the subtropical prison of Angola Penitentiary. The prison was once the site of a vast slave plantation and known as one of America's largest and most repressive institutions.

Wallace became a Panther while in the New Orleans Parish Jail, when he met the political prisoners known as the "New Orleans Panther 12." Woodfox was a member of the New York chapter before coming to New Orleans. King was an outspoken prison activist before his arrival at Angola. At Angola they established a branch of the Party, initiated political education classes, and organized against prison abuse.

The three men, now known the world over as the Angola 3, would be charged and convicted of the slaying of a prison guard at Angola, and the "evidence" used against them was their membership in the Party. The three men were convicted in 1972 and spent decades (over 40 years) in solitary confinement in Angola's holes. King had his conviction reversed in 2000 and was released in 2001. Wallace was released on October 1, 2013, and died just three days later. Woodfox finally gained freedom in February 2016 after more than 43 years in solitary confinement, the longest-ever in the US.[23]

While the Angola 3 and Jackson posed rigorous challenges to the state's repressive machinery, in later years, as the the Party left its guerrilla phase of resistance, many ex-Panthers, including leading memebers of the organization who ran afoul of Newton, would experience prison as *former* members, bereft of either the psychological or material support of the BPP.

## "Huey's Party"?

True to the patterns of Huey's youth, the Party chose to concentrate on the biggest bully on the block—the United States. The Black Panther Party opposed the war in Vietnam, as did many, many others. Yet none of the antiwar groups went as far as to offer troops to the Peoples Republic of Vietnam, the Black Panther Party did.

As the Party began to oppose nationalism, it took positions that reflected that perspective. If nationalism, per se, is wrong, then allegiance to the US nation is also wrong. Many of those in the antiwar movement were unprepared to take that next step.

That said, the antiwar movement was a burgeoning one that members of the government and the administration took seriously. Nixon aide Alexander Haig commented in an interview with the

French journal *Politique Internationale* that, "There is a Jane Fonda on every doorstep."[24] Fonda, at the time a popular Hollywood actress, was reviled by some Veterans of Foreign War (VFW) types as "Hanoi Jane" because of her antiwar activism and trips to Vietnam. Haig's comment may reflect a governmental paranoia, but among activists the FBI was intentionally stoking paranoia. The FBI directed agents to "enhance the paranoia endemic in these circles and...get the point across that there is an FBI agent behind every mailbox."[25]

The term "Huey's Party" arose when Big Bob Bay, one of Huey's personal bodyguards and a former Captain from West Oakland, became a personal emissary from Newton to the New York branch in the Bronx. Big Bob, as his name suggests, was a mountain of a man. He stood well over six foot four and tipped the scales at around 300 pounds. He didn't walk; he lumbered, from side to side, like a grizzly.

As one of Huey's oldest friends, and a dyed in-the-wool Panther, Big Bob regarded any deviation from proper Party ideology or form as more a personal than a political affront.

He became well-known among New York Panthers and dreaded for his fits of temper. He reflected an unbending allegiance to the Minister of Defense, and his countrified Californi-ese could be heard bellowing in offices throughout the five boroughs: "Nigga, I ain't lettin' you do nuthin' that'll fuck up this Party! Uh-Uhn! Not this Party, *not Huey P. Newton's Party!*"

Big Bob's reference was more than rhetorical, for, in fact, in essence, in people's heads, it *was* Huey's Party. He was the first Panther in the hearts and minds of his comrades.

We were molded in his image.

We read his words and tried to emulate his resistance.

This held true from members of the highest Party body, the Central Committee, to the lowest-level Panther-in-Training.

While this was not the Party's official position, it was how it lived in the real world.

That meant that Huey's political insights and developments became ours, to the extent that we could follow and understand them. When a major ideological shift was taking place, we followed it, even if we didn't particularly agree with it.

Huey had spoken—period.

That almost-blind faith in the guidance of Newton would have serious and long-lasting repercussions.

People read *The Black Panther* extremely closely to follow ideological developments.

When papers came in from the airport, fresh from the Party's printers, we would take the time, either in the office or in the field, to read the paper so that we wouldn't be caught sleeping. We never knew when a political opponent would try to engage us in ideological argument, so we had to be ready to defend the Party's positions. That meant we had to read our paper, preferably before we sold it to others. It also meant that we should read the publications of other groups to allow us to see where they were coming from. That habit came in handy to one young Panther assigned to paper-selling duty in a bustling section of the Bronx:

*The 3rd Avenue El in the Bronx was a major thoroughfare in the borough, and as such was a prime site for one trying to sell* The Black Panther. *I had recently been assigned to the Bronx office and in an attempt to sell my fifty copies, I chose a stop on the line where the foot traffic would be quite heavy, as people descended from the elevated train ride. At roughly the same time, another young Black man elected to stop at the busy corner with the intention of selling his wares.*

*His wares were essentially the same as mine—newspapers. There, however, the similarity ended, for it was clear from his product that competition was inevitable.*

*The young man wore a dark-green iridescent suit and a brightly colored bow tie. His hair was cut close to his scalp in the "hustler" style, with a thin part cut in, his face shaved hairless. He carried with him a multi-colored plastic shopping bag that appeared to be filled with copies of* Muhammad Speaks.

*As I surveyed his wares, he was surveying mine. We looked at each other and understood that neither would relinquish the corner to the other. And so, we began selling in earnest. Shouts of "Help us Free Huey!" mingled with "Salaam Aliekum, brother!" as we struggled to sell our product.*

*"Yho, brother! Find out what's happenin' that the white power structure ain't gonna tell ya! Check out* The Black Panther—*only a quarter!"*

*"Salaam Aliekum, Sister! Come on back to your own! Read* Muhammad Speaks! *Twenty-five cents!"*

*For nearly an hour the sales continued, fed and famished by the flow of passersby debarking from the trains hissing to a stop overhead. After a while, we got into a conversation:*

*"Brother, you got to get with the Honorable Elijah Muhammad, and stop following those devils like Marx and Lenin and 'em."*

*"Well, bro'—you should get with the Minister of Defense, Huey P. Newton, and the Black Panther Party."*

*"You should follow a Black man, brother, not some Jews like Marx and Lenin!"*

*"We revolutionaries, brother, and we study about revolutionaries from around the world. We don't care what race they is."*

*"I can see that, brother," glancing at a copy of* The Black Panther, *pointing to the cover picture of an Asian, full-haired man, "Who is that, brother?"*

*"That's Kim Il-Sung, the leader of North Korea, and a revolutionary."*

*"You see what I'm saying, brother? Here you go talking 'bout another guy! He ain't got nothin' to say to Black people, brother!"*

*"Well, if that's so, brother, why he in yho paper* Muhammad Speaks?*"*

*"What you talkin' 'bout, brother?" he asked, seemingly stunned by the question. I read and studied his paper quite regularly, for its layout, news, and commentary, but I doubted if he ever read any of ours. This seemed only logical for someone assigned to the East Coast Ministry of Information office, and I remembered reading this week's issue of* Muhammad Speaks.

*"Check it out, brother, in yho international news section."*

*In disbelief, he turned the pages until, sure enough, an article appeared bearing a photo of Kim Il-Sung. He looked at it, and then turned to me smiling.*

*"Yes, sir, brother. Yessir. Um-humm."*

*"And what we learned from him was the idea of* Júché, *a Korean word that means self-reliance!"*[26]

To the average Panther, even though he worked daily in the ghetto communities of North America, his thoughts were usually on something larger than himself. It meant being part of a worldwide movement against US imperialism, white supremacy, colonialism, and corrupting capitalism. We felt as if we were part of the peasant armies of Vietnam, the degraded Black miners of South Africa, the fedayeen in Palestine, the students storming in the streets of Paris, and the dispossessed of Latin America. As Huey Newton refined the ideology from revolutionary internationalism to intercommunalism these feelings of solidarity continued.

More than any other Panther, the work of Eldridge Cleaver seemed to prove this theory beyond question.

## The BPP Abroad

In July 1969, leading members of the Black Panther Party, led by Minister of Information Eldridge Cleaver, attended a Pan-African Cultural Festival in Algiers. Algeria would become home for the beleaguered Cleaver, who fled the US a year before to avoid a return to prison that he was convinced would result in his assassination. Out on bail for charges stemming from the April 6, 1968, shoot-out (which left the teenaged Hutton dead and Cleaver wounded), the Party's information chief had traveled around the world, his FBI wanted poster his initial "passport," in his lonely exile from his American homeland. On behalf of the Party, Eldridge went to Beijing and to North Korea's spartan Pyongyang with a media delegation.

The Algerian government, its memory still fresh of its own brutal struggles under French colonialism, looked on the Cleaver delegation with favor. An official international headquarters was established in 1970 which had all the trappings of an embassy. An embassy not on behalf of the US government, or even the American people, but a symbol of an independent Afro-America with the Black Panther Party in a representative capacity for the growing Black liberation movement.

Kathleen Neal Cleaver, Party Communications Secretary and Eldridge's wife, would later write of the office's impressive functions and scope:

> When the delegation returned to Algiers in September, the International Section of the Black Panther Party was formally opened. The Panthers invited representatives of all the liberation movements and socialist states to their villa, inaugurating their official establishment within the revolutionary diplomatic community in Algiers. The villa became a kind of embassy of the American revolution, receiving visitors from all over the world. But the Panthers found themselves essentially limited to serving as an information center, conveying news about revolutionary developments within the United States to their associates in Algiers and receiving information from all the movements represented in Algiers. The International Section of the Black Panther Party, however, turned into a magnet for an increasingly diverse crop of fugitives from the United States.[27]

The establishment of the international section in Algiers marked a coup for Eldridge just as the release on bail of Huey P. Newton on August 5 marked a major victory stateside. These events were high points of the Black Panther Party as a bona fide revolutionary organization of global import, and were the high watermark, too, of the American Black liberation movement. But all the news wasn't golden for Huey's Party. In July of 1969, the deeply negrophobic director of the FBI, J. Edgar Hoover, called the Panthers "the greatest threat to internal security of the country"[28] and those words were having a chilling effect.

The comments came from a man now known as a virulent, racist anti-Semite, for his career was based on deep, perpetual fear-mongering that played quite well among American nativists. Hoover's almost half-century of dominance by fear, subterfuge, and official criminality, reflected his powerful status as head of a de facto "ministry of internal security" that routinely ran roughshod over a slew of criminal and constitutional laws.[29]

When he spoke those words, however, they were far more than the dark obsessions of one old, somewhat twisted man; they reflected the aims of a powerful government agency that was created in his narrow and white supremacist image—the FBI.

Things were going well for the Party, and it was growing by leaps and bounds.

Things were going so well that they had to get worse.

## CHAPTER SIX

# The Empire Strikes Back: COINTELPRO

> History should teach us...that in times of high emotional excitement, minority parties and groups which advocate extremely unpopular social or governmental innovations will always be typed as criminal gangs and attempts will always be made to drive them out.
>
> —Hugo Black, Associate Justice, US Supreme Court[1]

**IF THE BLACK** Panther Party was a Black rebel band (and it was), the State would, as has historically been the case, respond with repression (and it did). From the highest levels of government came threats of destruction and wild, exaggerated claims of the violence posed by the Black Panther Party. The incoming US Attorney General, John Mitchell, a law partner of the persnickety Richard M. Nixon, vowed to "wipe out the Black Panther Party by the end of 1969."[2] Mitchell was the head of the government department encompassing the FBI, and his threat was not empty. The longtime head of the nation's premier law enforcement agency, J. Edgar Hoover utilized the enormous powers of his agency to put meat on the bones of Mitchell's threat.

Hoover skillfully utilized not only the powerful bureaucracy that he built and controlled, but also the vast powers of the predominantly white corporate press to demonize the Black Panther Party in the eyes of most of America. This clever, cunning, and quite bigoted man used one of the most powerful weapons ever in the scabbard of a politician—fear. The Black Panther Party,

Hoover claimed, "represents the greatest threat to the internal security of the country."[3] Why did he claim this?

If Hoover was to be believed, the Black Panthers were "the most violent of all" the Black militant groups, and he lamented "that the Communist Party has not been able to control" them. What peeved the "minister of internal security" was his observation that "black militants are more or less a law unto themselves and want no leadership other than their own." One wonders why Hoover, an ardent anticommunist, would decry the lack of *control* by the Communist Party, or their self-leadership? Moreover, he testified, "leaders and representatives of the Black Panther Party travel extensively all over the United States preaching the gospel of hate and violence, not only to ghetto residents, but to students in colleges, universities and high schools as well."[4]

What seemed to bother the pugnacious Hoover most, then, was the political independence of the Panthers (and other "black militants") and his inability to use them to prove his long-held pet theories of communist infiltration and foreign control of Black revolutionary political movements. What angered him further was the Party's growing influence, not over "ghetto residents" but on white youth in the nation's educational institutions.

Which was the real "greatest threat"?

For, if the FBI chief was correct that the Black Panthers were teaching a "gospel of hate," isn't it unlikely that such a doctrine would find support on college campuses, which in the late 1960s were certainly overwhelmingly white institutions? There is then, clearly, something else that motivated the State in its scorched-earth campaign against an entity it deemed the greatest threat to internal security.

The problem wasn't that the Black Panther Party was a "hate-based group," *but that it was not.*

It wasn't that the organization had an ideological affinity to Marxism-Leninism-Maoism. It wasn't that the Party was (in FBI-speak) "violence-prone."

These were mere pretexts.

Much to the chagrin of their nationalist contemporaries, the Black Panthers viewed themselves as internationalists and worked with people from a wide range of racial and ethnic groupings. Indeed, Asian-American activists played a pivotal role in the early Party's development with Richard Aoki's furnishing of Newton and Seale's first weapons.[5] Through the offices of its National Fronts Against Fascism, the Party had information and propaganda centers functioning in white communities. People who were reticent or afraid about going into the Black community could visit to read or purchase firsthand accounts of the revolution being waged in other parts of the Empire.

If you "hate" someone, you don't work with them.

One case study should give us some telling insight into whether it was the Black Panther Party or the groups that targeted them, the FBI and other government agencies, that operated as hate groups. Let us examine the remarkable career of Chairman Fred Hampton, the brilliant Chicago Panther and organizer of the Illinois chapter who, while barely twenty, had built one of the most impressive branches of the BPP in the nation.

As youth leaders in the Chicago NAACP, Hampton and his boyhood friend, Bobby Rush, felt that the integrationist, assimilationist-type group did not address sharply enough the challenges faced by the Black community. They were drawn to the open militance of the Black Panther Party, and that attraction would set the stage for a drama and political tragedy of epic proportions.

By all accounts, Hampton was a revolutionary who submitted his whole being to the ideology of the organization and the revolution. A gifted, engaging, and passionate speaker, Hampton's country-cadenced speech touched listeners with his own enthusiasm and youthful brio. He would organize, if given the opportunity, everybody, everywhere within earshot. He worked with the Young Lords, a street gang in Chicago, and inspired the young

Puerto Ricans to organize into a collective, political organization. The Young Lords Party was born. He did similar work among other ethnic groups.

Elaine Brown, with all her sophistication and worldly wisdom, found herself moved to tears when she and Chief of Staff David Hilliard saw this young Panther leader in action:

> Hundreds of Panthers were lined up in a West Side Chicago schoolyard, ready to start the day's work. "Chairman Fred" was making sure his chief of staff would see the good work the Illinois chapter was doing. Chicago Panthers, Fred explained, lined up that way every morning. It was a demonstration of discipline and commitment. Fred felt it was an inspirational way to get the day started. It was.
>
> "I ain't gon' die slippin' on no ice!" Fred shouted into a bullhorn, walking up and down the aisles of Panthers like a Baptist preacher.
>
> "I ain't gon' die slippin' on no ice!" Panthers shouted back.
>
> "I ain't gon' die in no airplane crash!"
>
> "I ain't gon' die in no airplane crash!" they responded in unison.
>
> "I'm gon' die for the People!" the chairman continued, his fist high, the steam of his breath bursting into the bitter early morning cold.
>
> "I'm gon' die for the People!" came the echo.
>
> " 'Cause I live for the People!"
>
> "...live for the People!"
>
> " 'Cause I'm high on the People!"
>
> "...high on the People!"
>
> " 'Cause I *love* the People!"
>
> "...*love* the People!"
>
> "Power to the People! Power to the People! Power to the People!"[6]

The legendary Chicago wind—the chilling, mighty Hawk—was cutting through the West Side at seven a.m., freezing Brown's cheeks, she recalls. But her cheeks were warmed by her tears as the surge of revolutionary love went through her like a wave.

But the FBI was also watching and listening. The organizing abilities of Hampton would fill them with alarm. Hampton worked with Puerto Ricans, Mexicans, Asians, even poor white greasers—anybody, everybody—to build revolution. He worked with Black apolitical gangs, such as the notorious Blackstone Rangers, and had almost effected an alliance, until their leader, Jeff Fort, had misgivings. Perhaps Fort felt Hampton was a challenge to his power; perhaps he intuited that a political affiliation would pose serious dangers to his organization. Perhaps it was the influence of letters like this one, sent, unbeknownst to him, from the FBI and authorized by J. Edgar Hoover on January 30, 1969:

> I'm not a Panther, or a Ranger, just black. From what I see these Panthers are out for themselves, not black people. I think you ought to know what they're up to, I know what I'd do if I was you. You might here [sic] from me again.[7]

At the same time that Fort was getting fake, FBI-generated *brownmail*, Panthers were getting mail from the same anonymous source, suggesting that Fort was planning to "off" Hampton.

To their credit, neither Fort nor Hampton reacted badly in response to these perceived provocations. Indeed, Hampton's courageous response was to go to Ranger headquarters to discuss this matter with Fort, and even though they discovered that neither had written the other, the damage was done. For, although this specific FBI *brownmail* attempt did not end in violence, it frustrated Hampton's objective of politicizing the Rangers and thereby bringing them, en masse, under Party discipline. Had he succeeded, over three thousand young men would have joined the Black Panther Party, and gangsters would have begun the transition to revolutionaries.

Both Hampton and Fort were the unwitting targets of the nefarious FBI COINTELPRO (COunter INTELligence PROgram) operation, ordered and authorized by Hoover.

While neither Hampton nor Fort were aware of the government activity tainting the wellsprings of their relationship, this was, in fact, one of hundreds of such operations occurring across America, designed with an overt political, and indeed racial, objective: to prevent Black unity and to prevent Black self-determination. In essence, the FBI functioned as political and race police—agents for the preservation of white supremacy.

What were the FBI's written, declared objectives?

> ... to prevent the coalition of black nationalist groups ... *prevent the rise of a "messiah"* who could unify and electrify the militant black nationalist movement ... prevent violence on the part of black nationalist groups ... prevent black nationalist groups and leaders from gaining respectability ... prevent the long-range growth of militant black nationalist organizations especially among the youth.[8]

Under declassified government documents obtained through the Freedom of Information Act in the mid 1970s, it was learned that the FBI began its intrusive spying, interference, and destabilization of Black groups before the founding of the Black Panther Party, and even the period of ascendancy of the Black Liberation movement. Although it used the lie of investigating hate groups to justify its efforts, the FBI also snooped on those Black leaders who were sworn to nonviolence, like the Rev. Martin Luther Kings (Junior and Senior!). According to the FBI's own records, they taped Dr. King's personal calls, sent him fake letters, threatened his life, tried to blackmail him, and even wrote him suggesting he commit suicide.

COINTELPRO, between 1956 and 1971, engaged in 295 actions against Black groups, most of them against the Black Panther Party.[9] The FBI engaged in covert criminal activities, according to FBI veteran Wesley Swearingen, who participated in illegal break-ins of properties owned by the members of the Nation of Islam. On the basis of Hoover's pretextual claim that the NOI "disavow[ed]" allegiance to the US, the Attorney General approved wire-tap surveillance. In December 1956 this was taken by

Hoover as a green light to run bag jobs, that is, illegal break-ins. Swearingen tells us:

> [T]he only plausible reason for the FBI to break into the homes of members of the Nation of Islam was Hoover's hatred for African Americans and Hoover's desire to keep Elijah Muhammad from becoming a messiah for African Americans.

> We bagged the residence of two Nation of Islam members and photographed membership lists and financial records, even though the Nation of Islam was not a threat to the U.S. government. I acted as the lookout for the bag jobs on members of the Nation of Islam while fellow agents broke into their homes.[10]

Let us not engage in the delusion that this action was undertaken by government agents who were performing a valuable national service for the greater good. Swearingen leaves no room to doubt whether he or his colleagues were knowingly ordered to violate the law against fellow American citizens:

> *We had no authority for the bag jobs* we did, and so we in the FBI were the ones who violated the Constitution. When we started bag jobs on a black religious organization, I knew then that the FBI was out of control, but I could not stop it because no one would have believed me—not even Hoover's most severe critics. *If I had said anything, Hoover would have had me prosecuted for violating local burglary laws.*[11]

The nation's premier law enforcement agency, one said to be investigating hate crimes, had itself been committing crimes motivated by hatred against Black Americans for decades. These crimes would pale beside other actions that the State would take against such alleged "citizens" in the years to come.

## War Against the People

In 1919, the first director of the Bureau of Investigation (the forerunner of the FBI), J.W. Flynn, aptly described his agency's objectives when he noted, "[the Bureau] required a vigorous and comprehensive investigation of anarchists and Bolshevists, along with kindred agitators—*advocating change in the present form of gov-*

*ernment*."[12] In the government's own terms, those who advocated change in government were perceived as enemies, and actions were taken against them as if they were such. Through intimidation and the fear of incurring the subtle wrath of the unsleeping State, the history of governmental crime against its own citizens has been allowed to be buried in the dust and detritus of time.

When such crimes perpetrated by the government do reach the light, they are quickly plunged into darkness. They are hidden in thick government tomes of roughly a thousand pages that the average American, much less the naive youth under the tutelage of a harried, overworked, and underpaid history teacher, will never read and perhaps will never know exist. These sources provide telling and damning evidence of the depths of the government's secret wars against its own civilians. They also testify to the abject impotence of the political branches, notably the US Congress, to take meaningful action to stem the crimson tide of criminal practices conducted by the government itself! In this light, one sees the real structure beneath the apparent one: a police substructure that acts as a social and, indeed, political power unto itself, without even a hint of control by the political branches, despite public protestations and claims to the contrary.

Bold though they may be, these facts can be supported by a simple reading of documents produced by the US government, made public in hearings before Senate subcommittees, or made public by citizens' groups who acted on their own to "blow the whistle" on this intolerable state of affairs.[13]

Let us examine the evidence.

The year was 1922, and a freshman senator, Burton K. Wheeler, was on his way to Washington from Montana, partly due to the campaign efforts of the Non-Partisan League, a left-leaning coalition of Montanans who stood for good government. Senator Wheeler, truly new to the ways of Washington, criticized the corruption of the US Department of Justice (DOJ) in speeches on the Senate floor. The Republican National Committee, apparently incensed at the whippersnapper's impertinence and armed with data supplied by the FBI, launched a series of attacks on Wheeler, among them the claim that while he was a US Attorney he had allowed Montana to become a "hotbed of treason and sedition." Meanwhile, G-men spied outside his home, while other FBI agents ransacked his offices on the Hill. Others tried to set him up with a pretty young trap in an Ohio hotel room. When these efforts failed, the DOJ launched a federal grand jury at him, and the freshman senator was indeed indicted for influence peddling to gain oil and gas leases for a friend.

It is worthwhile to note and here remember that this was a US senator, one of the most powerful figures in the pantheon of State power. Wheeler was eventually acquitted, and subsequent Senate hearings turned up the sources of the anti-Wheeler plot. The Bureau's director at the time, William J. Burns, testified that the Bureau was used in a vendetta against Wheeler because he criticized the Justice Department. Another witness told the committee that FBI agents openly acknowledged they wanted to "frame" the senator.[14] Members of Congress held hearings, several prominent people in the Bureau resigned, and all seemed right with the world. Yet the real question remained: what would have happened if the accused was not a member of the US Senate, but an average Joe? What if the FBI had been adroit enough to engineer a conviction in the senator's case? Indeed, what made the FBI and DOJ think they could do this, with virtual impunity, but their prior practice?

The powerful have resources that the powerless do not. The powerless suffer silently and often alone, and their hearings result in stone-faced denials or meaningless platitudes that preserve the prerogatives of power.

Preschool teacher Evelyn R. Sell was described by those who knew her as an intelligent, excellent teacher who was well qualified for her job. She also happened to be a socialist. She joined the Socialist Workers Party (SWP) in the late 1940s and had even run for various political posts under the banner of her group. This was a perfectly legal activity and a public one.

When she moved from Detroit, Michigan, and sought work in Austin, Texas, little did she know that the FBI and the Austin Police Department had engaged in an interstate, interagency conspiracy against her to ensure that she would not be hired for a job that even the FBI admitted she was "well qualified" for.

As documented in her FBI file of March 31, 1970, under the subtitle, "Evelyn Rose Sell, SM–SWP," which incidentally means, Subversive Matter–Socialist Workers Party, the Bureau comes to the following conclusion:

> The decision not to issue a new contract or consider the subject further for employment after the termination of her current contract is based upon information received from [deleted] the Austin Police Department.[15]

Austin's School Board president at the time, a Mr. M.K. Hage, Jr., said that knowledge that someone was a socialist was sufficient grounds to fire them.[16]

When Mrs. Sell had the good luck to be hired elsewhere in the same field, the FBI strenuously sought to have her dismissed, visiting her supervisors at least three times, according to her file entries. Sell would later explain that her employers resented the heavy-handed tactics of the Bureau. "The HOC (Human Opportunities Corporation, a Head Start–like agency) directors were outraged by the visits." Sell added, "One of them told me that he was seriously considering filing a lawsuit against the FBI because of the harassing visits."[17]

In her personal files sat a letter from the parents' council of the program, which read, in part:

> We wish to commend Mrs. Evelyn Sell ... for a job *well done!* The fairness and efficiency in her willingness to always make herself readily available if she could be of any help in any situation was quickly recognized.[18]

Mrs. Sell was seen as so much of an asset to the HOC that it was in their interest to ignore the whisperings of the FBI.

There were others, however, who were not as lucky as Mrs. Sell.

Morris Starsky was a professor of philosophy at Arizona State University. When a faculty committee at ASU met to consider whether to renew his teaching contract, the committee was influenced in its deliberations by the unseen presence of the FBI which sent an anonymous letter rife with slander against the educator.

An FBI memo of the period finds it "pretty obvious" who the target of their COINTELPRO ire in the area should be: "It is apparent that New Left organizations and activities in the Phoenix metropolitan area has received their inspiration and leadership almost exclusively from the members of the faculty in the Department of Philosophy at Arizona State University (ASU), chiefly assistant Professor MORRIS J. STARSKY."[19]

Without a doubt, Starsky was an outgoing, and active, activist. He helped organize ASU's first antiwar teach-in; he helped lead campus recognition for SDS (Students for a Democratic Society); he joined campus efforts to support the formation of a union for Chicanx laundry workers; and served as the faculty adviser for the Young Socialist Alliance and the Student Mobilization Committee (MOBE).

Members of ASU's administrative committees received slanderous letters signed by "A Concerned Alumnus" that were actually sent from agents of the FBI and personally approved by J. Edgar Hoover. Notwithstanding this heavy-handed and duplicitous activity, the committee recommended unanimously that Starsky not be dismissed, but the state's Board of Regents had other ideas and refused to renew his contract.

In July 1970, Professor Starsky was out of a job. He subsequently lost two teaching posts in California for political reasons. Starsky would later describe his experience as "sort of like being found innocent and executed anyway."[20]

He asks, "What teacher is safe? What ideas would not subject a teacher to this kind of attack? Only U.S. government-approved ideas."[21]

In such a climate, in such a world, how can it be said that there was even the merest shadow of academic freedom—or freedom period?

Cliff DeBerry was a Black laborer who was attracted to the socialist movement because he felt their ideas made sense. He was an average guy with high hopes for the future. What he didn't reckon on was the FBI.

When he joined the Socialist Workers Party and began speaking on their behalf in Harlem and in other communities, the agents of COINTELPRO took note and began to devise ways to scuttle his efforts, destabilize the growing coalition between Blacks and members of the SWP, and discredit the man.

When DeBerry became active in the labor movement and entered electoral politics in the SWP's name, the Bureau launched a self-described disruption program in October of 1963. Once again, an anonymous letter was prepared; this one revealed DeBerry had a prison record. The objective of the FBI is clearly reflected in a memorandum from the Director, to New York's Special Agent in Charge (SAC):

> On 10/14/63, the anonymous letter authorized in relet was prepared on a manual typewriter utilizing commercially purchased stationery. The letter was mailed 10/14/63 from a suburb of NYC.
>
> The Bureau will be advised if any tangible results are noted from this disruptive tactic.
>
> The NY Local of the SWP is presently running a candidate for the position of Councilman-at-large in the borough of Brooklyn. A review is being conducted of CLIFTON DE BERRY's file to determine if there is anything derogatory in his background which might cause embarrassment to the SWP if publicly used. It is noted that on a previous occasion it was possible to have printed in a daily NY newspaper the prison record of an SWP election candidate.

If a review of DE BERRY's file reflects a disruptive move is possible, the Bureau will be advised.[22]

The anonymous letters were routed to news media in New York in an attempt to scuttle the DeBerry/SWP campaign. DeBerry lost the election.

Nor was the FBI interested only in disrupting the political career of the candidate, but also his economic life. As he told fellow SWP members, "I would get a job, and it would only last three days. I would go from one job to another, and it would be the same story. The FBI would visit my boss, and I would be fired."[23]

Only when he found a stubborn employer, who refused to be cowed by the FBI, did DeBerry manage to hang on to a job. He learned the craft of painting, which became his lifelong trade. Still the Bureau snoops would turn up every three or four days to "check up" on him. He worked with Malcolm X during his Harlem years, as the radicalized minister tried to develop his political and religious organizations (the Muslim Mosque, Inc. and the Organization of Afro-American Unity). The FBI tried a number of tactics to divide DeBerry's group from the followers of Malcolm X.

A final example which examines a COINTELPRO attack on a Black nationalist group apart from the Panthers, reveals the breadth and depth of the State's reach. Having learned that the head of the Black Liberators, a Black nationalist group in St. Louis, was physically separated from his wife, the FBI prepared a macabre Valentine's Day present. The FBI memo of February 14, 1969, sets forth the following insidious COINTELPRO action:

> Enclosed for the Bureau are two copies and for Springfield one copy of a letter to "SISTER [rest of name deleted].
>
> The following counter-intelligence activity is being proposed by the St. Louis Division to be directed against [Name Deleted]. He is former [deleted] of the BLACK LIBERATORS (Bufile 157-10356), [rest of sentence, roughly page in length, one line deleted]. The activity *attempts to alienate him from his wife and cause suspicion among the BLACK LIBERATORS that they have a dangerous troublemaker in their midst.*

BACKGROUND:

[Name of target deleted] is currently separated from his wife, [name deleted] who lives with their two daughters in [deleted]. He occasionally sends her money and she appears to be a faithful, loving wife, who is apparently convinced that her husband is performing a vital service to the Black world and, therefore, she must endure this separation without bothering him. She is, to all indications, an intelligent, respectable young mother, who is a member of the AME Methodist Church in [the rest of the page, except for routing notations at the bottom, is deleted and blanked out].[24]

The rest of the memo is as remarkable, and as unseemly, as the foregoing. It dictates the text of a letter, to be inscribed with sloppy handwriting, intentional misspellings, and grammatical errors to "imitate that of the average Black Liberator member," and to be mailed to the leader's wife. It is intended to evoke jealousy in his wife by stating that the leader was cheating on her with other women. This COINTELPRO goes further as the St. Louis office recommends that the fake letter be photocopied and sent to the Liberator's office, to ensure that the leader knows it was written and that he suspects he was betrayed by one of his subordinates.

There is no reason to wonder as to what the objectives of the operation were. The proposal from the SAC in St. Louis to Hoover in Washington leaves little to speculation.

The following results are anticipated following the execution of the above-counter-intelligence activity:

1. Ill feeling and possibly a lasting distrust will be brought between [ blank] and his wife. The concern over what to do about it may detract from his time spent in the plots and plans of [deleted]. He may even decide to spend more time with his wife and children and less time in Black nationalist activity.

2. The Black Liberators will waste a great deal of time trying to discover the writer of the letter. It is possible that their not-too-subtle investigation will lose present members, and alienate potential ones.

3. Inasmuch as Black Liberator strength is ebbing at its lowest level, this action may well be the "death blow."[25]

The shortest month in the year would not pass before a letter was routed from the doddering Director of the FBI to the Special Agent in Charge of St. Louis, giving his baronial blessing to the enterprise. Hoover's approval for the operation warns the local office to be careful and use "precautions" to ensure that "this cannot be traced back to the Bureau."[26]

His only other substantive recommendation was that the local FBI office wait ten days between letters (apparently to make it appear that the letters were indeed mailed through the postal system by the people they appeared to come from).

There is little indication in these files, published as exhibits of the legendary Church Committee[27] hearings by the US Congress, whether the FBI succeeded in its "Anticipated Results" or whether they exceeded their expectations. What is clear is that the State, utilizing crude, incredibly slimy methods, came between man and wife, father and child, to cause marital and familial discord, because a man believed in Black nationalism.

In present day America, the charge that one is an enemy combatant results in the shackled, blindfolded, tortured, and denationalized captives of the US military base and mass outdoor brig at Guantanamo, Cuba. Yet decades before the USA PATRIOT Act, the assistant director of the FBI made plain his feelings about the tactics to be used, in a contemporary sounding phrase, against American citizens who "sought change in the present U.S. government."

William Sullivan, the number two man at the FBI and COINTELPRO chief, responded to the charge that the Bureau was "using techniques designed to destroy a person's family life."[28]

[T]his is a common practice, rough, dirty, tough, dirty business.... We are in it. To repeat, it is a rough, tough, dirty business and dangerous. *We have used that technique against foreign espionage agents, and they have used it against us.*[29]

A US senator questioning Sullivan seems incredulous at what the FBI Assistant Director is telling him:

Q: The same methods were brought home?

A: Yes; brought home against any organization against which we were targeting. We did not differentiate. This is a rough, tough business.

Q: Would it be safe to say that the techniques we learned in fighting Bundists and Silver Shirters, true espionage in World War II, came to be used, the techniques came to be used against some of our own American citizens?

A: That would be the correct deduction.[30]

If the tactics used against foreign nationals and enemies of the United States were utilized against American citizens, what does that say about the meaning of American citizenship? What does it say about the meaning of the State? The nature of the government? The nature of the security apparatus?

Senator Walter Mondale, a vocal and active member of the Church Committee, speaking for the record on the tactics used against the late Rev. Dr. Martin Luther King, Jr., seems particularly disturbed by the actions of the FBI. This series of questions and responses between Mondale and the committee's Chief Counsel, Frederick A. O. Schwarz, Jr., goes to the very heart of why the hearings were held in the first place—COINTELPRO's excesses and constitutional violations.

Senator MONDALE. Would it be fair to say that the tactics used against Dr. King had been borrowed from tactics used against foreign risks, spies, agents, and the rest, who could and did pose a threat?

Mr. SCHWARZ. Mr. Mondale, your own examination of Mr. Sullivan seems to have brought home that point as clear as it could be....

Senator MONDALE. I raised the Dr. King example because I think that is the classic example which shows all of the elements and the dangers involved in this tactic.

When did counterintelligence programs stop?

Mr. SCHWARZ. Well, *that is in question.*

In 1971, after they had been exposed through the media, there was an instruction that they would stop. The instruction says, however, "If anything like this is really important, please advise headquarters." And as I think some of the witnesses indicated, the line between counterintelligence and intensive investigation is one that really can not be drawn and has not been drawn.

Senator MONDALE. So are you saying we cannot be sure that COINTELPRO, in all of is [sic] elements has terminated?

Mr. SCHWARZ. I would not want to use that label, Senator, and I think that is a matter directed to the FBI witnesses. *But it is a problem when you have a Director of the FBI who declines to say that the activities were improper,* as he did when he testified in 1973.[31]

In 1943, during the later years of President Franklin D. Roosevelt's term, Attorney General Francis Biddle wrote a memorandum commanding his young subordinate, J. Edgar Hoover, to cease compiling security classifications of American citizens, asserting that the agency had no legal basis to prepare such lists. Biddle also called the records unreliable.

In clear, unambiguous terms, the Attorney General directed the Bureau's director to cease and desist from such record-keeping. Words like "compiling" and "records" serve to obscure the true nature of the activity whose initial use was the basis for determining whether to place people in secret internment camps during WWII.

Biddle, examining the program, found there was no statutory basis for it. Biddle's edict removes any serious question of the clarity of his cease and desist order:

> I am satisfied that they serve no useful purpose.... There is no statutory authorization or other present authorization for keeping a "custodial detention" list of citizens. The Department fulfills its proper functions by investigating the activities of persons who may have violated the law. It is not aimed in this work as to classifying persons as to dangerousness.[32]

What was Hoover's response? He directed his underlings to simply change the labels on the "Custodial Detention" files to "Security Matter" files. He issued a directive to his agents that the fact that the agency kept such files was "strictly confidential" and not to be disclosed to those outside of the Bureau.

Even his "superiors" in the Attorney General's office were not to be informed. Hoover directed his subordinates to only share security index data with authorized agents of military intelligence groups, who were known for their ability to keep secrets (even from other sectors of the executive branch).

This account just skims the surface of the history of a long-running, repressive regime established in the shadows of the US government. The government, armed with all the awesome powers at its command, destroyed the lives and livelihoods of thousands, nay, tens of thousands of people, who simply opposed the status quo and wished to change the way things were done in this country. We have only the haziest insight into the true scope of this program, for, as has been suggested, Senate hearings into the problem did not meaningfully resolve the problems. Indeed, at the time of the hearings, some five years after the startling revelations of COINTELPRO became public, senators and Senate staffers could not say with any degree of confidence that it had ended. It is easy therefore, to view the hearings themselves with a certain degree of cynicism. While they provided a riveting show, a thrilling political performance, a scripted pantomime of the workings of democracy, they remained, after all was said and done, mere performance. When the curtain came down on the show, the real world, with its painful ambiguities and chilling truths about power, race, and violent white supremacy, remained unchanged. Revelation is not transformation—it only looks like it.

After the revelations, the exposures, the hearings, what happened to those people who committed crimes against their fellow American citizens?

The department of the US government that calls itself Justice decided, some four years after the scandal broke, that *no one* would be held liable "in connection with the Federal Bureau of Investigation's fifteen-year campaign to disrupt the activities of suspected subversive organizations."[33] J. Stanley Pottinger, head of the Civil Rights Division of the DOJ, reported to the Attorney General that his office had found "no basis for criminal charges against any particular individuals involving particular incidents."[34] The government that murdered people, that hired others to murder people, that drove people into poorhouses, that split marriages asunder, that destroyed scores of livelihoods, had violated no "civil rights." The hearings were "punishment enough," the elite sniffed.

The efforts of the FBI against teachers, professors, workers, socialists, Black nationalists, and others (such as antiwar/peace activists) reveal the deep political nature of the agency, the Justice Department, and the United States government as a whole. Their objective was to criminalize dissent, and to instill the numbing fear of poverty into activists by running people out of their jobs solely on the basis of their political ideas. They were agents, neither of order, nor of law, but of capital. Anyone who merely questioned that arrangement, who thought that society could be organized on a more fair, rational basis, was seen as an enemy; in the words of the FBI itself, *no holds were barred.*[35]

The Bureau used its enormous power, influence, and contacts to intimidate politicians. It used the omnipresent press to hound people out of their jobs. It sabotaged allegedly free elections. It destroyed marriages. It shattered families. It fomented violence between political and social adversaries. And this is but the tip of the iceberg. If this is a law enforcement agency one shudders to think what a hate group would do.

## Objective: Neutralize

We have seen, earlier in this chapter, how the FBI was willing, way back in the 1950s, to violate the alleged constitutional rights of Black religious groups and leaders. If the FBI was willing to go to such lengths to undermine groups such as these, how did the agency regard the constitutional rights of Black militants?

As we shall see, the FBI fought them with a viciousness that has few parallels and with a lawlessness that is shocking. The misperception exists that the FBI did not cross the proverbial line, but only solicited violence. The FBI, in fact, solicited, instigated, aided, and abetted the murder of Black political opponents. This seemingly extraordinary claim is made by none other than a twenty-year veteran of the FBI, M. Wesley Swearingen:

> Soon after I had been assigned to the Los Angeles racial squad, I was told by a fellow agent, *Joel Ash*, that another on the squad, *Nick Galt*, had arranged for Galt's informers in the United Slaves [known popularly as the US organization] to assassinate Alprentice Carter, the Panthers' Los Angeles minister of defense, and John Huggins, the deputy minister of information. Following Galt's instructions, informants George Stiner and Larry Stiner shot them to death on the UCLA campus on January 17, 1969.
>
> I had thought Joel Ash had been kidding me because this was beyond any corruption or wrongdoing that I had witnessed or heard of by FBI agents.
>
> I later reviewed the Los Angeles files and verified that the Stiner brothers were FBI informants.... Hoover wanted the Panthers in jail or dead. That was why he had ordered biweekly reports from the field about the campaign against the Black Panther Party.[36]

According to Swearingen, the FBI "engineered" the Stiner brothers' prison break in 1974 and has protected them to the present (or disposed of them).[37]

The Stiner brothers were but two of the snitches the FBI employed to make Hoover's objective to see "the Panthers in jail or dead" a reality.

## The Snitch Game

Has there ever been a social movement that tried to transform the status quo that was not undermined by the use (one may even say misuse) of snitches? As we have seen in the long, tortured history of slave rebellions, snitches often sold out their fellows and betrayed communal liberation efforts for their own petty interests or because of their servile needs to please "Massa." That compulsion did not end when the formal institution of slavery ended, and it continues into the present era. During the radical 1960s, the reality of governmental infiltration into organizations and collectives was ever-present.

Nor did radicals and revolutionaries only have to live with the silent, hidden monitoring of their activities by an unknown observer. For the very nature of the "intelligence" enterprise was its lack of neutrality and its nakedly martial character. It was, in essence, a form of social, political, and economic warfare—an active campaign of State intrusion and antagonism, with clear objectives: to, in words drawn from FBI files, "disrupt," "discredit," and "neutralize" radical and especially Black nationalist (in COINTELPRO-ese "Black Hate") groups. In practice, this meant any group that disagreed with prevailing government policies on war, civil rights, Black empowerment, poverty, women's rights, and so forth.

What does this mean in the real world, where terms like neutralize have a . . . well, neutral, meaning?

If American history is any indication, bureaucratic terms and phrases often obscure far more than they reveal when they relate to State actions and intentions. In this context, where radical was but a synonym for subversive (or, in the now dated argot of the era, Communist-inspired), one who was deemed radical was considered a State enemy and could be treated accordingly.

An informant was often far more than one who merely provided the State with information on those classified as targets. His (or her) job was often to disrupt the normal functioning of organizations with a variety of tactics—creating dissension, lying, trickery, misdirection, and, if all else failed, violence (the elimination of targets by internal and external means).

## The First Snitch

Before the Black Panther Party had been in existence for a year, a young man joined who would be the first of many who would be swayed from defending the Party's program and interests and be persuaded to disrupt them instead.

Several courses shy of his law degree, Earl Anthony claimed to be the "eighth member" of the Party, when it was a tiny, regional group that could fill an efficiency apartment.[38]

When Anthony reported to his draft board in Van Nuys, California, he did so adorned in full BPP uniform and regalia. There he read a statement that warned, in no uncertain terms, that to draft him into the Vietnam War meant an eruption of a battlefield rebellion by a man who described himself as a "Communist" and a sworn member of "the Armed Revolutionary Black Panther Party."[39] Lest they missed his message, he became rather explicit:

> If they do send me to Vietnam, I will shoot my lieutenant and sergeant in the head once we get into the field, and escape over to the North Vietnamese. So I am telling the draft board... Hell, no, I won't go..."[40]

The five middle-aged white men on his draft board thought that perhaps Mr. Anthony was not the ideal candidate for the war then raging in Indochina and quickly dismissed him with no more questions.

Shortly after joining the Party, Anthony met two friends from law school who told him the people he was around were "Communists," as if to warn him. While Anthony didn't have to worry about the Vietnam War, his erstwhile "friends" from the FBI were another matter.

> A couple of weeks later, near the end of August, I was paid a surprise visited [sic] to my San Francisco apartment by Robert O'Connor and Ron Kizenski. No longer were we playing the "buddy buddy" rules. They were all business this time. They came right to the point: I was under investigation for the bombing of the Van Nuys draft board. I was stunned. Not only did I know nothing about the bombing, I hadn't even been told or heard on the news that the place had been bombed.
>
> Of course they said they didn't believe me, but would offer me a deal. They would not charge me if I would become an informant for the FBI inside the Black Panther Party. I start-

ed laughing, and instantly O'Connor threw a right fist upside my jaw, knocking me against the wall. Kizenski grabbed me, and O'Connor threw a series of rights and lefts, knocking me unconscious.

When I regained consciousness, they were still there, sitting down with guns drawn on me. Kizenski said something about them being Vietnam vets and that they didn't like my "smart-ass" attitude. They proposed their deal to me again. They would get the charges of bombing my draft board dropped, because no one was killed, if I became an FBI informant-agent-provocateur inside the Black Panther Party.

I agreed and as far as I know, became the first of dozens of Black Panthers who were to accept the same type of deal from the COINTELPRO division. Still others became local police informants. *There were soon so many of us that we were informing on each other.*[41]

Anthony claims he was sent down to organize the Los Angeles chapter of the BPP and was instructed by his handlers at the FBI to exacerbate discord between the newly organized Panther chapter and the US organization.

When rumors of his complicity led to charges of snitching for the FBI, Anthony hastily left the organization and began his government-supported career as author and playwright. The government sought to use him as an influential figure in the Black cultural scene, both as informant and as spokesman.

The path to informant/agent provocateur was frequently similar to Anthony's case. People facing serious jail terms came to an accommodation with the FBI and entered into a devil's bargain with the State. And as the evidence now overwhelmingly proves, these people didn't merely name names; many of them were asked, instructed, and ordered to cause serious damage to their organizations, and some snitches were government-supported psychopaths, who acted in ways that resulted in destruction and death.

## George Sams (a.k.a. "Madman")

Imagine a case where a man instigates others to torture and kill. Where a man, under the illusion of rank, riles the blood of others to slay a brother with the deadly libel that the victim is a "low-down, dirty, rotten snitch." Imagine that other young men, drunk on the opiate of revolutionary duty, carry out his will. Now imagine that it was later revealed that the man who issued the orders to kill was in fact the snitch. For young men and women in New Haven, Connecticut, they needn't have imagined because that precise scenario became stark, raving reality. On an early spring morning in 1969, the New Haven dailies hit with explosive headlines blaring "8 Panthers Held in Murder Plot."[42]

George Sams, claiming to represent the Central Committee and traveling from branch to branch, had appeared in New Haven and accused Alex Rackley, a young member of the New York branch of the Party, of being an informant. Under orders from Sams, Rackley was tortured and eventually taken into the woods outside of New Haven to be shot and killed. Once the story broke Sams vanished and FBI agents staged a series of raids across the nation—allegedly searching for Sams—hitting BPP offices in Washington, Denver, Indianapolis, Salt Lake City, Des Moines, Detroit, San Diego, and Chicago, demolishing office equipment, confiscating literature, swiping files and monies, and, of course, arresting scores of Black Panthers on false charges.

According to scholar and playwright Donald Freed, Sams's mysterious appearances across the nation seemed to presage pre-dawn raids by heavily armed city, state, and federal police forces. But for some strange reason, Freed notes, "Sams was never caught; he always managed to leave before the raids were made." In Chicago, Sams reportedly "walked, armed, through the police and FBI lines."[43]

Sams surfaced in Toronto before assuming his role as star witness for the prosecution in New Haven. During the first trial he admitted that he had instigated the beating and torture of Rackley and implicated Field Lt. Lonnie McLucas and Warren Kimbro for the actual murder. But Sams's duty wasn't done. His job was to help convict Bobby Seale, the Party's Chairman, and Ericka Huggins, the New Haven chapter's Deputy Chairman and the still-grieving widow of Jon Huggins, the Party's Deputy Minister of Information in LA, and by so doing, attempt to deliver a death blow to the Party.

On the stand, however, Sams seemed, well, not just unconvincing, but strangely incoherent. Under examination by defense attorney Charles Garry, Sams seemed unduly confrontational and somewhat given to going off on tangents:

Q: How old are you, Sir?

A: What did you say, Mr. Garry? What did you say?

Q: May the question be read back?

A: ... Today I became 25 years old.

Q: ... Before May 19, 1969, weren't you told by Mr. Seale that you are not to be around any of the Panther headquarters?

A: No, Sir.

Q: As a matter of fact, isn't it a fact, Sir, that you always made sure that you were never around when Mr. Seale was around any part of the party functions?

DA: I'm going to object to this.

THE COURT: Sustained.

Q: And isn't it true that on the nineteenth of May, 1969, you didn't go near Mr. Seale because you were afraid that Mr. Seale would know that you were there? ... Now, you said you first went to New York around the 12th of May?

A: Somewhere around the last of April; around the 12th of May ... [Garry shows him McLucas transcript.] ... Late April or May, I'm not sure.

Q: There's not a word in there about "late April" is there?

A: It could have been.

Q: ... You show me where it says "late April."

A: ... I'll tell you what, you look around somewhere else, Mr. Garry, and you will find it ... you are asking me specifically what happened, second-for-second ... I didn't keep up with the days, you know.

Q: Didn't you used to use heroin?

A: When I was about twelve, yes.

Q: Is it true that you said, "I have every intention of destroying the Party, the Party, period?"

A: No, Sir.

Q: So, if it's in this tape recording of yours, that's an incorrect transcription, is it?

THE WITNESS: Could I have some water?

Q: Are you taking Thorazine?

A: I don't know, Mr. Garry. I just go up to the Medic room and tell them, you know, describe to the doctor that I can't sleep, I'm suffering from some migraine headaches. And the doctor prescribes something for me, I don't go into asking him what he's giving me. And if he give me any drugs, and if it's too powerful—I think I have it in the record to the institution that I don't want any drugs. So the doctor just give me something to go to sleep. They don't work.

THE WITNESS: ... I have nicknames, like Crazy George, Madman, Detroit George—several names—I had the name Dingee Swahoo, which was an African name.

THE COURT: Dingee what?

THE WITNESS: Dingee Swahoo.

THE COURT: All right.

THE WITNESS: It's an African name, and I had the name that Chairman Bobby and David Hilliard gave me, which was Madman No. 1, which was in San Francisco. ... [44]

In a matter of minutes, Sams, the state's star witness, had admitted that he might be using the powerful mind-bending psychotropic medication Thorazine, offered a dizzying array of aliases,[45] and would, within moments, launch into a bizarre attack on Garry, which, when the attorney invites his response, claims that Garry is a secret member of the Party's highest executive body, the Central Committee.[46]

Sams did not help his case when he added that some of the other names he was known by were, "No. 1 Agent," "Rats," and "Snitch."[47]

This, in a torture–murder case, was the best the State could offer.

Before the trial had ended, the elusive Huey P. Newton would visit New Haven, speak at Yale, and sit in at the trial of his fellow comrades. Huey would ask the people's "pardon" for "our inexperience" for even allowing Sams in their presence and lamented the fact that one as ill as he was couldn't even get true psychological treatment in a society "as depraved as America." He did not hate the man, Newton explained; rather, he pitied him.[48]

On May 25, 1971, the "Trial of the Century" came to an unexpected denouement: a hung jury. Eleven of the twelve jurors had voted to acquit Seale; ten of twelve would have acquitted Huggins. When the defense presented motions to dismiss, the state, overwhelmed by the costs of security due to the huge crowds that attended, and the prospect of inflicting the "Madman" on other juries, quietly folded its deck.

The charges were dismissed against Huggins and Seale, but Lonnie McLucas, and Warren Kimbro wouldn't be so lucky. After a highly politicized trial, McLucas would be convicted of conspiracy to commit murder, and do four years of a 15-year sentence. Kimbro would plead to second degree, and like Sams, would be sentenced to life. In four years, however, Sams would be free. Through madness, or design, tragedy marred the newest chapter of the Party, touching, transforming, and, in a sense, damning all.

## Louis Tackwood

Few snitches played the extended, double-edged role of Agent/ Double Agent as did Louis Tackwood. As an informant formally deployed by the local Los Angeles Police Department's Criminal

Conspiracy Section (CCS), Tackwood had his hands in over a dozen area cases and worked to imprison and entrap many on the periphery of the Black Panther Party. The CCS was the LAPD equivalent of the Red Squad; a sort of local COINTELPRO unit. While not a Party member, like Sams or Anthony, he served to destabilize support groups.

Unlike Anthony, his predecessor, Louis came from a broken, utterly poor family. Raised by his grandmother in Louisiana, his family joined the swelling exodus from the South to the North and the West. Poverty contributed to his lumpen survival choices, and he began adulthood as an active gangster. As he entered into a life of petty crime, he learned he had the gift of gab—a quality that would come in handy in the dark and deceitful world of domestic spycraft as an informant agent provocateur for the LAPD.

Tackwood provides some insight into the complex characters that are sometimes drawn to the snitch game: their attraction to officialdom and their concomitant revulsion at their betrayal of their peers. When at the height of his powers, Tackwood became, what must be a rarity in his chosen field, a double agent who tried to play both sides of the fence—snitch on the movement and snitch on the cops. That said, Tackwood took a perverse pleasure and pride in the role he played for the CCS. As he describes his introduction to the CCS, he reveals his greed and, indeed, his "professional jealousy" at other snitches:

> My first meeting was held at the Glass House [Tackwood's name for CCS HQ in Central LA] on the third floor when I met the head man in charge of a new department called Criminal Conspiracy Section. His name is Lieutenant Keel. His partner was a Sgt. Sherrett. Before they started talking, they gave me a hundred dollars. Lt. Keel said, "Listen, man, you're just the man we want. You have all the experience we need. Stop working for S.I.I. [Tackwood originally informed for the LAPD's Special Identity and Investigations unit], and come to work for us." I said, "Well, yeah, the money looks good. Who are you?" Keel said, "Criminal Conspiracy Section." I found out later that's just what they're doing too. They spend all their time cooking up

criminal conspiracies against militants, particularly groups like the Panthers, Angela Davis, and people like that.[49]

As an SII snitch, Tackwood had worked on a variety of cases, but as a CCS operative, his targets became the leading Black activist figures in California—the entire state—wherever his expertise was in demand. According to Tackwood, the role he performed exceeded the usual snitch-informant gig:

> I served as a key instrument to these conspiracies, as did Melvin Smith and lots of others. They elevated a select number of informers to the level of agents. They no longer called us informers but special agents who were paid a lot of money for our assignments. One of the early agents to go to work for the special department was Melvin Smith, better known as Cotton, third man in command of the Los Angeles chapter of the Black Panthers. Supposedly, the man in charge of weapons, yeah, he was their weapons expert. He's the one who brought the automatic weapon to the Panther office the day before the raid. It was in his hands all the time when the shootout took place.
>
> *A select group; that's what we were. We were an elite corps.* Everything looked great.[50]

When Tackwood nonchalantly strolled into the offices of radicals affiliated with a group calling itself the Citizens Research and Investigation Committee (CRIC) and openly confessed to his role in conspiracies involving radical and revolutionary political groups in California, their minds were blown. They actually couldn't bring themselves to believe the guy (given the FBI's actions, people were quite paranoid). They suspected, given the times, that their tall, lean, Afroed Black visitor was trying to set them up for a bust. Though they taped his claims he sensed they didn't believe him, so he promptly picked up the phone, dialed the Glass House, and spoke conspiratorially with an LAPD sergeant—they laughed about one of their recent capers.

Still unconvinced, the radicals contacted the press, which had the resources and contacts to check the man's stories out. Shortly thereafter, they heard back from their press contacts (for *Newsweek*, the *Washington Post,* and the *Los Angeles Times*) that this guy was the genuine article. One press investigator found a parole officer's report that declared Tackwood was a reliable police informant; another traced his long criminal record, and marveled at the short time served. His name turned up in a slew of cases, not only those of political activists and revolutionaries, but average, everyday cases, with some of the "convicted" on the state's Death Row.

Why did he come to CRIC? Why now? It seemed that a recent police raid on Black Panther offices was one important factor. The December 8, 1969 raid was an urban war that lasted for hours. Tackwood, looking at the treatment of "Cotton" Smith, armed with the weapon that justified the raid, believed that the police tried to kill Smith, as well as Deputy Defense Minister Geronimo ji-Jaga and all the other Panther leaders during the raid. Tackwood reasoned that if the police would kill one of their highest placed agents, like Cotton, then he would fare little better when they wanted to make him disappear.

In any event, Tackwood's timing was exquisite: the LA District Attorney was trying the caged Panthers for their roles in the December 1969 raid, and was presenting Melvin "Cotton" Smith as a witness as if he had a genuine change of heart, and wasn't, in fact, a paid police informant placed in the Party to destroy it from within. When defense lawyers for the *Panther 13* received transcripts of Tackwood's revelations about Cotton, the case against them collapsed like a punctured balloon. The jury acquitted the Panthers of all major charges.

When the CCS learned their prize pigeon had sung to the movement, they hatched an elaborate plan to bring him back to their nest. They simply busted him. They knew that a snitch's greatest fear was prison, and so they left him sitting in jail for several days until he figured out the message.

After three days, they came to him with a form of redemption: set up his confederates in CRIC by claiming that they conspired to steal police documents. Not just any documents. They wanted him to testify that they were stealing LAPD identification papers to use to kill a number of cops. As Tackwood had crossed them, they reasoned, they would use him to double-cross his new found allies at CRIC. To make the ruse work, they had to set up others to give the alleged conspiracy legitimacy. Tackwood, ever the opportunist, seemed to get into the groove:

> That night around eleven o'clock, C.C.S. dropped me off at Newton Street [an LA police precinct]. There were only a few people there that time of night. I walked in and tell the cat I work for C.C.S., give him my code name, the whole shot, and I needed some money. The guy goes through all the motions, calls C.C.S., everything. They tell him to give me everything I need.
>
> No matter what it took, they should go out and arrest these people. Man, the dude snapped to attention when he heard that. There were six cops there just bullshitting on a coffee break. He broke in and told them, "Hey, go with this man."
>
> On the way down to the house, they picked up some more men. *They didn't know who I was, just that they were to take orders from me.* We set it up real nice. Cordoned off both ends of the street and eight came with me.
>
> We walked up to the back apartment building and I knocked. *When the lady asked who it was, I said, "The police."* You should hear every apartment door in the building slam shut. So I motion to the cops who came over, cocked their guns, told me to stand back and kicked the door in. We got inside but I didn't know which apartment Roy lived in. There were four of them. So, four cops, guns drawn, line up in front of each door, and bust in. There were some old people in one, two were empty, and Roy was in bed with his old lady.
>
> Cop says, "Your name Roy, dude?"
>
> Dude says, "Yeah."
>
> "Well, you better not breathe." He turns to me and asks, "Is this the one?"
>
> I say, "Yeah," but I don't know, I ain't never seen the dude before.

Cop said, "We're looking for a briefcase and some papers, right? ..."
Of course we couldn't find the papers so the cops asked me
"What shall we do now?"

"Arrest him," I said. "Handcuff him and take him."

"Her too?"

"No, she ain't the right one."[51]

Of course, there were no papers. Roy was merely a fall guy, a pimp, who had enemies among the police. The CCS plan was coming together, and warrants were being prepared for CRIC members that would demolish their attempts to publicize Tackwood's tales of government perfidy and political conspiracies. But Tackwood, in his own words, *crossed them*.[52] As a veteran of such proceedings, he knew that one thing was vital: he had to show up in court. Instead, he went to ground, and the case crumbled. The lesson of Cotton was not lost on him; he feared the CCS would betray him, so he flipped first.

The details of his last job, not to mention the lengths to which the police went to retain his services, to frame a pimp they didn't like, or to entrap and frame the CRIC activists, read like a television script. Except, of course, this was not TV. It was real life, a life concocted by State forces employed in political policing and repression, joined with the selfish, twisted motives of the bane of all progressive movements: the snitch. Tackwood was, to be sure, a piece of work, but his achievements would be dramatically, and tragically, exceeded by another member of the snitch club.

## William O'Neal

In the history of snitches, informants, and agents provocateurs, William O'Neal stands alone. A young Black man facing relatively minor charges of car theft and impersonating a federal officer, O'Neal was propositioned by Roy Mitchell, a Chicago FBI agent assigned to that city's Racial Matters Squad. Promised a monthly stipend and the dropping of all charges, O'Neal took the bait and made his way to Black Panther Party headquarters at 2350 Madison on the first day it officially opened and promptly submitted his application.

O'Neal was accepted and got in on the ground floor of the chapter's growth and soon emerged as a powerful and trusted cadre, rising to the ironic rank of Director of Security. He was assigned to be Chairman Fred Hampton's personal bodyguard. From this perch of power, the federally paid stool pigeon proceeded to sabotage every chapter activity that he could.

When Hampton was involved in tense, heated talks with members of the vast, well-armed Blackstone Rangers gang and the fledgling BPP was on the brink of effecting a merger that would have radicalized and drafted over three thousand youth into the Party, O'Neal intervened. O'Neal told his paymasters of the talks, and, as we have seen, a COINTELPRO letter was sent to Jeff Fort, then head of the gang claiming "there's supposed to be a hit out on you."[53] Several months later the FBI director continued to sew discord by authorizing the following letter:

Brother Hampton:

Just a word of warning. A Stone friend tells me [name deleted] wants the Panthers and is looking for somebody to get you out of the way. Brother Jeff [Fort] is supposed to be interested. I'm just a black man looking for blacks working together, not more of this gang banging.[54]

Thanks to intelligence provided by O'Neal, the FBI intervened and derailed this peace conference. It was not sufficient for the FBI to prevent these groups from coming together; O'Neal, perhaps in gratitude for a March 11 pay raise, personally instigated an armed clash between the two on April 12, 1969.[55]

Urged on by his handlers, O'Neal tried bolder and far more dangerous ways of sabotaging the BPP. At Mitchell's direction, O'Neal proposed a "security plan" that included nerve gas and the construction of an electric chair for Party backsliders. The Chairman and the Deputy Defense Minister, Bobby Rush, strongly opposed this idea and nixed it. When they were out of the office,

O'Neal bullwhipped a Party member whom he accused of being an "informer" against the organization.

By March 1969, O'Neal and his FBI handlers had concocted a plan to acquire an aircraft or a mortar to "bomb City Hall." Again Hampton and Rush rejected his "plan."

Several months later, when FBI agents raided the office on Monroe Street, it was because their agent provocateur had acquired arms illegally and stashed them at the office. Their other justification for the raid was because they were allegedly searching for fugitive (and FBI informant) George Sams. Well-publicized in June 1969, the raid was designed to isolate the BPP and gave the State the excuse to destroy Party property and try to destroy its hold on the radical imagination. At the time of the raids, Chicago's Special Agent in Charge, Marlin Johnson, was receiving directives from Hoover commanding him to order his minions to "destroy what the [BPP] stands for" and "eradicate its 'serve the people' programs."[56]

O'Neal would later provide the FBI with a floor plan of the Black Panther apartment where Hampton, his fiancée, Deborah Johnson, and other Party members slept during the night. Informed by O'Neal that arms were stored there, the FBI and its confederates in the state's Gang Intelligence Unit (GIU), the Illinois version of the Red Squad, had their pretexts for a raid. The FBI would recruit the shooters for this raid, and they had one primary objective—to kill Fred Hampton. They learned (again through O'Neal) that Hampton was so impressive that he was going to be elevated to the Party's Central Committee in California and be named Chief of Staff in place of David Hilliard. The FBI was determined to scuttle this plan, for they well knew Hampton's organizing abilities.

When Hampton, via Bobby Rush, first encountered the Party at 19 years of age he already had a remarkable history of activism behind him. While a student at Proviso East High School Hampton began to organize the NAACP "youth chapter" and saw its membership climb from 17 to some 700 members.[57] He worked with whites, Blacks, Latinx, Asians—everybody and anybody, if it furthered the movement, if it fueled the revolution. There was no way such a sublimely gifted organizer could escape the omnipresent gaze of the State—the snoops and spies of the FBI. This tall, handsome, personable, exuberant Panther posed a serious threat to the status quo, for he was, above all, a serious revolutionary.

In the early morning hours of December 4, 1969, the raid would be accomplished: Fred Hampton would be slain, Mark Clark would also be killed, and half a score of other Panthers would be wounded or imprisoned.

In Philadelphia, Captain Reggie called Rosemari Mealy to find out if any members of her radical Quaker commune were traveling to Chicago, and whether several Panthers could join them to represent the chapter in Fred's honor.

A group of us squeezed into a gray Saab and made the long trip to Chicago. Among those en route were Rosemari, Officer of the Day Rene Johnson, and myself.

When we arrived at the office, we were walked over to the apartment and saw the holes making the walls look like Swiss cheese. We saw the mattress, caked with blood, where Fred and his fiancée lay that fateful night, the bullet holes lining the walls, tactile markers of government hate.

Before the month had passed, O'Neal was sent his $300 bonus as a reward for a job well-done.[58] After O'Neal's betrayals, the Chicago Black Panther Party chapter, ripped apart by treachery, was never the same, and one of the most promising Panthers in the nation had his destiny torn from him.

In 1990, O'Neal committed suicide by running in front of a speeding car on Lakeshore Drive in Chicago. Hampton had become immortalized into legend as a loving "servant of the People," and O'Neal, as a snitch, was reviled.

## Protecting the Traitors

It would be misleading to suggest that snitches somehow got their comeuppance after their startling betrayals of the Party or their people. Truth be told, most did not. Some went on to public careers of influence and power, with none (but the espionage agencies) the wiser to their true identities or their treason to their fellows. Anthony, for example, wrote a book, *Picking Up the Gun,* that was widely seen as an insider's story that panned the Party as a violent, Communist-funded group. Readers of this tell-all weren't told quite all—they did not know that the author was an FBI informant and agent provocateur. He wrote and produced several plays that were performed in the Bay Area and New York, yet it is doubtful that his audiences knew the undercover role this Black cultural artist was performing.

George Sams's "life" sentence was decidedly short-lived. He was granted parole after four years in the joint and promptly went out and committed several other violent crimes.

Most snitches remain blacked-out smudges on faded FBI files, unknown to those they betrayed and those presumably closest to them. Anthony, for example, hid his snitch background for decades.

Every Panther, upon acceptance into the organization, was instructed to never speak with the FBI or any other agency. There was simply nothing to talk about. Some Panthers and others on the party's periphery ignored that sage advice and commenced making deals with the devil. Such decisions led to disaster, destruction, and death.

For the centuries-long, hard movement of Black people for liberation, the role of snitches made that trek all the more arduous.

## Media Wars

What began in Hoover's fevered imagination quickly took root in local and regional police departments, which viewed the Black

Panther Party as "the greatest threat" in their respective jurisdictions. With FBI intelligence and assistance, local police began to formulate and execute their own actions against these perceived "threat[s]." There was scarcely a city with a functioning BPP chapter that did not experience trumped-up arrests, police raids, firefights, and, in some instances, the death or wounding of Party members.

However, what made these raids and attacks acceptable to the public was the role of the American media. In a campaign of demonization and stigmatization, the FBI, working through its media "newsfriendlies," would circulate rumor, slander, innuendo, and lies to further COINTELPRO objectives—to "expose, disrupt, misdirect, discredit, or otherwise neutralize" the Black Panther Party and similar black nationalist, radical formations.[59] This negative reporting, which projected the Party as racist, violent, or criminal in nature, served to justify virtually any repression that the State could dream up. Such treatment incensed New York Panther Assata Shakur:

> What made me maddest was the media treatment of the BPP, which gave the impression that the Party was racist and violent. And it worked. The pigs would burst into a Panther office, shoot first, and ask questions later. The press always reported that the police had "uncovered" a large arsenal of weapons. Later, when the "arsenal" turned out to be a few legally registered rifles and shotguns, the press never printed a word.[60]

While negative media accounts angered Panthers and served to legitimize State attacks on them, the press reports and consequent repression had other, unanticipated effects: it deepened and broadened support among Blacks. Historian Howard Zinn notes that, "A secret FBI report to President Nixon in 1970 said 'a recent poll indicates that approximately 25% of the black population has a great respect for the Black Panther Party, including 43% of blacks under 21 years of age.'"[61]

A contemporary public opinion poll for the Harris organization revealed far greater support. Asked whether the Panthers gave

Black persons an individual sense of pride by standing up for the rights of Blacks, 66 percent agreed. When asked, "Even if you disagree with the views of the Panthers, has the violence against them led you to believe that Black people must stand together to protect themselves?" a whopping 86 percent of black respondents were in agreement.[62]

Although such advances came in result to tremendous loss, they show a significant percentage of Black Americans were becoming open to the positions of the Black Panther Party.

While Blacks may have felt a growing solidarity in the face of the fierce and deadly State repression of the Party, their white fellow citizens did not share their views. Whites saw it as something happening to "them," not to "us." Black feminist scholar Joy James notes:

> However, no concerted national outrage emerged in response to the state's violent repression of black insurgency.... The lack of concern was partly tied to ignorance and partly the consequence of negative media depictions of black revolutionaries.[63]

James then cites the 1976 Church Committee report:

> The FBI has attempted covertly to influence the public's perception of persons and organizations by disseminating derogatory information to the press, either anonymously or through "friendly" news contacts.[64]

The role of the media has often been overlooked in the police-Panther conflict, especially during the extremely bloody 1968–70 period. By the end of 1970 an estimated twenty-eight armed clashes occurred, and an estimated nineteen Panthers were slain by state forces.[65] The news reports which, no matter the circumstances, inevitably supported the government (consider the murder of Fred Hampton), bespeak a profound conservatism of the press that prevails in spite of any given reporter's political views. Journalism professor Jack Lule, who uses the influence of social and cultural myths to analyze the media comes to a similar conclusion:

Coverage of radical politics thus raises difficult issues. Social institutions—including the news—might be under violent attack. Publishers, editors, and reporters, no different from most people who grow up in a society, often share most of society's cultural and political beliefs. How do newspapers respond to people who challenge fundamental beliefs?

Some writers already have looked at this issue. They harshly criticize news coverage of radical politics. They argue that news coverage seeks to delegitimize and disarm perceived threats to social order. They find that although journalists themselves are often seen as politically liberal in their beliefs, the news media are a conservative ideological force. News media serve, in this view, as "agents of social control" who preserve "the status quo by providing unsympathetic coverage to those whose behavior threatens it...."

Black political leaders in particular attract negative coverage, critics say. The news degrades black activists and situates moderate black leaders on more "legitimate" middle ground. From coverage of Malcolm X to that of the Black Panthers, of Louis Farrakhan, and of Al Sharpton, stories of black leaders who espouse controversial views reflect a troubled relationship among the news, race, and politics.[66]

The acclaimed Black novelist and former journalist Ishmael Reed decries this deep bias in favor of the State, and deep antipathy against African Americans as a kind of "White nationalist journalis[m]."[67]

The role of the American media is reminiscent of that played by the radical press in eighteenth century, pre-Revolutionary France. In that era, the government was said to be comprised of three estates: the monarchy, the nobility, and the elite of the Church. The press was so powerful, so influential, however, that it came to be seen as a branch of government, or, as it was called, the fourth estate.

The American media plays a somewhat similar role by supporting the *status quo,* no matter what. When the State commits crimes, such acts are not so described, but are referred to as "excesses." While the toll of assassinations, exile, and incarcerations have garnered some attention from radical scholars, there is little research on how FBI, and local police actions, caused activists to be fired, to be denied employment, to lose housing, scholarships, and other social provisions. How many suffered divorce? Suicide?

Jean Seberg is perhaps little known in this age of actress-celebrities like Jennifer "J.Lo" Lopez, or Madonna. Ms. Seberg was an artist of some note in the 1960s, but the FBI was more interested in her political sympathies. When she dared make contributions to the Black Panther defense fund, she earned the twisted ire of the FBI, which launched into a vicious media attack.

Swearingen reports the agency went ballistic when it suspected the actress of having an affair with a high-ranking Panther member. He later reported, in a sworn affidavit, that the racism of his fellow FBI workers was intense, and it compelled them to the unthinkable. "In the view of the Bureau," he later related,

> Jean was giving aid and comfort to the enemy, the BPP ... The giving of her white body to a black man was an unbearable thought for many of the white agents. An agent was overheard to say, a few days after I arrived in Los Angeles from New York, "I wonder how she'd like to gobble up my dick while I shove my .38 up that black bastard's ass."[68]

The FBI contacted its media "friendlies" to issue gossip items about her. The *Los Angeles Times* printed the gossip, and Seberg, who, as the FBI knew, was emotionally unstable, went into a terrible emotional spiral. She was about six months pregnant when she attempted suicide by taking sleeping pills. This caused her to go into labor prematurely and the fetus died. The shattered woman attempted suicide annually around the time of the miscarriage, and finally succeeded in 1979. Her ex-husband, Romaine Gary, later took his own life.

## Uncovering COINTELPRO

The American people did not learn about the infamous COINTELPRO violations because of the investigative prowess of the vaunted press. No government agency sounded the alarm on this outrageous and long-standing program, which reveals the government's utter disregard for the Constitution and other laws. The Senate, with all its pomp and ceremony, didn't stop it.

The acronym COINTELPRO would not be known to us today were it not for the efforts of a secret group of radicals who broke into an FBI storage facility in Media, Pennsylvania, on March 8, 1971. This anonymous group of antiwar and anti-imperialist activists broke in, under cover of night, photocopied the files that they found there, and later mailed copies to dozens of activists, organizations, and news media. In short, it wasn't "the media" that broke COINTELPRO, but Media.

The group, calling itself the Citizen's Commission to Investigate the FBI, shared an edited representation of their files with an antiwar periodical called *WIN* magazine, which devoted an entire issue to the files, reprinting many of them verbatim. These acts, more than anything else, opened the window of light on the repressive nature of the FBI, the megalomania of Hoover, and the government's secret war against peace and antiwar activists, civil rights organizations, feminists, socialists, Black nationalists, and other social groups.

There are, of course, lessons to be learned from these events. One may not wisely rely on government, nor on other elite, allied agencies, to defend the people from the crimes of government. Further, it takes actions from the outside to reveal what takes place on the inside. This cannot be seriously questioned in light of the Media, Pennsylvania, and the CRIC/Tackwood revelations.

The Media raiders found that the vast majority of FBI efforts were dedicated to the surveillance of political activists, some 40 percent—the largest single grouping. Thirty percent of the files were administrative, training, or routine materials; 25 percent of the files dealt with bank robberies; 20 percent involved murders, rapes, and interstate theft cases; 7 percent dealt with draft resistance-type cases, and 1 percent (1 percent!) dealt with organized crime, primarily gambling-related.[69] This reveals, better than anything, the true nature of the beast.

Consider, as a kind of leitmotif, the case of Dick Gregory, a caustic comedian of the 1960s, who was attracted to the Civil Rights movement and to Martin Luther King. He transformed his performances from racially tinged comedy to socially insightful speeches and once dared to speak out against the violent criminality of the US Mafia. In a Chicago speech, Gregory reportedly stated that the "syndicate" were "the filthiest snakes that exist on this earth."[70] In light of the prominence of the FBI as a major US law enforcement agency, one might think that the heads of the agency would wholeheartedly concur with Gregory's assessment and perhaps even applaud his anticrime sentiments. The Bureau's response, however, was telling.

It came in a memo dated May 5, 1968, where the FBI, calling Gregory a "militant black nationalist," directed its agents to:

> Consider the use of this statement in developing a counterintelligence operation to alert [the crime syndicate] La Cosa Nostra (LCN) to Gregory's attack on LCN. It is noted that other speeches by Gregory also contain attacks on the LCN. No counterintelligence action should be taken without Bureau authority.[71]

Affixed to the May memo was a note saying that "Richard Claxton Gregory" had previously referred to the FBI in a derogatory manner (as well as the director, of course). Director Hoover promptly gave his OK to the COINTEL operation, which consisted of anonymous letters routed to various Mafiosi in Chicago, Gregory's hometown. Did the FBI think the Mafia would boycott Gregory's speeches or stop laughing at his jokes?

The FBI, in this and hundreds of other such operations, was fomenting violence between people and hoped that the syndicate would rid them of the "militant black nationalist" who dared to criticize the high lord director.

Senator Walter Mondale put things in frighteningly clear perspective when he opined in the midst of the Church Committee hearings:

We heard that the FBI, to protect the country against those it believed had totalitarian political views, employed the tactics of totalitarian societies against American citizens. We heard that the FBI attempted to destroy one of our greatest leaders in the field of civil rights and then replace him with someone of the FBI's choosing.

From the evidence the committee has obtained, it is clear that the FBI for decades has conducted surveillance over the personal and political activities of millions of Americans. Evidently, no meeting was too small, no group too insignificant to escape their attention … the FBI created indexes, *more commonly called enemies lists,* on thousands of Americans, targeted many of the Americans on these lists for special harassment.[72]

One wonders, who were really the subversives of American democracy?

*Being a teenager in the national headquarters of the Black Panther Party, even as a tall, older-looking-than-you-really-are teenager, was mostly great fun. It was, of course, work, hours spent writing, editing, reading, studying, and learning. But it was also talking to older Panthers who always took the time to teach their younger brother about anything his ever-hungry curiosity could dream about. Mojo, a true Black Southerner, had an uncanny skill at hambone. What's hambone? That's taking two spoons and, using them like a percussive instrument, hitting your body, your thighs, and your chest rhythmically to create wonderful music. Mojo was a one-man orchestra! But I, woefully uncoordinated, try as I might, couldn't even get a good "thump!" going. It was most frustrating.*

*Teenagers, being naturally curious, always want to touch things. One day, after I had done my writing, editing, and justifying, I ambled up to the second floor, and what would I see but a group of radios standing on a table in the conference room, emitting a dull, unformed static. "Hey!" I thought, "let's get some music on this joint!" I walked over to the radios, and, one by one, I tried to dial in a Bay Area music station and maybe hear some James Brown, Curtis Mayfield, or the Temptations. Coming from Philly, I knew where the Black radio stations were clustered on the dial, and my months in the Bronx schooled me on where WLIB was stationed, but this was northern California.*

*Where were the good RnB stations? I turned and turned the dials of these funny-lookin' radios, but, except for a few pops and hisses, I got nothing. As I was deep into my dialing I heard a rough voice bark out an order, "Boy! Getta fuck away from them radios!"*

*I stood up erect, and stared into the face of an LA Panther who had been at Headquarters for a few days. I knew him from rumor, and from articles in* The Black Panther. *This was Melvin "Cotton" Smith, perhaps the oldest member of the Black Panther Party. Smith was a tall, thin, bald-headed man with a deeply lined face. As one of the youngest Panthers, I looked up to him with true admiration for he seemed to be old enough to be, not merely an older brother or sister, but my parent. For him to be a Panther! I thought he was extraordinary. Yet, here he was, glaring at me as if I had stolen something. I was terrified. He glared at me, and called in June Hilliard to report, with a tone that only made me grow in discomfort, that I was "tampering" with these radios. June looked at me for a few minutes, and asked me what I was doing. I told him the truth, that I was looking for some music stations to listen to, but I didn't know where to find them out here. He smiled a half-smile, and whispered to me that they were "special" radios that were "tuned in" to our troops "in the field." He said they couldn't pick up regular radio stations, and if I saw them again, just to ignore them. As June was calmly explaining things to me, "Cotton" continued to glare, as if I was guilty of a major Party infraction.*

*Years later, after the Media raid lead to the uncovering of the COINTELPRO files, I would learn why Cotton had that perpetually worried look on his face, and, perhaps, why he reacted so strongly to my meddling with his radios. He was an undercover plant and agent-provocateur. I wondered if I had inadvertently thrown off one of his snitching efforts. He was but one of a half-dozen Panthers who I knew who would later be revealed as traitors to the Party and their People.*

## CHAPTER SEVEN

# A Woman's Party

Women ran the BPP pretty much. I don't know how it got to be a male's party or thought of as being a male's party.
—Frankye Malika Adams, Member, Black Panther Party

**THE GREAT AFRICAN** American educator and civil rights leader Mary McLeod Bethune (1875–1955), a major force in the Black women's club movement in the 1920s and 30s, called on women to "go to the front and take our rightful place; fight our battles and claim our victories."[1] Women tried to do this in the heyday of the Black Liberation movement, as well as during the Civil Rights movement, with various degrees of success. In these movements, women generally were relegated to subordinate roles and were virtually invisible within the hierarchy of the organizations, even though they provided the bulk of the membership and labor. This phenomenon in part led the Student Nonviolent Coordinating Committee (SNCC) founder Ella Baker (1903–1986) to observe that "strong people don't need strong leaders" and to advocate the collectivist model of leadership over the prevailing messianic style of the period. In essence, Baker was arguing against civil rights organizations mirroring the Black church model—a predominantly female membership with a predominantly male clergy—and for the inclusion of women in the leadership of these organizations. Baker was also questioning the hierarchical nature of these groups' leadership.

The Black Liberation movement, typified by groups such as the Republic of New Afrika (RNA), the Congress of Racial Equality (CORE), the Junta of Militant Organizations (JOMO), the Revolutionary Action Movement (RAM), the US organization, the Black Panther Party, and a multitude of local groups, by not drawing on the Black church as a base, did not inherit the structural defect Baker observed. That said, much of the movement was indeed deeply macho in orientation and treated women in many of these groups in a distinctly secondary and disrespectful fashion. This is seen in the popular saying attributed to Kwame Turé (né Stokely Carmichael) that "the only position for a woman in the movement is prone."

It is with a focus on these macho and misogynist attitudes that much of the popular press has examined the role of Black women in the Black Panther Party. In *The Shadow of the Panther*, Hugh Pearson, who had no discernable background in the Black Liberation movement, and therefore no firsthand knowledge of what he wrote, damned the Black Panther Party's "routine" mistreatment of women as both wide-ranging and "flagrant."[2] Pearson relied on three BPP insiders, "those who would never forgive Huey for what he did to the party," and on "nonblacks who had been affiliated with Newton and the party," whom he found to be the "easiest" sources for him to interview. It is not surprising that he comes to flawed conclusions based upon these limited and biased sources.[3]

Historian and scholar Errol A. Henderson is quite critical of Pearson on this score.[4] Other scholars have deemed Pearson's work "flawed" and "biased journalis[m]."[5] Black studies professor Reginald Major was even more critical, calling it "stealth history," which "has a distinctive political objective, to dampen, discredit and demonize the revolutionary potential of African-Americans."[6] Kathleen Cleaver questions the whole enterprise surrounding the portrayal of women in the Black Panther Party:

> Well, ask yourself, where did the image of the Black Panther Party that you have in your head come from? Did you read

those articles planted by the FBI in the newspaper?...How many photographs of women Panthers have you seen? Think about this: how many newspaper photographers were women? How many newspaper editors were women? How many newscasters were women? How many television producers were women? How many magazine, book, newspaper publishers? Who was making the decisions about what information gets circulated, and when that decision gets made, who do you think they decide to present?...Could it be the images and stories of the Black Panthers that you've seen and heard were geared to something other than conveying what was actually going on?[7]

While it may be proper to be sharply critical of the Black Liberation movement generally, it is also proper to give credit where it is due. For the undeniable truth is that the Black Panther Party, for ideological reasons and for reasons of sheer survival, gave the women of the BPP far more opportunities to lead and to influence the organization than any of its contemporaries, in white or Black radical formations.

A comparison with contemporary society as a whole also reflects positively upon the BPP. Eldridge Cleaver wrote, "[W]e have to recognize our women as our equals...revolutionary standards of principles demand that we go to great lengths to see that disciplinary action is taken on all levels against those who manifest male chauvinism behavior."[8] And:

> I'm aware that it has been a problem in all organizations in Babylon to structure our struggle in such a way that our sisters, our women are liberated and made equal in our struggle...I know that the Minister of Defense, Huey P. Newton has spoken out many times that the male chauvinism that is rampant in Babylon in general, is also rampant in our own ranks."[9]

And point seven of the BPP 8 Points of Attention in the Party's rules states, "Do not take liberties with women,"[10] showing an awareness that sexual misconduct must be confronted within the Party. Kathleen Cleaver writes, "In 1970 the Black Panther Party took a formal position on the liberation of women. Did the U.S. Congress make any statement on the liberation of women?...Did the Oakland police issue a position against gender discrimination?"[11]

This writer knows of no other instances of radical groups of the period, especially those projected as having a predominantly male membership, that had women in the leadership to the extent the Black Panther Party did. During its time, the BPP had women in leadership positions in the internal organization and the regional offices, and even as the leader of the total organization.

Afeni Shakur (known to millions of youth as the mother of the late rapper Tupac Shakur) was appointed to a position of responsibility in the Harlem branch that she felt she was ill-chosen for. She felt she was neither "brilliant" nor had the "leadership ability" to function properly as section leader.[12] It is an interesting psychological insight that people seldom perceive themselves as others do, but unless Shakur is projecting a false sense of self-effacement, it reflects a startling imbalance between what she and others perceived in her. Several committed Party members who worked alongside her were struck by her utter brilliance and her radiant sense of self as she went about her daily duties. Safiya A. Bukhari, who held various posts in the Party and later commanded units of the Black Liberation Army (BLA), met and interacted with a broad range of Panthers, from all across the country, some famous and others not as well-known. While she found them all to be impressive individuals, she was deeply struck by Afeni Shakur. She would later write of her "exposure to an elfin, dark skinned woman with a very short afro":

> Afeni Shakur walked tall and proud among these people. She emitted an inner strength and assuredness that made me say to myself, *This is a Black woman worthy of respect.*
>
> Other than my grandmother on [my] mother's side, to that point I had not met a woman that I could look up to.... At that time when I needed it most Afeni Shakur exemplified the strength and dignity amid chaos that I needed to see.[13]

Afeni, taught by teachers and others in the white power structure that she was not worthy of much, probably saw herself as they did. But to those around her, another Afeni was visible. Indeed, Bukhari notes that "Afeni never knew she was having this effect on me."[14] Yet this writer can safely state that Bukhari was far from alone in her response.

Other Party members saw something in Afeni that she may not have seen in herself. She was promoted from the ranks despite her objections when two leading Panthers were busted on old bench warrants that predated their BPP membership. Afeni would later recount, "…and every time I'd tell them that I shouldn't be in any position like that, they would just look at me and tell me there's nobody else to do it. That's how they justified it."[15] Jamal Joseph, who at sixteen was among the youngest members of the New York Panthers, would later list three women as some of his "most important teachers and best friends" and as people who taught him to oppose male chauvinism and value the wisdom of women: Assata Shakur, Janet Cyril (one of the founders of the Brooklyn branch), and Afeni Shakur.[16]

How did Afeni Shakur, as an angry, alienated, desperately poor girl from North Carolina, living in the cold, hellish Big Apple, get interested in the BPP? She heard someone she described as a "cute little nigger," who later turned out to be Bobby Seale, giving a roaring street corner soapbox speech at 125th Street and Seventh Avenue about something called the Black Panthers.[17] She was so moved that she searched out the address of the Harlem branch office, attended a Political Education class, and promptly joined. The way this young woman was treated was an important factor in why she joined:

> When I first met Sekou [Odinga] and Lumumba [Shakur] it was the first time in my life that I ever met men who didn't abuse women. As simple as that. It had nothing to do with anything about political movements. It was just that *never in my life had I met men who didn't abuse women*, and who loved women because they were women and because they were people.[18]

This observation is a telling one, for if, as Pearson avers, the BPP abused women in a manner that was "flagrant," widespread, and "routine," then the impressions of a young, naive, beautiful woman, who entered at the Party's ground level in one of the largest BPP chapters in the nation, would have been far more negative.

Afeni would later be numbered among the famous *Panther 21*, leading Party members who were targeted by the State for removal, incarceration, and attempted neutralization via government frame-up. The *Panther 21* were indicted on April 2, 1969, on a plethora of weapons, attempted bombing, conspiracy, and related charges. The *Panther 21* received that name because of the twenty-one names on the original indictment. Three of the Panthers were never caught, two were severed from the case because of age, one for health reasons, and two were already being held in New Jersey for other charges. Two years after the initial arrest the thirteen remaining defendants were acquitted of all 156 counts. Despite their eventual acquittal the Party suffered, during a critical period, the loss of some of its best and brightest members' organizing efforts and social presence.

In Brooklyn, another Panther member, Frankye Malika Adams, challenged the preeminent idea that the Black Panther Party was a man's thing:

> [W]omen ran the BPP pretty much. I don't know how it came to be a male's party or thought of as being a male's party. Because these things, when you really look at it in terms of society, these things are looked on as being women things, you know, feeding children, taking care of the sick, and uh, so. Yeah, we did that. We actually ran the BPP's programs.[19]

Adams's insights reveal a perspective that reflects what every Panther actually experienced daily, feeding thousands of Black schoolchildren across the nation, providing free medical services to the ghetto poor, in some cities offering free shoes and clothing to people, and the like. Armed conflict, despite its salience in press reports, was actually a rare occurrence.

Indeed, if a more balanced account of the Oakland office was written, it would significantly undermine Pearson's central thesis that the sexual abuse of Party women was "flagrant," wide-ranging, and "routine."[20] Furthermore, a systematic review of the treatment of women in Oakland would have, at the very least, examined the experience of the first woman to join the Party, Oakland native Tarika Lewis, as she lived, struggled, and worked as the only female in an otherwise all-male milieu.

As a woman, Lewis was not pampered and was subject to the same organizational regulations as her male comrades. In addition to regular attendance in PE classes, she trained in usage, cleaning, disassembly, and reassembly of small arms.

In her first year of service, the bright young recruit made rapid advancements in rank, and was appointed to teach Political Education classes. That said, she still faced macho posturing and resistance, which she handled with style. "When the guys came up to me and said 'I ain't gonna do what you tell me to do 'cause you a sister,' I invited 'em to come on out to the weapons range and I could outshoot 'em."[21] Such a Panther, woman or no, would earn the respect of her comrades because of her undeniable abilities and demonstrated performance.

Other examples, gleaned from the public record, were equally accessible to the principled researcher, and their omission from Pearson's work denotes either an intentional denial of the positive role women played in the Party or a willful ignorance. Moreover, according to BPP Chairman Seale, a year after the BPP's founding, women comprised almost 60 percent of the membership.[22]

This is not to suggest, by any means, that sexism was not a serious problem in the Party, nor that it did not hamper Party growth, development, and maturation. What is clear, however, is that sexism did not exist in a vacuum. As a prominent feature of the dominant social order, how could it not exist in a social, political formation that was drawn from that order, albeit from that order's subaltern strata?

For men who, often for the first time in their lives, exercised extraordinary power over others, sexism became a tool of sexual dominance over subordinates, as one young Panther, Regina Jennings, recounted:

> All I wanted was to be a soldier. I did not want to be romantically linked with any of my comrades, and even though I gave my entire life to the Party—my time, my energy, my will, my clothes, and my skills, yet my captain wanted more. My captain wanted me.... I lacked maturity and the skill necessary to challenge authoritarian men, so I searched for ways to circumvent the sexism of my captain. I was determined not to leave the Party because I felt there was no other place in America where I could fully be my Black revolutionary self.... After a year of transforming myself into a young woman who cared deeply for my people and becoming a fixture within Oakland and enjoying all of its rights and privileges, I found that my captain searched for greater ways to push me out of the Party.... There were women who came through the Party and would immediately leave because of the vulgar male behavior. There were women in the Party like me who tried to hold on because we understood the power, the significance, and the need for our organization. Black men, who had been too long without some form of power, lacked the background to understand and rework their double standard toward the female cadre. Perhaps, if the Party had external observers—community elders who respected our platform—much unfair practices against women may not have occurred.[23]

Jennings's example is all the more tragic when one examines the remarkable origins of her membership. Imagine the idealism and determination of a sixteen-year-old, jumping on a plane from her native Philadelphia, flying to California, and marching into the Oakland office of the Black Panther Party announcing an intention to join the controversial organization. When asked why she wanted to join, the teenager answered with youthful brio: "I wanna kill all the White people; that's why."[24]

It took a mature Panther to see the jewel beneath the drug-addicted wild child before him. This Officer of the Day took down Jenning's particulars, suggested she return in a few days (sober), and accepted her for membership. When she returned still under the influence, they took her in, cured her of her addiction, and filled her drug-free void "with a pure and noble love for my people."[25]

Even given her experience with her dense and dishonorable captain, Jennings reminds us that this was not the norm within the Party, for "all men in the Party were not sexist. In fact, many fought with me against the foolishness of our captain. These men were also ostracized by the leadership."[26] Jennings's experience teaches us that while sexism certainly existed in the Party and poisoned some interactions between male and female comrades, it was most often a feature of imbalanced power relations between the higher and lower ranks.

Indeed, the rise and fall of former Party chief Elaine Brown, and an account of her life on the "throne," is a riveting tale of gender politics, power dynamics, color consciousness, and sexual dominance exhibited by her when she was, as Huey's lover, given the top post upon his exile.[27]

Brown demonstrated, upon her elevation, that the abuse of power was not solely a male prerogative. She brooked no questioning of her role and relished the opportunity to "discipline" a member of the Los Angeles underground who had beaten her up several years earlier. Brown ordered him to Oakland, ostensibly for a "meeting," disarmed him, and proceeded to ruthlessly teach him who was boss:

> "Right now, I'm going to give you an opportunity to apologize, and to acknowledge the leadership of this party."
>
> "You mean, to say I'm sorry I kicked your ass," he interrupted.
>
> "I'm through, Larry," I said, getting up from my chair, scraping it along the floor with my foot as I rose.
>
> Big Bob reached over, lifted Steve from the couch, and slammed his solid body to the floor.... Four men were upon him now.... Steve struggled for survival under the many feet stomping him.... Their punishment became unmerciful.... Blood was everywhere. Steve's face disappeared.[28]

Was this a kind of "reverse sexism" (to borrow a phrase)? Hardly. For sexism is the systematic, as opposed to the incidental, devaluation of a person because of one's sex. Was this an abuse of one's power and rank for personal purposes? Of that there can be little doubt.

Brown's account also reveals the dual nature of sexism and the ability it gave women to use their sexuality to gain influence, access, rank, and power. Brown was prepared to use this tool when necessary. Sexism also fed into what might be called "light-skin privilege," or the ability for lighter-complected women in the Party to acquire the attention of men in the Party hierarchy that sisters of darker hues, with superior work ethics, could not.

Former Black Panther Safiya A. Bukhari had a sterling career, not only in the Party, but in the Party's military successor, the BLA. While criticizing men who brought "their sexist attitudes into the organization," she also is critical of those women who "utiliz[ed] their femininity as a way to achieve rank and stature within the Party."[29]

Bukhari did not enter the Party as a wild-eyed youth. She came from an upward-bound family of ten children, and was a bourgeois-oriented Black college student. Her sorority chose to begin a study of poverty among children in Harlem. Safiya approached the project with skepticism, for she did not really believe such conditions existed in America. Raised by parents who were "strict," "religious" folks (she doesn't describe her parents as conservative, but they clearly were), her first response to the sorority project is breathtaking, especially when one considers her later political development:

> Personally, I'd never even thought of people in the United States being disadvantaged, but only too lazy to work and "make it." ...

> A few of us were sent to Harlem to investigate the situation. We talked to people on the street, in the welfare centers, from door to door, and watched them work and play, loiter on the corners and in the bars. What we came away with was a story of humili-

ation, degradation, deprivation and waste that started in infancy and lasted until death ... in too many cases, at an early age.[30]

Even after seeing these conditions, she looked at them with a kind of professional detachment: "I didn't see this as affecting me personally, only as a sorority project ... sort of as a tourist who takes pity on the less fortunate."[31]

She heard of the Black Panther Free Breakfast for Children program and found it a valuable and viable program to address the widespread poverty and hunger among the very young. So she and some of her sorority sisters promptly offered their services to help the program. This support still took the form of charity rather than political support.

> I couldn't get into the politics of the Black Panther Party, but I could volunteer to feed some hungry children; you see, children deserve a good start and you have to feed them for them to live to learn. It's hard to think of reading and arithmetic when your stomach's growling.[32]

This essential conservatism, this deeply apolitical stance, would have been right at home in the women's club movement of an earlier era when Black women of means and learning launched social uplift-type programs for their poorer, less educated sisters. And this would probably have been the limit of the involvement of this up-and-coming sorority sister with the Black Panthers, had not the State intervened.

Their intervention, though petty and minor, shocked her. As she volunteered for the free breakfast program, she was dismayed to see attendance begin to diminish and couldn't understand why. When the trend continued, she went out into the community and talked to parents and learned that many of them were told by police that the people at the breakfast program were "feeding them poisoned food":

> It's one thing to hear about underhanded things the police do—you can ignore it then—but it's totally different to experience it for yourself—you either lie to yourself or face it. I chose to face it and find out why the police felt it was so important

to keep Black children from being fed that they told lies. I went back to the Black Panther Party and started attending some of their Community Political Education classes.[33]

The crude attempt by the State to cripple a vital self-help community program only served to attract Bukhari to the ideology and politics of an organization that she had hitherto been studiously avoiding. But she still was not a Panther. She was just an angry Black woman who was intrigued when she learned how the cops would lie to destroy something that was doing such obvious good.

She wondered, "Why?"

## Personal Engagement

It is said that small incidents can have profound repercussions. Consider what next happened to Bukhari. Her proud, independent, analytical nature would not allow her to fully embrace the Black Panthers, yet she had begun to listen to their message. Shortly after her unsettling experience with the cops regarding the breakfast program, she and a friend were walking down 42nd Street in Midtown when they noticed a crowd gathering. Rushing to see what was happening, they came upon a dispute between two cops and a Panther with a bundle of newspapers under his arm. As she stopped to listen, she learned that the cops were telling the young man that he couldn't sell the papers on the corner, while the Panther was insisting that he could. The sober, conservative sorority sister chimed in instinctively, informing the cops that the guy had a constitutional right to disseminate political literature anywhere. Instead of responding to the young lady's legal argument, the cops demanded identification and, moments later, arrested her, her friend, and the Panther selling papers.

While en route to the station, Bukhari could only believe that this was a minor misunderstanding that would be cleared up once the police listened to reason. When her girlfriend started to speak about her illegal arrest, and as the car began to pull away from the milling crowd, the cop threatened to stick his nightstick up in her unless she shut her mouth. Then he proceeded to give an unsolicited speech to a captive audience about what was wrong with Black people.

At the Fourteenth Precinct, they were separated, stripped, and searched. She distinctly remembered a male cop telling the female cop doing the searching to wash her hands to make sure she didn't catch something. Bukhari was livid. She was also determined:

> That night, I went to see my mother, explained to her about the bust and about a decision I'd made. Momma and Daddy were in the kitchen when I got there—Daddy sitting at the table and Momma cooking. I remember telling them about the bust and them saying nothing. Then I told them about how the police had acted and them still saying nothing. Then I told them that I couldn't sit still and allow the police to get away with that. I had to stand up for my rights as a human being. I remember my mother saying, "… if you think it's right, then do it." I went back to Harlem and joined the Black Panther Party.[34]

The Party gained a hard-working, tough-minded, intelligent, and committed young woman as comrade because of petty lies and attempts at harassment by the police. After all was said and done, Bukhari ended up organizing hundreds, if not thousands of others, and being appointed section leader for parts of Harlem. She would go on to establish a liberation school, and later, after the Party was ripped apart by division, she would command an armed unit of the Black Liberation Army. Police repression and threats did more than push her to join the Black Panther Party; they brought out the commitment and determination of a revolutionary.

She spent a long and brutal stint in prison, at one time facing forty years, and the death penalty, for work done while in the BLA underground. As a woman who joined a predominantly male-membered group, who rose in leadership in both the Ministry of Information of the Party and the BLA, her insights into the problem of sexism should prove invaluable.

Bukhari would be the last to be an apologist for the organization. In an article written in response to the well-publicized *New York Times* op-ed piece co-authored by former Panther chief Elaine Brown and acclaimed novelist Alice Walker, Bukhari strived to put the issue of sexism within the BPP into its proper, and historical, context. Bukhari, in her "On the Question of Sexism Within the Black Panther Party,"[35] recounts a people's history of severely damaged, and intentionally sabotaged, familial relations. Under a system of chattel slavery and the unrelenting violence used to enforce it, she argues, Black men and Black women were compelled to construct relationships that could be severed at whim and over which little appreciable control could be exercised. Men could find favor if they impregnated women (thereby increasing the slave stock), and, similarly, women were favored if they delivered such stock (thus increasing white wealth). These socially and psychologically deformed, and deforming, practices, which took place in North America for well over two centuries, continue to live in the Black psyche long after the legal cessation of formal slavery and even after the century of legal apartheid that followed. It follows in Black consciousness even today, as she explains:

> The error everyone seems to be making, supporters and detractors of the Black Panther Party alike, is separating the Party from its time and roots and looking at it in a vacuum. Quite clearly, the Black Panther Party came out of the Black community and its experiences. The membership of the Black Panther Party was recruited from the ghettoes of the inner cities. The Party itself was founded ... by two Black men who came straight out of the ghetto and met on the campus of Merritt College....

> Which brings us back to 1966 and the founding of the Black Panther Party. Nothing had changed in terms of the quality of life in the Black community and racism in this country. We were still slaves in every way except we were no longer bound and shackled. We still didn't have a culture. Our Africanism and sense of identity were gone and had been replaced by western civilization. We were busy trying to be like the rest of the peo-

ple in America. We had taken on the persona of sexist America, but with a Black hue. It was into this that the Black Panther Party was founded, declaring that we were revolutionaries and a revolutionary had no gender.[36]

Bukhari does not claim that some Black women were not wrongly treated, in either the community or the organization. That was a given, in light of the historical processes that led to the Party's development. That the Party intentionally concentrated on those elements of the community considered to be lumpen also ensured that the least enlightened on gender issues would be widely recruited into the organization. Yet, she argues, much of the popular media would never give the Black Panther Party the credit it rightly deserves for the trailblazing it performed:

> The simple fact that the Black Panther Party had the courage to address the question in the first place was a monumental step forward. In a time when the other nationalist organizations were defining the role of women as barefoot and pregnant and in the kitchen, women in the Black Panther Party were working right alongside men, being assigned sections to organize just like the men, and receiving the same training as the men. Further, the decision as to what a person did within the ranks of the Black Panther Party was determined not by gender, but by ability.[37]

Bukhari's memory of the service of other women reads like a roster of pride in their accomplishments, though it is not without criticism:

> In its brief seven year history (1966–1973)[38] women had been involved on every level in the Black Panther Party. There were women like Audrea Jones, who founded the Boston chapter of the Black Panther Party, women like Brenda Hyson, who was the OD (Officer of the Day) in the Brooklyn office of the Black Panther Party, women like Peaches, who fought side-by-side with Geronimo Pratt in the Southern California Chapter of the Black Panther Party, Kathleen Cleaver, who was on the Central Committee, and Sister Rivera who was one of the motivators behind the office in Mt. Vernon, NY. By the same token, there were problems with men who brought their sexist attitudes into the organization. Some of the men refused to

take direction (orders) from women. Even though we had a framework established to deal with that, because of liberalism and cowardice, as well as fear, a lot of times the framework was not utilized.

The other side of the coin was women who sought to circumvent the principled method of work by utilizing their femininity as a way to achieve rank and stature within the Party. They also utilized their sexuality to get out of work and certain responsibilities. This unprincipled behavior within the Party (just as on the streets) undermined the work of other sisters who struggled to deal in a principled manner. Thus, there were three evils that had to be struggled with, male chauvinism, female passivity and ultrafemininity (the "I'm only a female" syndrome).[39]

Finally, Bukhari was critical of those who, from their positions of relative and temporal safety, deign to criticize the Party for failure to live up to its theoretical construct of ideals whilst involved in a bitter and brutal life and death struggle:

It is easy to decry the sexism of the leadership of the Black Panther Party from afar, without having struggled along with them.... While the Party was dealing with the issue of politically educating its ranks it was also feeding hungry children, establishing liberation schools, organizing tenants, welfare mothers, and establishing free health clinics. Simultaneously, the Black Panther Party was under attack from the local, state and federal government. Offices of the Black Panther Party from California to Louisiana, from Texas to Michigan, all across the country were under physical attack and Panthers were being killed and imprisoned. We were not theorizing about struggle, we were in constant struggle on all levels.[40]

At least one scholar who looked at the Party's history on the question of women came away with a similar conclusion. Indeed, Nikhil Pal Singh wrote of the Party's 1970 call in support of both women's liberation and gay liberation, as an "astonishing leap, given the period."[41]

## The Hard Life of Panther Women

Some women had, relatively speaking, privileged lives in the Party, primarily due to their or their mate being in the upper ranks of the Party. Such privileges often took the form of exposure to opportunity, such as for travel or nicer living accommodations.

Barbara Easley Cox, for example, the wife of revered Field Marshall D.C., was considerably more privileged than the average sister in the organization, a fact she freely conceded in recent correspondence.[42] It did not hurt matters that she also came from the original West Coast core of the BPP. Although she hailed from Philadelphia, Cox worked and lived in San Francisco, Oakland, New York, and for a time in Algiers, Pyongyang (North Korea), Frankfurt, and Paris. In recent years, she has lived in Amsterdam. She speaks of her years after the Party as a continuance of a journey started then. She writes, "I received and got a lot of respect, [that] I am not certain I always deserved. [H]owever, I earned it over the last 35 years and will not let anyone diminish our/my value as a part of history." She doesn't rest on her historical experiences, adding, "[W]e are still here[—]black and strong...if I can help one young person to forge forward, keep the faith, give strength to or clear up his/her direction, I live to do the job, anywhere time or place."[43]

Cox was privileged to experience so much of the world and to live, perhaps, in greater luxury than her Panther sisters. It is necessary here, however, to qualify the term privileged. For, as the experiences of Afeni Shakur and Ericka Huggins show, Panther women and those associated with the Party were also privileged to the full force of State repression. The State was fully willing, if it could, to send such women to prison for the rest of their lives. As Eldridge wrote about Ericka Huggins, "So they didn't put her in a powder puffed cell. They did not make life easy for her. But the pigs recognized a revolutionary woman to be just as much a threat as a revolutionary man."[44]

Most Panther women were not extended such privileges as Cox and other women in the Party's upper ranks enjoyed and made choices that reflected that absence. Naima Major's struggle is more representative of the life of a Black Panther woman.

A precocious teenager, Major left home at seventeen (she uses the word "fled" to describe her exodus). It was 1968, and the bright youngster, a National Negro Scholar, had recently graduated from high school. But she wasn't really interested in college, which seemed to bore her. Her story is so compelling, that I will not paraphrase it, but allow her to present what is, after all, her story:

> [I fled] to San Francisco/Oakland looking for the BPP office and ended up at the campaign office of Eldridge Cleaver. I was 17, had no family there, knew no one except my roommate, a Spelman College dropout, also on the run from petit bourgeois mediocrity.
>
> I went to a Free Huey Rally at the federal building in SF, and met many brave Panthers. Went on a mission with Kathleen Cleaver in Hunter's Point because my beloved was one of her self-appointed guards. Captured body and soul by the rally and the love and energy of black people. My favorite retort to almost anything soon became, "And how does that free the people?" I was dogmatic and insufferable, but could dance you down at a house party!
>
> Found the Panther before I found the office. Married the handsome, temperamental revolutionary because he showed up at my door with a swaddling baby named BJ, Baby Jesus, because we weren't sure who the father was. BJ's mother of the immaculate conception was on her way to Corona State Prison for Women, and my beloved, one of her lovers, was trying to care for the baby. Need I say more? What's not to love? I devoted the next 5–6 years of my life to him and the party, two of them visiting Soledad Prison where my beloved was held on a sentence of 6 months to life. He was 19. Imagine that. I was pregnant. My beloved was released after 22 months by a mass civil action initiated by Huey P. Newton from behind prison walls and Senator Mervyn Dymally to get scores of young Panthers in California released from wrongful convictions and

these draconian sentences for minor or first time offenses. We lost BJ in 1969 right before my beloved was sentenced. I never saw him again. We saw his mother after she was released, she was 16 when she entered, 21 when she was released. You can see her and BJ in Pirkle Jones' collection of photographs ... BJ's mother died, mysteriously, some say, in Los Angeles a few years later. BJ is grown up somewhere in San Francisco; he doesn't know us. I pray he doesn't hate us.

Despite these heartbreaking setbacks, Major soldiered on, as did thousands of young women like her. She did political work, and studied revolutionaries, like all other Panthers. She fought her way through, with grit and will:

> Devoted to the black revolution and the ten point program, I commenced with baby in sling to doing the hard community work required of all Panthers, organizing poor women like myself, planning and supporting free schools, writing letters for people who couldn't write, demanding decent housing for people who were afraid of the landlord, helping get the newspaper out, health cadres, food cadres, you name it. Did some dangerous work too, and studied Hegel, Marx, Lenin, Fanon, Mao like a religious zealot, mostly with the brothers. Fought with them over Bakunin and Stalin. Just because I was the only woman in my group, husband gone, baby at the breast, nobody cut me any slack, but nobody molested me either. I had to learn what the brothers learned. Learned well. Fought well. Knew then and still know how to choose my battles. I know I saved some lives. Indeed my own. I wanted to live for the revolution, not die for it. The people became personal instead of theoretical.

> My beloved came home just in time for hell on earth. The so-called split tore the Fillmore and West Oakland communities apart and almost destroyed my whole family, which included a nursing baby and a toddler at that time. Never mind that. We persevered against all odds and with uncommon sense, supported the International Chapter in Algeria and wherever with money and supplies. *Does anyone remember a shoot to kill order against all SF Panthers and left adventurists? I Do.* Terrible times.

> Poor as we were and living under siege sending baby clothes and money overseas! Wrote propaganda, a number of things.... Forced underground in New York City, east coast Panthers and

Muslims took care of me and my family—we didn't get out much but we never missed a meal. Fled NYC back to California, joined the Nation of Islam because they offered us shelter when no one else could or would. As a Muslim woman, I was forced out of the NOI by fundamentalism—which I recognized even then—plus greed, economic exploitation, stupidity and COINTELPRO-type activities.[45]

Major experienced many things, but a privileged life wasn't one of them. She went back to school, educated their children, and keeps her inner life shining with poetry, literature, and film studies. She describes herself as "the proud mother of three free black people" and is the grandmother of four. She is a founding member of the Keep Ya' Head Up foundation, a supportive collective of ex-Panther women.

Despite it all—the loss, the pain, the betrayals, and the political reversals, she continues to aspire to the revolutionary, humanistic ideal, saying, simply, "I want to be like Che." She works today in the nonprofit sector.

Although her name may be little known by those who have read the popular literature produced around the Black Panther Party, her story is actually closer to the norm of a woman's life in the Party. Hard work. Hard study. Jailed lovers. Survival. Striving. Times of promise. Times of terror. Resistance to male chauvinism.

And hope.

It is telling that Major, although decades have passed since she was a member of the BPP, is still an organizer, who works collectively to assist those who lived similar lives.

Rosemari Mealy had no intention of joining the Black Panther Party. In the late 1960s she lived in a predominantly Quaker commune in West Philadelphia, and was quite busy living her life and working on antiwar, draft resistance, and Black economic justice issues.

She had worked as a community activist with the Civil Rights movement, as an actress in the Black Arts movement, and was one of the few woman members of the Black

Economic Development Conference (BEDC), a group led by activist Muhamad Kenyatta that petitioned wealthy white churches for economic reparations to the Black community. Although she studied Marxist writers, she was also a mother of a young child and the dangerous life of a Black Panther was not attractive to her. Indeed, "the last thing" on her mind was to join the BPP.

Then, in December 1969, the phone rang. Young Fred Hampton, in Chicago, was murdered in his bed by state and federal police.

Captain Reggie had often called on her for help getting leaflets printed, and she had struggled with members of the commune to help the Party in this effort. Some of the radical Quakers found the Party's determination to defend itself with arms in stark contrast with their commitment to nonviolence.

This time Reggie called, not for help in printing leaflets, but to find out if any members of the commune were traveling to Chicago, and if several Panthers could join them to represent the chapter in Fred's honor.

While some members of the commune had misgivings, several agreed, and made the long trip to Chicago. Rosemari left Philadelphia a member of a mostly white commune; she returned a member of the Black Panther Party.

For members of the Party the visit to the Windy city was traumatic, though it deepened our determination for we knew that any of us could be slain like Fred.

For Rosemari:

> Fred Hampton's murder by the Chicago police propelled my political activism to the next stage ... That experience in retrospect would always have the most profound of all impacts in my life. In the Party, I used all my contacts ... to build networks and support between a sector of Philadelphia society who had so often denounced the actions and tactics of the Party. Since my life was so engaged by the collective experiences of prior movements and living arrangements, I sort of took my place naturally alongside those of different age, class, and similar, as

well as not-so-similar, life experiences. I sold papers, organized against police killings of Black youth, and wrote articles for the newspaper about what was happening in Philadelphia.[46]

As an experienced organizer, the Party found her skills valuable and shortly thereafter, she was transferred to New Haven to help with the case of Bobby Seale and Ericka Huggins.

When Huey visited the chapter, as the Lieutenant of Information, Rosemari was selected to speak to him and deliver some of the chapter's most pressing complaints to the one man who could unilaterally solve them.

The Huey she met wasn't the Huey she expected, and when she voiced the chapter's complaints he responded by expelling her from the Party. The next issue of *The Black Panther* would announce her expulsion and denounce her as an "enemy of the People," along with the *New York 21* and those assigned to the International Section in Algiers.

She left the city and, to ensure her survival, went underground. She survived to see her son reach manhood. She went on to marry, write several books, earn a law degree, and work as a radio journalist. Since the first edition of this book she has continued to teach and has earned a Ph.D.

Angela Y. Davis, who joined the LA chapter before her rise as an icon of the Black freedom movement, also experienced the hard reality of how arbitrary Party power could be. She reports that "Bunchy" Carter, before his martyrdom and hagiography, ordered the expulsion of all the women in the LA chapter. He later allowed some to rejoin, but for many, this behavior proved that the BPP—or, notably, its LA chapter—wasn't right for them.[47]

The Party may no longer exist, yet much of the spirit, the essence of collective resistance, of community service, of perseverance, continues in the lives of people like Major, Jennings, Mealy, and others who aspired to change the realities into which they and their people were born.

They were, without question, the very best of the Black Panther Party.

# Memories

*When I read or hear critics employ their projections against the BPP on charges of sexism I can barely conceal a chuckle, for my memories of women in the Party were of able, determined, and powerful revolutionaries who fought with and for their brothers like lionesses.*

*Women in the Party in which I spent several years of my youth were not dainty, shrinking violets. They were, of course, of various backgrounds and, as is common in Black America, of every which hue.*

*They were also tough women.*

*We lived in spartan, virtually bare "Panther pads," where we fell onto mattresses at the end of a long day's work.*

*Whether I was in Philadelphia, the Bronx, or in Berkeley, California, I was under the authority of a female Panther who ran a tight and efficient operation.*

*Although no woman helped found the Philadelphia branch and none held office, the national office sent a woman invested with the rank of Deputy Field Marshal, which meant she had immense power in the city.*

*Her name was Sister Love.*

*She spoke with that common black Californi-ese that had deep roots in the US South. She looked into every nook and cranny of the branch and occasionally cracked her whip by ordering the branch leadership to correct some defect or close some loophole in office security. As an outsider, and as a woman, she evoked mixed emotions in us. On the one hand, there was clear resentment at her presence and, yes, her power; on the other, there was a profound respect, for, we reasoned, if she was sent by "the Coast," by friends and comrades of our beloved Minister of Defense, Huey P. Newton, then she had to be most extraordinary.*

*In the Bronx, Sister Bernice ran the office of the East Coast Ministry of Information with all the tenderness of a drill sergeant. She could be mercurial. At one moment she could be whispering encouragement to you as you worked on a project, but in the next she would bark out, "drop down and give me twenty!" and stand there, her dark bespectacled face an impassive mask of obsidian, as she counted out the pushups: "1, 2, ... 17, 17 1/2—give me a real pushup, nigga—18, 19, 20." The office was a beehive of Panther productivity, and she, Sister Bernice, was the undisputed queen.*

*At the Party's national headquarters in northern California, a phalanx of women ran the Party offices, answering phones, paying bills, and generally taking care of the business of a large, national organization. When I arrived, I was stunned by the normality of it, the everydayness of it. This, the national office of the notorious Black Panther Party, with its offices, phones, typewriters, and related paraphernalia, could have been the offices of the Chamber of Commerce. It was a business office, peopled with competent, efficient, and attractive young women. With perhaps one difference: some of these women wore pistols.*

*There was an additional difference: almost all of the women were light-complected. The men, by contrast, were generally brown to dark brown to jet black, like Mojo.*

*On the second floor were the offices, layout area, and composition machinery for the Party's acclaimed weekly journal,* The Black Panther. *I was assigned to assist the editor, Judi Douglas, and do anything necessary to help the paper. My boss was a gentle woman, with a soft, southern accent, who patiently helped the young Panther from Philadelphia write pieces worthy of the paper. She was a selfless and dedicated teacher.*

*On both coasts, in cities of different rhythms and pace, one found confident, capable, proud, and inspiring women, who commanded respect, camaraderie, intense loyalty, and sisterly love.*

*We knew from experience that they would be treated as viciously as we if they fell into the hands of the enemy, and we loved them all the more for their courage and their sacrifice. We knew, and could recite, the names of our sisters who were political prisoners of the pigs, and their names were like a mantra of resistance: Ericka Huggins, Angela Davis, Afeni Shakur, Joan Bird....*

*As for sex, women chose their partners as freely as the men, and many could and did say no.*

*One night, Sheila came into my room and asked, matter-of-factly, "Do you wanna do it?" As I looked at this girl, her copper-colored Afro like a soft halo circling her pretty face, her eyes like green jade, standing in the doorway with panties on, I almost stuttered. But deeper than my desire was a burning guilt, for earlier in the day, our deputy chief of staff, June Hilliard, had dressed down a brother for going to a whorehouse:*

*"Mojo, don't you know it's a breach of security for you to relate to a woman outside the party?"*

*"But, June—I know, brother, but—but—"*

*"But, what, Mojo?"*

*"Won't nobody give me none," he admitted, shyly.*

*"Mojo—either work wit' yo rap, or work with yo hand, bro'—What can I tell ya, man? But, you just cain't be relating to sistas in no who'house—that's a security risk, brother."*

*"Yes, sir, June. I hear you, man."*

*Mojo gave an empty laugh and walked away, his head down in a wreath of sadness.*

*I thought of Mojo as Sheila stood there, inviting me to her garden of celestial delights, and I think a groan escaped from my lips.*

*"Well, do you want to relate to me?"*

*"Oh, I do—but, that thing with Mojo—"*

*"What about Mojo?"*

*"Well, the brother hadda go to whorehouse, 'cuz none of the sistas would relate to him—and that's fucked up!"*

*"And that's my problem?"*

*"Naw, but—"*

*"'But,' shit! This my pussy! I give it, or don't, when I want to, hear me?"*

*"I hear you, sista—"*

*"Now, tell me—Do you want this pussy, or not?"*

*I wanted it. I wanted it so bad I could taste it. But it would have tasted like a betrayal to my brother, Mojo. I was, first and foremost, a Black Panther. A true revolutionary would choose loyalty over desire. "Not," I answered.*

*"Fuck you, then," she raged, her green eyes shooting darts at the fool who would turn down her sublime offering. She made a neat pivot and turned and a luscious ass undulated out of my room and into the darkness of history.*

*"I am a revolutionary!"*

*"I want for my brotha, what I want for myself."*

*"I am a Black Panther!"*

*I repeated these mottoes to myself, over and over.*

*Under the motto, almost in counterpoint, came another message:*

*"Mumia—You let that—get away? Youza stoo-pid muthafucka, boy!"*

*I rolled over on my side, the floor feeling firm and unforgiving through the thin, worn sleeping bag, which did little to camouflage the California night's cool, and soon plunged into slumber, dreaming about Sheila.*[48]

To be a Panther meant something extraordinary in 1970, and one felt immensely honored to know, work with, and love these tough, committed women. These were, as Elaine Brown would later recount, "hard" women who were seen as "soldiers, comrades—not pretty little things."[49] They were, to use Eldridge Cleaver's words, our "other half," who fought as "strongly and enthusiastically as we [did] ... in the struggle":[50]

> Because the liberation of women is one of the most important issues facing the world today.... [T]he.... demand for liberation of women in Babylon is the issue that is going to explode, and if we're not careful it's going to destroy our ranks, destroy our organization, because women want to be liberated just as all oppressed people want to be liberated.[51]

In the ranks and offices of the Black Panther Party, women were far more than mere appendages of male ego and power, they were valued and respected comrades who demonstrated daily the truth of the adage, "a revolutionary has no gender."

## CHAPTER EIGHT

# A Panther's Life

Indeed, we are all—Black and white alike—ill in the same way, mortally ill. But before we die, how shall we live? I say with hope and dignity; and if premature death is a result, that death has a meaning reactionary suicide can never have. It is the price of self-respect.

Revolutionary suicide does not mean that I and my comrades have a death wish; it means just the opposite. We have such a strong desire to live with hope and human dignity that existence without them is impossible. When reactionary forces crush us, we must move against these forces, even at the risk of death. We will have to be driven out with a stick....

—Huey P. Newton[1]

**TENS OF THOUSANDS** of ghetto souls came into contact with the Party daily. Elementary school students attended the morning breakfast programs, adult poor came for the free clothing and free shoes programs, the ill came to the Party's People's Medical Centers across the nation for sickle cell anemia testing, and treatment for high-blood pressure, sexually transmitted diseases, and other fairly simple ailments. To this number must be added those many people who bought the Party's newspaper, *The Black Panther,* on ghetto street corners, in bars, in beauty parlors, and outside high schools.

Who were these people called Black Panthers?

Much has been written about Party leadership, its so-called stars: the photogenic Newton, the charismatic (Eldridge) and brilliant (Kathleen) Cleavers, the ambitious and talented Elaine

Brown, the long-suffering Geronimo, and the like. As leaders, many of these people formed the Party's public profile and came to typify a Black Panther in much of the public mind.

Most people, indeed most Panthers, never came into intimate contact with such people, for they usually traveled in rarefied, higher strata than did the average Panther.

The average young man or woman in the Black Panther Party was between seventeen and twenty-two years old, lived in a collective home with other Panthers, worked long and hard days (and sometimes nights) doing necessary Party work without pay, and owned nothing. Except to their neighbors, and, of course, the ubiquitous police (and their snitches), most Panthers lived in relative obscurity and rarely, if ever, got their picture in the paper (in either the bourgeois press or the Party press). Friends, comrades, and lovers were primarily other Party members.

With very little exception, other than the folks who participated in the various programs, most Panthers spent every waking hour with other Panthers. The people looked up to and admired were the leadership, but close, loving relationships, of true care and concern, were with fellow Panthers. They were our confidants, our counselors, our comrades—those we could be easy and relaxed around.

The average Panther rose at dawn and retired at dusk and did whatever job needed to be done to keep the programs going for the people, from brothers and sisters cooking breakfast for the school kids, to going door-to-door to gather signatures for petitions, to gathering clothes for the free clothing program, to procuring donated supplies from neighboring merchants.

The average Panther's life was long, hard, and filled with work.

A Philadelphia-born member of the Oakland branch was struck by the deep poverty she found among Party members in West Oakland:

Many of the brothers were hunters so they cut up the deer meat in the back of the office. I almost fainted. The Panther men in particular laughed at my reaction, but after it was cooked, I refused to eat the meat. Knowing that I was very hungry, some of them chased me around the office and playfully urged me to sample the spicy scented deer. Ironically, as we fed hungry children breakfast, and later gave out bags of groceries to the poor, oftentimes Panthers themselves had little food and certainly little money. We lived mostly off paper sales. We sold each Panther paper for twenty-five cents and kept ten cents for ourselves.[2]

While that division of the paper sales money may have been the case for her chapter, it differed in other places. In some chapters, where Panther members lived communally and ate Party dinners, it was argued that the additional dime should be donated to the office, for the Party met all of the essential needs of its full-time members. That was certainly the case for the Philadelphia office.

People could be affiliated with the Party in the following ways:

Party supporter: This person might buy a paper or attend a rally organized by the Party, but was not a member.

Community worker: This person might donate time to Party efforts, as some non-Panthers would assist in the breakfast program, for example, or assist the Party in administering Party programs. Often, this person would be unable to secure parental permission to formally join the Party, but would help in some form; as students who sold the paper at their school, for example.

Panther-in-training (PIT): These were probationary members, who were expected to memorize the Ten-Point Program and Platform; they were expected to obtain a copy of the Red Book by Mao Tse-Tung and to learn from it the Three Main Rules of Discipline and to memorize them. These PITs would also be required to attend a given number of Political Education (PE) classes, to learn more about the Party. If a PIT failed to attend required PE classes, he or she would be counseled and if unresponsive, could be dropped from consideration for full membership.

Black Panther: These persons were expected to use any and all of their skills or expertise to help build and protect the organization and further its aims and objectives as determined by local, regional, and national leadership. They were traditionally full-time Party operatives, who spent virtually seven days a week conducting Party business.

Being a Black Panther, for many members, was never a single thing; indeed, it was many things, at different times, in different places. Panthers were taught to eschew what was called careerism and to shun compartmentalist thinking. This meant that one should not perceive any given rank as one's own, nor to look at things from a narrow, linear perspective, but from a broad one, asking, "What is in the best interest of the Party?" Individualism, like careerism, was seen as a negative, bourgeois trait that was criticized. The highest achievement was for a brother or sister to think in collectivist terms, as in *we* not *I*.

This way of thinking fostered humility, self-sacrifice, and discipline in Party ranks. It promoted the best interests of the collective, rather than arrogance and egotism, which threatened cohesion and working relationships.

In this environment, the Party became the central focus in the lives of thousands of Panthers across the nation, and an extraordinary morale and sense of unity of purpose were engendered. Thus, there were few things more exciting than meeting a fellow Panther from another part of the country.

Although there is considerable linguistic diversity in Black America, these regional forms of speech did not divide Panthers, but acted as bonds of affection between brothers and sisters. The deep, southern drawls of our North Carolinian or Virginian comrades drew smiles from Pennsylvanians or New Yorkers in the Party. Similarly, when we met Panthers from New Haven or Boston who wanted to drive a "cah" to the "bah," we found ourselves rolling on the ground, giddy with laughter, and really with a kind of amazement that Black people—Black Panthers—really talked like that. In many of these informal settings, Panthers learned from other Panthers how life was lived in different parts of this vast nation.

That joy, however, was tempered by gritty moments of terror. The slaughters of the sleeping Fred Hampton and Mark Clark in a Panther pad in Chicago on December 4, 1969, had sent a disturbing message to Panthers all across the nation: we will kill you in your sleep with impunity.

Some chapters had more intense relationships with the police than others, with the aggressive Los Angeles chapter finding an equally aggressive adversary in the Los Angeles Police Department. Panthers trying to sell papers, an action allegedly protected by the First Amendment, learned otherwise in the wilds of LA when met by members of the LAPD. In 1968, a sixteen-year-old Panther named Flores Forbes

> was stopped by the LAPD while selling Black Panther newspapers almost every single day. The cops insulted me, beat me, and, usually, dislodged my papers from under my arm, causing them to fly all over the streets of South Central Los Angeles. Even when I invoked the principles and guidelines of the *Pocket Lawyer of Legal First Aid,* the cops would bristle. "Nigger, you, your mama, and them other Black motherfuckers in the country have no constitutional rights that we recognize."[3]

How can one claim that the infamous *Dred Scott* opinion is truly ancient history and not the ever-present law of the land?

Forbes had an extraordinary career in the Party, one that lasted almost a decade and that took him from LA to the Party headquarters in northern California, to the homes of the highest ranked members of the organization. He rose from a rank-and-file member who sold Panther papers seven days a week and served free breakfasts to school kids, to Officer of the Day (OD) of both the LA office and, later, the San Francisco office. He was assigned to the Ministry of Information and worked as a community news reporter; he later served as Assistant Chief of Staff of the entire Party in 1974.

Now an urban planner and scholar, Forbes has written what may be the most remarkable, certainly the most detailed, and chilling account of a raid on a Black Panther office ever yet published in the non-BPP press. As a contributor to the anthology *Police Brutality,* he does not fall into the easy trap of macho posturing, but freely reports his moments of high anxiety and even fear while the office was under siege—an unexpected, unprovoked attack that came about a year and a half after the infamous LAPD paramilitary assault on another LA Panther office on December 8, 1969.

In Forbes's account, the late September day in 1971 was unremarkable. The office was filling with members returning from selling BPP newspapers. The OD, Sheldon Jones, left his desk to perform a security check of the premises and the surrounding area. The residential building was an office to be sure, but largely indistinguishable from the single family, detached, three bedroom homes in this South Central neighborhood.

What set the house apart, however, was a bright, powder blue and black sign erected in the front yard designating the site as the Southern California chapter of the Black Panther Party. What also distinguished the home was that it was prepared for war. In a bedroom, off to the side, a locked cabinet stood, stocked with riot pump shotguns, an AR-180, and a number of handguns. Its walls were packed with earth, and trenches lined the four sides of the house. Gun ports were placed discreetly at eight locations and an "eagle's nest," installed by a Vietnam veteran named Simba, sat in the attic. Forbes writes:

> We had been "tunneling for freedom" for the past two months. We dug straight down through the floor of a closet in one of our bedrooms for about ten feet and then hollowed out an area, like a vestibule that had two tunnels heading in different directions.... Each of the tunnels went directly to an exit under our neighbors' homes....[4]

Forbes further explained that as the OD made his daily rounds of the property he was seized and surrounded by six to eight cops, who trained their weapons on him and disarmed him. A Panther sister inside witnessed Jones's seizure and alerted the others:

> I started to hear the pounding of feet and the jingling of keys on the right side of the office. The police were outflanking us and taking up positions in our neighbor's yard. I could also hear the heavy engines from LAPD squad cars roaring through the alley. They literally shook the house. I noticed, as had everyone else, that the police in the front street were positioning themselves behind their cars with revolvers and riot shotguns … [I] was somewhat alarmed at the speed with which everything unfolded and the precision displayed by this group of cops. I asked myself a very personal question, "Was this it?"[5]

The Panthers reported to their Defense Captain, who unlocked the gun cabinet and distributed weapons to disciplined Panthers standing in line. He also checked to see if every Panther knew his proper defensive position, to which each promptly reported.

Forbes was assigned to the trenches, in the northeast corridor, a hot, dirty, and dusty area:

> I started to sweat profusely. Nevertheless, I loaded the shotgun, chambering the last round—a rifled slug. I set my bandolier down in the dirt and waited, still sweating. From my vantage point, I could see our front yard, grass level. I removed the screen from my gun port, exposing the wire mesh that remained to protect me from tear gas canisters. I put the barrel of my shotgun near, but not completely out of, the gun port. Everything got quiet in the office, which made me believe we were all in position and ready to defend ourselves. To me at that moment, this was what it was all about: taking a stand and letting the state know that somewhere in our community a group of people were prepared to fight and die, if necessary.
>
> The house started to rattle. The trees in our yard and across the street started to swirl. The once still grass began to flutter. It was the LAPD's chopper descending slowly and then drawing to a hover over the office. In the street outside the office and over the sound of the chopper, I could hear hundreds of our neighbors shouting and yelling at the police, who had once more invaded our community as if they were an occupying army in a foreign land.[6]

For about a half hour, both sides remained armed and waiting for action, nerves a-jangle with tension. That day, however, it did not come.

The cops pulled back, and before long the order to stand down was given. Panthers climbed up from the dark, dusty tunnels, turned in their weapons to their captain, and lived to fight another day.

According to Forbes, such faux attacks occurred weekly or biweekly in the LA area.

At first blush, it would seem like the LAPD staged dry runs to keep Panthers off-balance or to give their personnel on-site training for real raids to come. But as Forbes explains, these raids had a draining effect on the Party. A week after the raid four Panthers deserted. The LAPD managed to hurt the LA chapter without firing a single shot.

The infamous raid of December 8, 1969, on the chapter's former headquarters on LA's Central Avenue featured the first time that an American police department utilized a Special Weapons And Tactics (SWAT) unit. For six long, harrowing hours, LA Panthers and the LAPD traded gunfire.

The LA chapter was led and defended by the legendary Geronimo ji-Jaga, who fortified the headquarters and set up defensive positions. Ji-Jaga [né Pratt] drew on lessons learned while fighting for the Empire in Vietnam. Upon his return, he was drafted into the Black Panther Party and served as Deputy Minister of Defense of the Southern California Chapter. Miraculously, because of the office's defensive preparations no one died from the December 8 police assault. Two Panthers and two cops were wounded.

Ironically, the Panthers suffered most when the public and media showed up and they surrendered to the police. Many, both men and women, were brutally beaten by the cops. The cops had their special targets of vengeance, like Paul Redd, the chapter's youthful Deputy Minister of Culture, a gifted artist whose work earned the praise of those who saw it in the national *Black Pan-*

*ther* newspaper and regional party publications. It earned him as
well the enmity of the State. When he was arrested and his name
learned, the members of the LAPD brutally broke the fingers of
his right hand. Undaunted, Redd learned to draft art with his left.

Though some left the Party, many Panthers withstood the
attempted intimidations and State terrorism that was trained on
Black revolutionaries for a very simple reason. Many had harsh
memories of police violence or indignities that predated their
membership in the Party. They therefore reasoned that the vicious, brutal behavior would not ease if they left the Party, but
might in fact worsen if the Party didn't exist, and could not openly
oppose it.

When Forbes reflected on his earliest childhood memories,
they are marred by his contact with racist cops. As a twelve-year-
old boy, riding around his neighborhood on a bike, Forbes was
picked up by two white cops and ordered to get into the black and
white. He was terrified and did as he was told:

> They drove me up the hill on Market Street toward San Diego.
> After a ten or fifteen-minute ride, they pulled into a residential
> area just short of downtown and drove up to several other po-
> lice officers and a young White couple. The car stopped, and
> the cop on the passenger side got out and walked over to the
> group of people. After a few brief words, which I could not
> hear, the officer pointed toward me sitting in the back seat,
> explaining something to them as he pointed. The cop and the
> couple walked over to the car and peered in. By this time my
> entire body was shaking with fear. All I could think about was
> going home and never riding my bike again. The couple looked
> at each other and spoke a few more words I couldn't hear (they
> never rolled the window down). The White man stood back
> from the window, shaking his head from side to side. He then
> took his woman by the hand and walked back toward the six or
> so policemen and they huddled again. The policeman returned
> to the car. They drove me back to Forty-Seventh Street and
> pulled into the parking lot where I had been kidnapped.

> A huge crowd had gathered in the parking lot, and standing in
> the center was my mother. The policeman stopped, got out,

went around to open the trunk and got my bike, while the other cop opened the back door to let me out. Man was I glad! My mother, with the crowd of neighbors in tow, approached the cop asking, "What are you doing with Flores? Did he do anything wrong?"

The cop who had my bike told my mother, "Back away bitch, this is official police business."[7]

Forbes saw a rage in his mother's face that he never saw before. That fear and rage was doubtless a factor in Forbes's decision some four years later to join the Black Panther Party.

## A Philadelphia Story

Philadelphia, with its vast Black population, was a rich recruitment pool and a responsive propagation ground for the Black Panther Party.

We were gifted with a smart, levelheaded defense captain, Reggie Schell, and the over-the-top presence of the late Frank Rizzo as a political adversary. Most of the members were of high school–graduate age, with a smattering of military veterans among the officers and senior members.

Rizzo, as police commissioner in the 1970s and later mayor of Philadelphia, was an ambitious politician who knew well the value of appealing directly to white ethnics by engaging in repressive tactics against Black citizens. In one of his mayoral campaigns, he urged his supporters to "vote white." Members of the Party could always count on Rizzo to do, or say, something provocative and controversial, which would rebound to the organization's benefit.

Despite the ever-present repression, the police harassments, and the arrests, the city's chapter blossomed as Black youth flocked to the offices to join the Party. We had Panther supporters in most of the city high schools, selling and sharing the newspapers. By fall 1970, we fed kids in four sites throughout the city; across from the main office in North Philadelphia on Columbia Avenue in a storefront next to a supermarket; in West Philadelphia, in a church near Party headquarters; in Germantown; and in a community center in South Philadelphia. Soon, another center would open on Susquehanna Avenue, the second in North Philadelphia.

Hundreds of children were fed well, thanks to their elders in the Black Panther Party.

For most Panthers, the day began shortly after daybreak, as we awoke in our communal apartments, grabbed a quick munch, and rushed to our offices.

There, the Officer of the Day would assign Panthers to various duties throughout the day. Some were sent to high schools. Others would be sent out to sell papers. Still others would be sent out to have petitions signed. The time of a Panther would always be spent working for the Revolution.

Sometimes our work routine would change if we were relayed orders that originated from National. Such was the case in the fall of 1970, when the Revolutionary People's Constitutional Convention was planned for Philadelphia, and thousands of radicals and revolutionaries were expected to attend. This was supposed to be the Party's clarion call to all radicals to converge in a convention to write a new egalitarian, liberational Constitution for a Revolutionary New America.

Several days before the event, a group of young Blacks, who were not Panthers, engaged in a deadly shoot-out with members of the Philadelphia Park police. Rizzo seized on this event to justify an unprovoked series of raids against local offices of the Black Panther Party. The predawn raids were Rizzo's attempt to destabilize and humiliate the Panthers as well as to derail the imminent convention. Captain Reggie recalls:

> About five o'clock that morning I was asleep, and somebody woke me up (we used to pull guard duty in the Panthers anyway) and said, "They're here." I looked out the window, and they're lined up across the street with submachine guns, shotguns; they're in the alley. I saw the head man clearly, he had a pistol and a gas mask strapped to his leg; he was bending down, and

then all hell broke loose. Finally, we had children in there and the gas got to them too much so we had to come out.

Each cop took an individual Panther and placed their pistol up back of our neck and told us to walk down the street backward. They told us if we stumble or fall they're gonna kill us. Then they lined us up against the wall and a cop with a .45 sub would fire over our heads so the bricks started falling down. Most of us had been in bed, and they just ripped the goddamn clothes off everybody, women and men. They had the gun, they'd just snatch your pants down and they took pictures of us like that.

Then they put us in a wagon and took us down to the police station. We were handcuffed and running down this little driveway; when we got to the other end of it, a cop would come by with a stick and he'd punch us, beat us. Some of us were bleeding; I know I was bleeding, but really I thought it would be a whole lot worse.[8]

Rizzo had his photo op: embarrassed, naked Panthers. But it had the opposite effect he intended. Support for the Panthers was wide and deep, the fruit of anger and outrage unleashed by the publication of the photos in the media. Community groups protested and some sued the city for their sanctioning of such police tactics against Black Philadelphians. Progressive attorneys organized legal defense and bail hearings for the imprisoned Panthers, some of whom had $100,000 bail.

On September 4, 1970, the registration for the convention opened, and over six thousand people came from across the country in support. One contemporary observer, the late Rev. Paul Washington, would term the Philadelphia Panthers "essentially a nonviolent movement."[9] He came to know, respect, and admire Captain Reggie for his sincerity and his down-to-earth style. Captain Reggie could be tough and gruff, as well as sensitive and even silly. He knew that people were motivated by hope and strengthened by love. He knew, instinctively, that people were drawn to the Party by boundless youthful idealism and that therefore the fear tactics that often accompanied paramilitary organizations would not work with the young people around him. We were there to serve our people, to defend our people, and to protect our community. We were servants of the people. Those ideas sparked us and carried us through dark days and too-short nights.

*Being a Panther in Philadelphia was a unique challenge. One was home, but not at home. For "home" meant where Panthers dwelled, not where one's mother lived or where one's biological brothers and sisters lived.*

*It meant living in a family of several hundred young men and women, all dedicated to building, defending, or promoting the revolutionary collective. With offices in several sections of the nation's fourth largest city, the BPP was in contact with broad segments of the Black community on a frequent and daily basis: in North Philadelphia, through the two offices at 1928 West Columbia Avenue and 2935 West Columbia Avenue; in West Philadelphia, through the office at 3625 Wallace Street; and in Germantown, through the office at 428 West Queen Lane. There was a free breakfast program for schoolchildren in a South Philadelphia community center and near all major offices.*

*The offices were like buzzing beehives of Black resistance. It was always busy, as people piled in starting at its 7:30 a.m. opening time and continuing 'till after nightfall. People came with every problem imaginable, and because our sworn duty was to serve the people, we took our commitment seriously.*

*Early in the morning, we might get visits from nearby merchants, who just wanted to chat. We welcomed such visits, for they normalized our presence in the neighborhood, and they cemented relationships with businesspeople who had a stake in the area. When people had been badly treated by the cops or if parents were demanding a traffic light to slow traffic on North Philly streets where their children played, they came to our offices. In short, whatever our people's problems were, they became our problems. We didn't preach to the people; we worked with them. Some of us worked hard to develop relationships with our neighbors, because we knew that they knew the neighborhood intimately and they could teach us things about it. Throughout the early afternoon, we would get visits from school kids, not those of breakfast school age, but junior high and high school kids, who wanted to sell the paper in their schools. We would caution them to be careful, to only take as many as they were fairly certain they could sell, and ask them to return to the office 20 cents on each paper sold before the week was out.*

*One of our closest neighbors were the Siedlers, a family who ran a children's clothing store across the street from us. They were an older couple, affectionately called Mom and Pop Siedler, who lived in an apartment overtop their Columbia Avenue storefront. Although they were white, they were warm and supportive, and as they were apparently well-read in Marxist literature, we held political discussions with them after the office was closed. One of our sisters, a mother with a young child, stayed with them, as it seemed far more conducive to their well-being than the rough and tumble and dangerous Panther pad where we lived communally. Although unstated, we knew that the cops would be more hesitant to raid a home where white merchants lived, than a Black Panther apartment building, where we were known to be well-armed. The sister was the wife of a well-known Panther from the West Coast who left the country surreptitiously, so we were grateful for the Siedlers' generosity and kindness. Unfortunately, all did not go well for the Siedlers as Pop (Bill) was killed during a robbery of the downstairs store. We shared our grief with Mom (Miriam) at the tragic loss of her mate.*

*As an officer, it was disconcerting to have older members come to me with Party, and even personal, problems. I had to dispel the suspicion that I was a young snot, convince them instead that I had the confidence of the chapter and Party leadership, and thus had a duty to try to do my level best to help any Panther brother or sister, older or younger, who came for help, and if unable to do so, to refer them to other leaders in the organization.*

*The days were full, the nights too short, and the fellowship was electric with Black love and die-hard commitment.*

*One could be transferred in the blink of an eye, for reasons that were beyond one's ken. A Panther accepted this with equanimity or even looked forward to it with anticipation.*

*I was excited when transferred to the BPP Ministry of Information in the Bronx, New York. The size and scale of New York's five boroughs were stunning. It would take a vast metropolis like New York to make a city like Philadelphia seem small and somewhat parochial.*

*The people of the Bronx were outgoing and warm in their response. Once, while we were racing from our home on Kelly Street to the office on Boston Road near Prospect, we hailed a cab, and as all five of us couldn't fit in the back, the cabbie, a middle-aged guy who spoke with Spanish-accented, broken English, invited one of us into the front seat, where he and his woman sat. He was a happy, gregarious man who exuded an infectious* joi de vivre. *He passed around hot, steaming English muffins to his riders and chatted amiably with us in a way that warmed us despite the biting New York winter all about us. I couldn't help thinking that we wouldn't have received such warm hospitality if we were in the city that claims to be reflective of brotherly love. Philadelphia never seemed smaller or meaner.*

*New York's branches were also unique in the racial composition of party members, for it was the only site where Puerto Ricans served as Panthers. While they seemed to make up a higher percentage in Brooklyn, there were also some in our Bronx and Harlem branches. Some were former members of the Young Lords Party, who, because of their African heritage or their radicalism, felt more at home* en el Partido Pantero Negro. *They gave the Party a deeper penetration in the communities of color in New York and served with both pride and distinction.*

*New York seemed like an ethnic and cultural stew that was far more varied and textured than its Oakland-based progenitor. In New York, for example, a significant portion of Panthers were Sunni Muslims, as many of them had either known personally, or profoundly respected the Sunni-convert, Al Hajji Malik El-Shabazz (Malcolm X). Indeed, Dr. Curtis Powell (one of the famed New York* Panther 21*) met and talked with Malcolm in Paris after his pilgrimage to Mecca. Fellow* Panther 21 *veteran Richard Harris heard Malcolm preach as a Black Muslim minister at the Newark Temple.*

*Consequently, the National Office saw the New York branch as somewhat skewed, perhaps tacking toward the dreaded heresy of "cultural nationalism." New York Panthers boasted African or Islamic-oriented names, had Hispanic names or accents, often wore African or traditional garb, and were riotously independent. The secular, uniformed center in California looked at New York as a wildly undisciplined little brother (with, incidentally, a larger membership).*

*If Philadelphia was busy, then New York was a frenzy.*

*Everywhere one turned there was something new to learn about this vast tableau. In Philadelphia, Broad Street was the main artery, dissecting the city into North and South Philadelphia. If you knew Broad Street, you knew Philadelphia. What in the name of heaven did one do in New York, where five huge cities (they called them boroughs, but they looked like cities to me) converged into an amorphous, octopus-like mass of confusion. Manhattan? The Bronx? Harlem? Queens? Staten Island? IRT? IND? New York was a vast puzzle that a young Philadelphia Panther tried to solve daily. Native New Yorkers rarely helped, for they assumed that anybody with half a brain would know, almost instinctively, what the IND or IRT lines meant in the subways. I had to learn how to ask questions and how to pick up keys for what train went where, and when. It was dizzying and challenging.*

*More than once I dozed during a subway ride, only to wake on a darkened car, out in some huge, dark subway yard, and have to find my way back. Many times I spent hours walking from place to place, selling papers or traveling from our office to the apartment. I was more confident in my walking than engaging the alphabet soup of the subway and El system.*

*After several months in the bustling city, several of us were informed we would be leaving that very night for the West Coast. Brad, Stephanie, and I were driven to New York's LaGuardia Airport, given cash for tickets, and told to catch the next flight to San Francisco, California. Brad, Stephanie, and I were artists and writers for Party leaflets and other media that came through the Ministry of Information. We were all excited about going out West, I, perhaps more than my comrades, because I had never flown before. We had no real luggage (as Panthers, we owned little), but Stephanie had a carry-on bag for her cosmetics, a few dresses, and other female necessaries. A chocolate-skinned, deeply dimpled, slender young woman, Stephanie was one of the few Panther women who seemed to utilize makeup.*

*As we were boarding the plane, a strange thing happened to us. We were walking down the accordion-like feeder tube to the plane, when the stewardess closed the door abruptly and a troop of armed men in dark suits appeared, as if they were waiting for us. They leaped at us as if we were the Al Capone gang, instead of Black Panther artists and writers. They rifled through what bags we had, searched us as if they expected to find a bazooka, and spoke nastily to us, in the way cops do to spark angry responses, "We gotcha now, nigger!" We looked at each other, our eyes betraying exasperation and muffled laughter. When they found no weapons, they seemed deeply disappointed and somewhat deflated; they stormed away, leaving threats instead of the expected arrests. Almost as if on cue, the blonde stewardess reopened the door of the plane, and with a fake Barbie-doll smile, welcomed three tousled Panthers aboard her flight, the New York-to-San Francisco overnight. To ease the tension of my first flight, I plucked a tightly wound joint out of my jacket pocket and lit it up, drawing a deep draught of the pungent herb into my lungs. Almost before I could taste it, a stewardess appeared at my elbow to announce, "Smoking marijuana on board American Airlines is a violation of—" and she cited a statute. "Please put it out, sir!" she perkily ordered. I almost choked. I was so rattled that I did exactly that and rode across the country at night, marveling at the sheer vastness of the nation, its cities flashing by beneath us like a distant swarm of lightning bugs.*

*We shed our stifling winter gear at the door of the plane; the California warmth of March 1970 greeted us as we alighted from the silver-skinned bird. The heat, compared to the icy temperatures of the Bronx, was almost unbearable. Stephanie was sent to the San Francisco office, I to the national office, and Brad I know not where.*

*Upon arrival, I was sent to the office of Judi Douglass, editor of* The Black Panther, *to assist her in any form she wished. She was a sweet, gentle woman, with a soft, southern accent, who seemed to always possess an aura of sadness about her.*

*But it was a rare Panther who did one job. I wrote; I read; I edited; I shoveled sand for our sandbags; I sold papers; I worked security; I did all that I was ordered to do.*

*One night, I was posted to night watch, a job requiring one to stand armed and to watch the rear of the national office on Shattuck Avenue for any incursion from the police. My job was to watch the side alleys, the rear concrete yard, and the rooftops; the side alleys, the rear yard, and the rooftops;*

*the side alleys, the rear yard, and the rooftops; the side alleys, the rear yard and the rooftops.... and all of a sudden, I felt a dull thump, and it felt like I got hit in the head with a hammer. I fell. I looked, surprised, at Willie Dawkins and was about to ask him what happened:*

*"Willie! What the— ?"*

*"Nigga! Wachu mean, 'What the—?' Nigga! You was 'sleep! Don't you know you sleepin' ona job coulda got us killed? What if the pigs had vamped?"*

*"Sleep? Huh? Wachu mean?—I—uh—?"*

*"Nigga—I called you four times! Four times! You didn't hear me, did you?"*

*"But I wasn't 'sleep, man—"*

*"Then how'd I getcha gun? Huh?"*

*I then saw that it wasn't a hammer that hit me but the butt of a shotgun. I was asleep? I was asleep. Standing up. On post. On night watch. I had dreamed that I was awake, watching the side alleys, the rear yard, and the rooftops. Willie was right. I had endangered every Panther asleep within the walls. My head ringing, crestfallen I apologized to Willie.*

*"Nigga, don't be sorry—be alert!"*

*The national office of the Black Panther Party had its share of unexpected guests.*

*One day Chief Hilliard came up to me and in a low voice, drew my attention to a little white guy standing around the office, his arms clasped behind his back. The Chief told me to escort him around the office, saying, "He's French. He wrote some shit,* The Blacks, *or something about Blacks. Show this motherfucker around, ok?" I readily agreed, and he handed me a slim worn paperback with the title* The Blacks *emblazoned on its cover, written by someone named Jean Genet.*

*There, in front of me, stood a diminutive, elderly white man, bald, with very short gray hair fringed around the base of his head. His eyes were blue and seemed full of joy. He wore a weathered, cracked, brown leather, bombardier-style jacket and bluish-gray corduroys that sang with his every step. He apparently spoke no English, and I, not a word of French.*

*How were we to communicate? Oh, boy.*

*I figured simple sign language would suffice, and, as I looked into his eyes, I sensed deep intelligence. I motioned for him to wait, as I read the back cover of his book. I learned he was a playwright and did a serious bit in a French prison. His work was called emblematic of something termed "the theatre of the absurd." Hmmm? I hadn't the faintest idea of what the "theatre of the absurd" was, but I somehow felt that any white dude who wrote a play about Black folks had to be alright. Moreover, I had little choice but to obey the Chief. So I resolved to do my best. I escorted the short guy around the office, introduced him to several Panthers, and showed him the production facilities of* The Black Panther *newspaper. I explained that the white dude came all the way from France to see us, and some were duly impressed. (Most weren't, though—they had no idea who he was!) When I returned from the brief tour and left him again in the company of the Chief, Hilliard seemed peeved, but I shall never forget the broad smile and twinkle of joy on Genet's face. He seemed more honored to be in the company of the Black Panthers than if he were accorded an honor guard by the president of the United States.*

*I later learned that he had entered the US illegally and toured on the Party's behalf both in the States and abroad. Refused a visa by the United States, Genet spent several weeks in the US, even attending the murder trial in New Haven, Connecticut, of Chairman Bobby Seale and Captain Ericka Huggins, and he gave speeches at Yale, Columbia, and other colleges.*

*While Bobby and Ericka's fate hung in the courtroom, Genet spoke to over twenty thousand people on May 2, 1970, on the Green at Yale:*

> As for Bobby Seale, I repeat, there must not be another Dreyfus Affair. Therefore, I count on you, on all of you, to spread the contestation abroad, to speak of Bobby Seale in your families, in the universities, in your courses and classrooms: you must contest and occasionally contradict your professors and the police themselves.

And, I say it once more, for it is important, what is at stake are no longer symbolic gestures, but real actions. And if it comes to this—I mean, if the Black Panther Party asks it of you—you must desert your universities, leave your classrooms in order to carry the word across America in favor of Bobby Seale and against racism.

The life of Bobby Seale, the existence of the Black Panther Party, come first, ahead of your diplomas. You must now—and you have the physical, material, and intellectual means to do so—you must now face life directly and no longer in comfortable aquariums—I mean the American universities—which raise goldfish capable of no more than blowing bubbles.

The life of Bobby Seale depends on you. Your real life depends on the Black Panther Party.[10]

*Genet left America as he arrived, illegally, returning to his native France in May 1970.*

*I often wonder why his wordless visit stands so stark in my memory.*

*It is not because he was the only white visitor to the office. He wasn't.*

*Several white radicals came by, some fairly often, but almost all of them radiated fear and discomfiture in the office. Genet seemed oddly at home and at ease around the office. As a former prisoner, and a homosexual, perhaps he saw himself as the perennial outsider, the consummate outlaw. I could tell by his body language, by the openness of his face, by his vibration, that he really dug being in the office. It gave him a kick. He looked like a little boy who had found his favorite toy. He did not fear us. Strangely, he seemed to feel as one with us. His Yale speech certainly showed deep support for the significance of the Party in American life.*

*Perhaps, as an outsider, he perceived these other outsiders as insiders?[11]*

## CHAPTER NINE

# The Split

Society in every state is a blessing, but government even in its best state is but a necessary evil; in its worst state an intolerable one; for when we suffer, or are exposed to the same miseries by *a government,* which we might expect in a country *without government,* our calamity is heightened by reflecting that we furnish the means by which we suffer.

—Thomas Paine, American Revolutionary, *Common Sense*[1]

**THE HIDDEN HAND** of COINTELPRO is often felt in the loss of life, of liberty, and the like. These are indeed dire measurements of the project, but there are other measures, infinitely more difficult to gauge, of its woefully widespread and deleterious effects.

These secondary and tertiary effects of the government's illegal campaign against Black political opponents split asunder one of the nation's most vigorous and ambitious revolutionary organizations—the Black Panther Party—a shattering that disproved the mathematical axiom that the whole is equal to the sum of its parts.

For, in severing the Party and dismembering its remnants, it forced the very notion, not to mention the expression, of revolutionary internationalism underground, denying an oppressed people their inherent right of self-determination, and derailing their struggle for true, independent self-expression, and yes, sovereignty, free from the constraints of the oppressor nation.

Using brutal police repression on the one hand, and false, deceptive *brownmail* on the other, the State utilized a divide-and-conquer tactic that worked surprisingly well.

Here are the basic five techniques employed in domestic espionage.

Surveillance: Direct visual spying on people; mail-snooping and monitoring of conversations, either by phone taps or the planting of mics inserted in adjacent rooms or buildings.

Infiltration: Seeding groups with police agents or using members for purposes of internal surveillance or as agents provocateurs to entrap others in illegal acts.

Intelligence-gathering: The gathering and compiling of data to use in destabilization efforts.

Destabilization: Any effort that derails, disrupts, frustrates, or weakens the organization's ability to function or fulfill collective objectives.

Neutralization: A bureaucratic euphemism for the murder, elimination, or removal of political opponents; the forcing of an organization to cease its operations or to disband.

The FBI, through its infamous COINTELPRO operations, did all that it could to disrupt the Black Panther Party. An FBI memo from 1970 reports:

> A wide variety of alleged authentic police or FBI material could be carefully selected or prepared for furnishing to the Panthers. Reports, blind memoranda, LHMs [letterhead memoranda] and other alleged police or FBI documents could be prepared pinpointing Panthers as police or FBI informants; ridiculing or discrediting Panther leaders through their ineptness or personal escapades; espousing personal philosophies and promoting factionalism among BPP members; indicating electronic coverage where none exists; outlining fictitious plans for police raids or other counteractions; revealing misuse or misappropriation of Panther funds; pointing out instances of political disruptive material and disinformation; etc. *The nature of the disruptive material and disinformation "leaked" would only be limited by the collection ability of your sources* and the need to insure the protection of their security.[2]

This memo delineates the FBI's intent to snitch-jacket Panthers, that is, to falsely portray Panthers as snitches, and, by so doing, to threaten their continued performance in the Party by exposing them to improper expulsion, heated conflicts with other Party members, and perhaps worse. No one, outside of the FBI, that is, really knows how many Panthers unjustly suffered from such submissions.

The other serious, and certainly anticipated, effect of such insidious operations as FBI snitch-jacketing was that it frayed and eroded trust between comrades. This aura of distrust was one of Hoover's prime objectives, for amidst such widespread distrust and incipient paranoia, no organization could meaningfully function.

It is necessary here to state the obvious: the FBI's objective was not to disrupt the breakfast program, to interrupt membership drives, to cripple *Black Panther* newspaper sales, or even to kill or imprison Party operatives. These were mere incidentals. The primary objective was the destruction of the Black Panther Party as an independent Black radical presence in the American body politic.

Former New York Panther leader and long-time political prisoner Dhoruba bin Wahad has described the State's counterintelligence program as "a domestic war program, a program aimed at countering the rise of black militancy, black independent political thought."[3] As usual, the outspoken bin Wahad got it exactly right.

The East-West split had many beginnings, some known, some unknown, with the State skillfully manipulating the noxious toxins of ego, pride, and envy among key Party officials. Hoover authorized false letters to all of these leaders, ostensibly from the others. Each letter was critical of another Party leader for some perceived fault or flaw.

Such letters, because of the hierarchical nature of the Party and the aura of paranoia that permeated the time—fueled by the incessant military attacks on Party offices and homes—seemed like another form of attack and, to some, treason.

Despite the ideological claim that the Party functioned under the principle of criticism and self-criticism, the Party hierarchy in fact functioned much like any other group in bourgeois society, that is, according to the principle of power dynamics: those who have power strive mightily to keep it—period.

So when Huey received letters full of criticism of his leadership, he struck out at those he thought were angling to undermine his rule of the organization. When Eldridge received letters critical of Huey's leadership, he felt a sense of affirmation. Neither apparently questioned the authorship of this critical correspondence.

Why would they? Why *should* they?

Neither they nor their subordinates had any real idea of the existence, and definitely not the extent, of government brownmail and other assorted dirty tricks. If someone had suggested that the government, the American government, was involved in writing poison pen letters pretending to be who they were not, most would have laughed, ridiculing the person as a fan of James Bond films or as paranoid.

It is ironic that revolutionaries, who swore an oath to replace the incumbent government, would yet still believe, essentially, that there were limits to what that government would do to preserve its hold on power.

This begins to make sense when one considers the deepest philosophical roots of the Party. While some might identify the philosophical basis as Marxism, or its later variation, Maoism, others would prefer Black nationalism, Black revolutionary internationalism, or, as we have suggested, Malcolmism.

None of these truly answer the question, for while they identify a stage of the Party's ideological development, the underlying philosophical approach, as based in Huey as the heart of the Party, was essentially a legalist one.

An examination of the early history of the Party, reveals, even in the events that evoked the most coverage in the corporate press, an intensely legalistic perspective. Huey was deeply influenced by the letter of the law.

Few researchers, scholars, or historians have fully analyzed this facet of Huey's worldview, preferring instead to project him as the outlaw.

This may be seen in the way that two seminal events, the BPP's armed monitoring of the Oakland police and the BPP armed demonstration in Sacramento on May 2, 1967, were told by the government and by the press.

The tone set by the State, and subsequently carried by much of the white press, may be seen in the following quote from the US House Subcommittee on Internal Security Report on the Black Panther Party:

> On May 2, 1967, twenty-four members of the Black Panther Party *invaded* the California State Assembly at Sacramento while it was in session. The *invaders* were armed with rifles, shotguns, and pistols, and claimed they were there to protest a gun registration law. Security guards seized the weapons, unloaded them, and returned them to the panthers, who then walked out of the building.[4]

This account, based on the congressional testimony of Director J. Edgar Hoover, aside from its factual inaccuracy, reflects the slant adopted by much of the corporate media, which places the Panthers in the role of invaders or, by implication, outsiders. One would suppose they were aliens, not citizens who were entitled to exercise their constitutional and statutory rights as such. The account also doesn't give the slightest hint that these men were behaving in ways that were legal in California, in regard to both arms possession and their open display. In fact, had their actions not been legal they would not have been at the state house protesting, for the purpose of the new law they were opposing was to *outlaw* such behavior.

Huey, who constantly studied California law books, turned to the myths and language of the law constantly, and these ideas in turn influenced his outlook long before his introduction to Fanon. We know the value Newton placed on legal concepts because we see it in many of the platforms set out in the Black Panther Party's Ten-Point Platform and Program. The US Constitution is specifically cited three times, its language, "fair and impartial," is borrowed directly, and the Declaration of Independence is partially excerpted verbatim in the "What We Believe" section of the tenth point.

This legalistic bent was not only in the mind of the founder of the Black Panther Party, but shared by many Panthers who emulated and admired Huey. Not surprisingly, David R. Papke, a law professor who has studied Newton's writings and his early courtroom adventures, found him to have the mental makings of a potentially "fine lawyer."[5] While Papke doubtless meant it as a compliment, it also had a negative connotation: legalists believe that there are legal limits beyond which the State may not go.

To the average Panther, a young man or woman of seventeen to twenty years of age, there really was no frame of reference that would alert them to the level of "dirty tricks" that the State was capable.

Former Panther and former political prisoner Assata Shakur, perhaps spoke for many when she mused:

> No one could have known that the FBI's COINTELPRO was attempting to destroy the Black Panther Party in particular and the Black Liberation Movement in general, using divide-and-conquer tactics. The FBI's program consisted of turning members of organizations against each other, pitting one Black organization against another.[6]

Why could no one have known?

There may be several reasons: youthful naïveté, a strong sense of legalism, or perhaps, as the former political prisoner Geronimo ji-Jaga would tell a German journalist, Panthers didn't really think that what they were doing could be seen as wrong and, further, they didn't think they were important enough to warrant that kind of intense government scrutiny or that level of government repression.[7]

What was quite unknown at the time was that the FBI held secret files on some two million Americans, from the paranoid, drug-addicted Elvis Presley to the absent-minded Albert Einstein.[8] Few Americans, Black or white, had any idea of the scope of FBI and other governmental spying, infiltration, and destabilization of organizations engaged in (allegedly) constitutionally protected activities and organizing efforts, such as the anti–Vietnam War, woman's liberation, and Civil Rights movements. If one wrote a letter to the editor of a newspaper or made a phone call to a "target," a file was opened and one's life could be irreparably and surreptitiously damaged.

## Letters from the Feds

Party leaders regularly received mail from various Party offices and the community. It is a telling reflection of the times that a leader really would have no immediate way of knowing whether the writer of the letter was a cherished comrade, or an agent of the FBI. The following is the full text of a letter mailed to the Minister of Information, Eldridge Cleaver, at his Algerian offices in early 1971:

> Eldridge,
>
> John Seale told me Huey talked to you Friday and what he had to say. I am disgusted with things here and the fact that you are being ignored. I am loyal to the Party and it makes me mad to learn that Huey now has to lie to you. I am referring to his fancy new apartment which he refers to as the throne. I think you should know that he picked the place out himself, not the Central Committee, and the high rent is from Party funds and not paid by anyone else. Many of the others are upset about this waste of money. It is needed for other Party work here and also in Algeria.

It seems the least Huey could do is furnish you the money and live with the rest of us. Since Huey will lie to you about this, you can see how it is with him. You would be amazed at what is actually happening.

I wish there was some way I could get in touch with you but in view of Huey's orders it is not possible, You should really know what's happening and statements about you. I can't risk a call as it would mean certain expulsion. You should think a great deal before sending Kathleen. If I could talk to you I could tell you why I don't think you should.

Big Man[9]

The apparent writer was a "big man" named Elbert Howard, who edited *The Black Panther* for a time (and was known by the nickname Big Man).

But Big Man Howard, FBI files reveal, never wrote this letter. Its recipient, Eldridge Cleaver, did not know this, and thus the fake letter achieved its desired objectives. It insinuated itself between Cleaver and Newton, and it encouraged Eldridge to discourage his wife, Kathleen, from coming to the US to, among other things, speak at the Washington segment of the Revolutionary People's Constitutional Convention (RPCC).

Newton wanted Kathleen Cleaver to help promote a number of Party projects, including the support of the imprisoned and endangered Bobby Seale and Ericka Huggins, for whom a series of rallies were planned. Newton knew that this attractive, articulate, and knowledgeable Panther leader could move and electrify a crowd, something the introspective Minister of Defense never truly mastered. He realized that he spoke in a "dull fashion," and he perhaps remembered the disquieting events in Philadelphia months before and had no wish to replicate them.[10]

When the RPCC's Washington session began, Newton had no idea why the Party's Communication Secretary hadn't communicated with him and had not appeared, as promised and advertised. Huey felt this was further evidence that the Cleavers were trying to seize control of the Party.

This important Party project, which sought to create a broader, institutionalized revolutionary structure, foundered in its crib, at least in part because Kathleen didn't appear. The Party could not seize the moment to spark the vast throng, who either attended or followed the events of the RPCC, into action.

Kathleen apparently didn't appear because Eldridge didn't want her to appear, and Eldridge didn't want her to appear because he was being flooded with false, COINTEL-initiated correspondence that played on his ego and his fears and, given his extreme degree of isolation in Algiers, *he believed to be true.*

Indeed, this was the FBI's explicit intent, as seen by a December 1970 memo that instructed its agents to:

> [W]rite numerous letters to Cleaver criticizing Newton for his lack of leadership. It is felt that, if Cleaver received a sufficient number of complaints regarding Newton it might... create dissension that later could be more fully exploited.[11]

Their diabolical plan seemed to be working to perfection.

There was another reason why enmity was building between the Minister of Defense and the Minister of Information. Newton, again apparently believing the plethora of reports coming to him, began to order purges of anyone that he suspected might challenge his authority.

After the LA chapter's defense against the quasi-military forces of the LAPD, Geronimo emerged as a hero among Panthers. He was deeply respected for bringing out his troops alive and giving the State up to six hours of resistance. When the State's undercover efforts were exposed at the subsequent trial of the LA Panthers and the jury tossed their case, they emerged from the joint to a hero's welcome. *The Black Panther* called Geronimo's actions representative of "the essence of a revolutionary."[12] Geronimo's 1970 release, however, would mark a fateful turning point for him and the Party. Upon his release, he went underground and set up a secret camp in Texas where he used his Vietnam-acquired skills to train an underground military force for the Black Panther Party. However, shortly after an emissary from Hilliard arrived at their location, the place was swarmed by CSS agents, the Panthers were busted, and Geronimo was immediately returned to Los Angeles.

While Geronimo was awaiting trial in December, he came across an article in *The Black Panther* denouncing him and claiming he was working for the CIA.[13] Geronimo ji-Jaga, once a hero called "the essence of a revolutionary," had been labeled an "enemy of the people" and purged from the Black Panther Party.

The report that Geronimo was now considered an enemy rocked the organization. Within weeks of the Geronimo purge, members of the New York–based *Panther 21* also found themselves labeled enemies. Some of these "enemies" were facing serious charges at the hands of the State. The timing was ugly. By February 1971, it was clear that a split was weaving its way through the Party, as respected comrades were praised one week, only to be condemned the next.

It was maddening.

Letters from the FBI to leading Party members sparked increased paranoia and higher spirals of instability and danger. Who knew who was writing to whom?

Letters signed by prominent Party members flowed to the exiled, isolated Minister of Information, who badly wanted to get back into the swing of things in the States. The letters virtually dripped with vitriol for the equally isolated (in his penthouse apartment) Minister of Defense. What is lamentable is that there is every indication that Cleaver and Newton believed the accounts coming to them, never questioning their authenticity.

Consider the following examples, the first allegedly from an influential Party member, Connie Matthews—a brilliant, able activist who served as Newton's personal secretary:

> I know you have not been told what has been happening lately.... Things around headquarters are dreadfully disorganized with the comrade commander not making proper deci-

sions. The newspaper is in a shambles. No one knows who is in charge. The foreign department gets no support. Brothers and sisters are accused of all sorts of things.

I am disturbed because I, myself, do not know which way to turn.... If only you were here to inject some strength into the movement, or to give some advice. One of two steps must be taken soon and both are drastic. We must either *get rid of the supreme commander* [a BPP reference to Huey Newton], or get rid of the disloyal members.... Huey is really all we have right now and we can't let him down, regardless of how poorly he is acting, *unless you feel otherwise.*[14]

One of Cleaver's white supporters, "Algonquin J. Fuller" who claimed to be a member of Youth Against War and Fascism in New York, sent the following letter to Algiers:

Let me tell you what has happened to our brothers in the Party since you have left and that "Pretty Nigger Newton" in his funky clothes has been running things....

Brother Eldridge, to me as an outsider but one who believes in the revolution, it seems that the Panthers need a leader in America who will bring the Party back to the People.

Brother Newton has failed you and the Party. The Panthers do not need a "day time revolutionary, a night time party goer and African fashion model as a leader."

They need the leadership which only you can provide.[15]

Through their contacts within and without, the FBI learned that letters such as these were getting to Cleaver and that he thought they were genuine.

Their files reveal a Bureau that was almost giddy with glee at their apparent success, with one file noting "Cleaver has never previously disclosed to BPP officials the receipt of prior COIN-TELPRO letters."[16]

Shortly after the February 1971 so-called "Big Man" letter, what was originally the private province of correspondence became public proof of a conflict between the two most influential members of the Party.

Newton phoned Algiers to invite Cleaver to join him in a television call-in show later in the day. Cleaver readily agreed. When the station's call got through, Cleaver's voice was angry and tight, and he launched into a furious, on-air verbal attack on the Party's Central Committee. He demanded that Newton dismiss the Chief-of-Staff, David Hilliard. Newton responded in kind by attacking Cleaver personally, calling him a "punk" and a "coward."

The breach was complete.

This was far more than a falling-out between two hard-headed men. It signified the rending of the organization itself, a split that would tear east from west.

As Cleaver fell under the spell of COINTEL-produced correspondence, so too did Newton succumb to the lure of letters surreptitiously scripted by the invisible agents of the State. As the founder and the head of the Party, Newton undoubtedly received the lion's share of brownmail. In his 1980 doctoral thesis (in which he referred to himself in the third person), Newton recounts the time he received a sheaf of documents from Philadelphia:

> The Philadelphia FBI field office prepared and sent to Newton a fictitious Black Panther Party directive, supposedly prepared by the Philadelphia Black Panther Office, which questioned Newton's leadership abilities; accompanying it was a cover letter purportedly from an anonymous Party supporter accusing the Philadelphia chapter of "slandering its leaders in private." FBI headquarters, in approving this operation, noted that prior COINTELPRO action which "anonymously advised the national headquarters that food, clothing, and drugs collected for BPP community programs were being stolen by BPP members" had resulted in criticism of the Philadelphia chapter by the national office, transfer of members, "and the national office has even considered closing the Philadelphia chapter." The memorandum concluded, "we want to keep this dissension going."[17]

If the Philadelphia chapter had it rough, what of the members of the biggest chapter in the nation—New York?

New York arguably boasted the most influential and certainly best-known Panthers outside of the California chapters. They were an astute bunch who published a remarkable collective auto-biography from prison, a kind of political memoir that sold briskly in the nation's mass media hub. The New York Panthers were immensely popular, not just in the ghettos and barrios of New York, but throughout the country.

Leading New York Panthers like Dhoruba bin Wahad, Afeni Shakur, Michael "Cetawayo" Tabor, Lumumba Shakur, Zayd Malik Shakur, and Beth Mitchell had the good looks, oratorical skills, and charismatic presence that the media seemed to love. It was precisely these qualities that made some of the New York Panthers prime targets for FBI and government neutralization. The somewhat California-centric Party could not help being challenged by the growing prominence of its eastern half, and the agents of COINTELPRO were there to exploit this incipient envy.

Not content with their neutralization of the *Panther 21* by unjust incarceration, the FBI, learning that the group made public a letter critical of Newton's increasingly autocratic rule, proceeded to produce and send other letters, in the name of the *21,* to Eldridge and Huey, each critical of the other. Huey expelled the authors (all but Dhoruba and Cetawayo, who were out on bail, and thus hadn't signed the letters), sending New York to the brink of revolt. Meanwhile, the FBI wrote this letter to the international office in Algiers:

> As you are aware, we of the Panther 21 have always been loyal to the Party and continue to feel a close allegiance to you and the ideology of the Party which has always developed mainly through your efforts.

> We know that you have never let us down and have always inspired us through your participation in the vanguard party. As the leading theoretician of the party's philosophy and as a brother among brother [sic], we urge you to make your influence felt. We think that The Rage [that is, Eldridge Cleaver] is

the only person strong enough to pull this factionalized party back together....

You are our remaining hope in our struggle to fight oppression within and without the Party.[18]

One Harlem Panther, Assata Shakur, would still simmer at the mass expulsion of the *21* many years later and expressed wonder at the efforts of the government to destroy the Black Panther Party:

Zayd [Malik Shakur, New York's Deputy Minister of Information] was acting as peacemaker between Huey and the Panther 21, furiously trying to get Huey to rescind his expulsion order. Zayd felt that to take any position in reference to the problems might jeopardize his role and result in dire consequences for the Panther 21. Cetawayo and Doruba, who had not been expelled because they were out on bail and had not signed the letter, were also attempting to get the Panther 21 reinstated. Huey wanted them to support the expulsion and the expelled Panthers wanted them to criticize Huey's actions.[19]

Their efforts, while undoubtedly noble, did not fit the frenetic temper of the times. Theirs was a call to reason and restraint, in an era of paranoia and widespread distrust:

Like Zayd, Cet and Dhoruba honestly believed they could straighten out the madness. And were it not for the FBI, they probably would have. Nobody could possibly have known that the FBI had sent a phony letter to Eldridge Cleaver in Algiers, "signed" by the Panther 21, criticizing Huey Newton's leadership. No one could have known that the FBI had sent a letter to Huey's brother saying the New York Panthers were plotting to kill him.... Huey ended up suspending Cet and Dhoruba from the Party, branded them as "enemies of the people," and caused them to go into hiding, in fear of their very lives. No one had the slightest idea that this whole scenario was carefully manipulated and orchestrated by the FBI.[20]

The FBI, having achieved their objectives of splitting apart the two most influential Panther chapters in the nation, was thrilled at the level of their success. By March 1971, a new range of orders went into the field, based upon the same tactics that were used previously:

> Since the differences between Newton and Cleaver now appear to be irreconcilable, no further counter-intelligence activity in this regard will be undertaken at this time and now new targets must be established. David Hilliard and Egbert [sic] "Big Man" Howard of national headquarters and Bob Rush of the Chicago B.P. Chapter are likely future targets....

> Hilliard's key position at the National Headquarters makes him an outstanding target. Howard and Rush are also key Panther functionaries ... making them prime targets.[21]

That the FBI began to target other, second-tier Panthers suggests that the emphasis on Newton and Cleaver was based upon the leaders' Party-wide and national influence, rather than their discrete personalities. Yet both men were fashioned in ways that made them particularly vulnerable to the FBI shenanigans. Both were remarkable men, with abilities and strengths that made them indispensable for the tasks thrust upon them by history. Yet, like all other mortals, they had vulnerabilities, weaknesses, and tendencies that, when exploited, could open the door to disaster. Some of these traits are revealed by how the two men fell into the traps prepared for them by the class enemy—the State.

## The Power of Personality

It is beyond dispute that Huey P. Newton was a man of signal brilliance and truly remarkable courage. In many ways, the Black Panther Party came into being because of his will, and his strength. While those are positive attributes, they also had negative aspects. Huey, while nominally ranked below the Chairman, was, in fact and in our consciousness, the first Panther, the de facto Leader. Thus he was the first among unequals. He was a model that all Panthers aspired to.

Eldridge Cleaver, as an ex-convict and author, brought to the Party more than his writing skills and his notoriety. An adept and exciting speaker, Eldridge brought a public strength to the Party that it lacked, given Huey's real aversion to public speaking. His criminal background, indeed, gave the Party a kind of street credibility to its claimed lumpen origins.

Eldridge also brought to the Party his contacts in the white radical fringe that did not really warm to Huey.

Yet the Cleaver-Newton alliance had its fault lines, and ego was one of them. It is apparent when one reads the letters from the FBI to Eldridge that each of them appeals to his ego, with almost saccharin pleas like "only you can provide the leadership" that the Party needs and suggestions to get rid of Huey and the like.

For someone who was some 7,000 miles away from home, in exile, who dearly wanted to come home to the States, the letters to Cleaver must have been heady stuff.

As for Huey, it appears the Minister of Defense had several traits that first exploded in his conflict with Eldridge and later with other, mostly eastern, Panthers.

In his earliest years of adolescence, Huey fought hard, mostly against his fellows in the neighborhood, and suspected anyone who he didn't know was friend to be his enemy.[22] Can we say that this formative experience and youthful inclination simply disappeared when he created the Party as a young, angry man?

It appears that this deep, instinctual way of knowing, or of fearing the unknown, may have been a powerful factor in Huey's relationships with other Panthers. Consider this: when Huey went to prison in 1967, he had a personal connection with every man or woman who was a member of the Black Panther Party. Usually he or Bobby knew them from the neighborhood and had recruited them. If they didn't know them, then they certainly knew of them or knew the people who recruited them. Three years later, free on appeal in 1970, the Party he knew was tremendously transformed. There were now branches and chapters not in three geographically close cities (Oakland, San Francisco, and Richmond), but in over forty-three. The largest chapters were in Los Angeles, Chicago, and New York. Huey didn't know any of these people. He never rapped with them. He knew of them, certainly, but he must have wondered where they stood, or where they would stand, in times of strife and battle.

Could he trust them?

Conversely, to many of the young men and women who joined the Party in other parts of the nation, Huey was the brother on the posters on our office walls. He stood, steely-eyed, beside a flint-jawed Bobby Seale, a shotgun in his grasp. Or he sat, like an African warlord, in a wispy wicker chair, a shotgun in one hand and a spear in the other. They did not know him. They only knew his image.

There were few of the real human ties of sympathy and concern that grew from shared struggles on the ground.

Huey tended to make leaders of those people that he knew from his pre-Party street life, his homies and friends. While these were undoubtedly people that he trusted, they often were people who were, quite frankly, ill equipped to handle the pressures and stresses of directing and managing an international organization.

What appears to have happened is that guys whom Huey trusted tended to carry Huey's water, rather than question his decisions on matters involving Party discipline. They became, not his comrades, but his emissaries, instruments of his will. It was to men such as these that the term Huey's Party had meaning and verity.

David Hilliard's autobiography is instructive in this regard in at least two respects. He writes that he was stumped by the central work of Fanon, *The Wretched of the Earth,* which was so important to the founders of the Party. He also describes an event in which he, drunken and frustrated, walks out of his home and takes a potshot at a passing cop car, an expression of his giving vent to "the madness."[23]

While this behavior perhaps reflects the actions of a drunkard, therefore somewhat mitigating the charge, it raises justifiable questions about his ability to effectively manage the affairs of the nation's largest Black revolutionary organization. It suggests that Hilliard was in over his head. Shortly thereafter, Hilliard is counseled by Seale, who explains to him the rudimentary notion of the revolutionary process as an extended one, and not an emotional or instantaneous response to external stimuli. David listens as if it's the first time he has heard such ideas.[24] Clearly, then, while Hilliard may have held Huey's trust and his affection, it is doubtful that he possessed the managerial or interpersonal skills necessary for a group composed of young, angry Black people who wanted to fight to bring freedom to their people. That didn't mean, of course, that David was somehow stupid or didn't learn the lessons needed to do the task. It means only that Hilliard's prerequisite for the job was his deep, personal loyalty to Huey, and while that served Huey's interests, it did not necessarily serve the interests of a growing, changing Black revolutionary political party.

It seems easy, in time's hindsight, to be critical of Huey for appointing people who seemed ill equipped for the job. It is also somewhat unfair for us to do this, especially given the ungodly levels of repression visited upon the Party at the time. There were raids all across the nation, some fatal. The Party was under direct and sustained military and political attacks. That is to say, it was not an easy task. Further, where was Huey to find the people more prepared for the job? Put an ad in the campus newspaper at Howard University? Put an ad in *The Black Panther?*

At the time, perhaps the best-educated Panther may also have been its most treacherous—Earl Anthony. Anthony, who was several credits short of his law degree when he joined the Party, would go down in history as the Party's first snitch. It is bad enough that he was given the rank of Captain and was sent to help organize the LA chapter. Even though he was intelligent enough to take on the task of Chief-of-Staff, there was also the growing suspicion that he was not cool—they didn't think he was a snitch exactly, but fishy in some way. If he had been given the rank of

Chief-of-Staff, the disaster that befell the Party might have been even more tragic.

As a rule, given the Party's rhetoric about being a lumpen group, credentials didn't really matter. What mattered was your heart. What mattered was your will.

Yet Huey's parochial instincts; his dis-ease with the new, the unknown, also fed into his behavior toward the end of 1970 and 1971. He essentially distrusted those folks whom he didn't know. Thus, he looked at Panthers in New York and Philadelphia with a jaundiced eye. When he felt he received less than total obedience, he expelled. Period.

While it is undoubtedly true that between Cleaver and Newton there was considerable ideological dissonance, it is also true that one's ideology arose from one's ideation, that is, one's world view, and one's perspective on the world. To suppose that all political ideas arise from the calm, untroubled realm of logic without the influence of one's inner life is to suppose that all that men do in the realm of politics is logical. History, with all of its inexactitudes, gives us sufficient evidence to the contrary. Can anyone claim that the mania of the Nazis regarding Jews during the Reich was logical? With the exception of the value of defining an "other" for the Nazis to focus on, there is little real doubt that the enmity visited upon the Jews came from a psychosocial place where logic doesn't dwell.

Ideologically, Cleaver was a devotee of the paramilitary *foco*, a form of organization typified by the urban guerrilla campaigns waged throughout much of Latin America. He wanted the BPP to form the nucleus of such groups as a New World Liberation Front in the US. While this certainly was a direction that was approached by the Party in the late 1960s, and perhaps early 1970s, by 1971, it was not the direction Newton would advocate. Indeed, by 1972 the BPP, which remained under his control, would opt for an electoral strategy, as Bobby Seale and other leading members ran for local and regional offices in Oakland and its environs.

A 1972 order of the Central Committee commanded all Panthers to centralize in Oakland to support the campaign of Bobby Seale for Mayor of Oakland (and related campaigns for various offices on his slate). The order meant that Panthers from across the country had to close their local offices, close their local community survival programs, and, essentially, leave for Oakland. For some Panthers, this was simply unacceptable. Many people left the Party.

Audrea Jones from Massachusetts was not one of them. She followed the directive of the Central Committee but not without misgivings. She was one of the few women who captained a chapter and was thus deeply involved in the Party's community operations.

She submitted to the will of the Central Committee and joined the Party's efforts in the Bay Area to consolidate power in the birthplace of the organization. Years later, she would state that the decision by the Party was a serious tactical error:

> It [the closing of all chapters outside California] was a major mistake. I think that it was a major mistake. It was a national organization with viable structures in communities. I think people felt abandoned by that. There was great support for the Party in local chapters and branches. People had ... put themselves out to be part of that. To just close down clinics and close down breakfast programs. I mean the whole idea was to organize these things to the extent that things could be taken over. But there was a hole left.[25]

The 1972–73 centralization of the Party in Oakland had another impact that was perhaps unforeseen by the Central Committee: it communicated to many common people that the Party was in decline. Why else, people wondered, would the Panthers close down their community programs? Therefore the centralization contributed to the Party's own demise.

It was a continuing diminution, a devolving of sorts, that seemed to suggest that the much-reported split was a reality. Perception became reality. That perception was, if anything, strengthened when Seale lost the mayor's race, albeit after a surprisingly strong showing.

## Huey's Return to "The Good Old Days"

According to several published accounts, it was Huey's insistence on the centralization of the Party in Oakland, over the objections of Chairman Bobby, that swung the Central Committee on the question.[26]

While there were arguments for the centralization, it would appear that the main reason was Newton's determination to recreate the Party of his pre-prison memory: to bring all Panthers to Oakland; to close down all other offices; to re-create a smaller, more manageable Party.

To know them.

To test them.

To determine, once and for all, were they friend or foe?

What Huey had demonstrated in his life experience was an extraordinary will. It took will to found the Party. It took will to build the Party. Perhaps his will would allow him to rebuild the Party.

This was not to be.

The split left several groups vying for the legitimacy of the original Black Panther Party—a western branch centralized in the port city of Oakland; an eastern branch headquartered in the Bronx, New York; and the Black Liberation Army, which drew from the remnants of both.

Within weeks of the Newton/Cleaver breach, Panthers began to die, this time not from the fire of the class enemy, the State, but by the hands of their erstwhile brothers.

Robert Webb, an ex-GI who returned from war for the Empire determined to battle for the liberation of Black people in the US through the Black Panther Party, was shot to death while standing on the corner of 125th Street and Seventh Avenue in Harlem on March 6, 1971, perhaps because, as a western Panther, he dared to ally himself with members from the East.

Six weeks later, Sam Napier, a gentle man who was Distribution Manager for *The Black Panther* newspaper, was tortured to death in a grimy apartment in New York in retaliation for Webb's slaying. Both Webb and Napier were much-loved and well-respected members of the Party, and their loss precipitated an exodus from the Party of members who felt disgusted at the in-fighting.

The losses of Webb and Napier marked the depths to which interparty rivalry had fallen. Their deaths marked far more than the passing of two dedicated revolutionaries.

It marked the shattered dreams of hundreds of Panthers, who watched as the Party of their dreams become the abode of their darkest nightmares.

Men like Webb, Napier, Fred Bennett, and others known and unknown became unwitting martyrs to madness, while the FBI, and those who sponsored them, cackled with glee.

The split became a divide, which became a rending, which yawned into a canyon.

Like a ruminant, like a wild animal born in the bush with the scent of the predator on the wind, the Black Panther Party sprang into being quickly and rapidly found its footing, running across the vastness of the nation with the swiftness of an African gazelle. It grew quickly and knew its strength in its ability to reproduce itself over forty times in forty different places.

Quietly, under cloak of darkness, the hunter lay, feeding poison into the waters and death into the air.

It awoke one day to find its body severed in twain, pain searing the breach, but miraculously, incredibly, still alive.

Dulled by agony, less than its former self, smaller, less vital, but, for now, alive.

## CHAPTER TEN

# One, Two, Many Parties

> There is a tide in the affairs of men
> Which, taken at the flood, leads on to fortune;
> Omitted, all the voyage of their life
> Is bound in shallows and in miseries.
>
> On such a full sea are we now afloat,
> And we must take the current when it serves,
> Or lose our ventures.
>
> —William Shakespeare, *Julius Caesar* (Brutus to Cassius)

**TO MANY BLACK** and white radical youth of today, the very existence of the Black Panther Party seems almost miraculous. To many of the young people who worked, lived, and loved in the Party, however, the Party was not a miracle, but a bright, shining reality, one born of radical necessity.

It was the stuff of bitter hopes, of frustrated dreams, a will-o'-the-wisp of Black desires that caught on the wind's ragged updrafts, and spread like a fire in the mind, across vast distances.

In the years preceding the birth of the Party, famed Black labor leader and 1963 March on Washington organizer Bayard Rustin would argue that southern Blacks had no intention of leaving their traditional, albeit troubled, home in the Democratic Party:

> Southern Negroes, despite exhortations from SNCC to organize themselves into a Black Panther Party, are going to stay in the Democratic Party—to them it is the party of progress, the

New Deal, the New Frontier, and the Great Society—and they are right to stay.[1]

For the most part, of course, Rustin's insight has stood the test of time; however, within months of his writing, there was indeed a Black Panther Party with Blacks as fervent members in the North, the South, the West, and the East. All were united under the inspiring vision of Huey P. Newton and by Malcolm's post-NOI powerful exhortations to revolution.

With the whole world seemingly embroiled in revolutionary and anticolonial struggle, and given the oppressive nature of Black existence, it seemed not only logical but inevitable that Blacks in America would launch mass movements of rebellion. The Black Panther Party, as the embodiment of that rebelliousness, seemed as natural as rain showers in April.

Within a decade of its flowering however, the split dealt a serious blow to the BPP. For a time, like jealous, bickering twins vying for a prince's throne, the two sides were locked in conflict; each strove to prove it was the legitimate heir to the name of the Black Panther Party.

Newton, ever the Nietzschean, sought to actuate his own will to power, sought to minimize the damage by denying the very existence of a split. He termed it a "ghost split" that was more media creation than material reality.[2] In a sense, he was correct. Broadly speaking, however, he was not.

For there can be no question that the antagonistic media delighted in projecting and exacerbating any hint of conflict between members and even supporters of the Black Panther Party.

Yet, there *was* a split.

Cleaver, raging and fuming in Algiers, announced he would lead the "real Black Panther Party" from his redoubt in North Africa. Newton would dismiss him as "an ultraleft sorcerer's apprentice with a gift of verbal magic."[3]

Truth be told, the bulk of the organization remained firmly in Newton's grasp. Newton also held on to the Party's crown jewel,

*The Black Panther* newspaper. The paper was valuable, not merely because of the financial resources it generated, but because it directly communicated with hundreds of thousands of people, weekly, unmediated by the establishment media.

Yet, by mid 1971, it became clear that some who resigned from the organization resigned from its western branch and affiliated with the wing of the East Coast Black Panther Party, headquartered in Harlem and the Bronx. Panthers in the East published *Right On! Black Community News Service,* a Black Panther newspaper in everything but name.

Like any divorce, parting was not sweet sorrow.

Panthers, feeling either deeply wounded or deeply betrayed, turned their volcanic anger, their frustrated rage, and their misguided vengeance on each other, with predictably disastrous results. Selling a newspaper, whether East or West, became a serious matter. Indeed, walking the streets became problematic, as shown by the noted killing of the diminutive Robert Webb and echoed by the killing of Sam Napier. They were but part of half a score of Panthers who appeared to have met their ends at the hands of other Panthers.

The fate of Webb and others like him showed that the split was far more than Newton's "ghost split."

This was a split of the spirit.

There was, in fact, more than one split; there were several. In each, a new organ came into being to give voice to the alienation that arose between former comrades. As *Right On!* marked the emergence of the East Coast Black Panther Party, a new journal, *Babylon! Revolutionary People's Communication Network,* reflected the emergence of a formation to the left of the East Coast Party, more in line with Cleaver's exhortations to present a more radical, more militant, and more confrontational profile.

But, as Safiya Bukhari recalls, Cleaver's influence, at least in the East Coast, New York–based formation, had its limits. She recalls receiving an unexpected transatlantic phone call that broke into a tense, nerve-wracking night:

> This particular night I was on security at the Harlem office, along with two other people when the phone rang. When I answered the phone an operator said, *Your overseas party is on the line. Go ahead please.* I said *I didn't make an overseas call.* I didn't make one but Eldridge Cleaver was on the line from Algeria. Neither one of us had placed the call, but we knew who had. It seems the government or somebody wanted us to talk about something.
>
> We decided to talk despite not initiating the call. Eldridge took the opportunity to tell me that it was time to escalate the struggle. He said it was time to take it to the streets and that's what I should tell people to do. I said, NO! I was not going to tell people to do that. I told Eldridge that the conditions were not right and I was not going to encourage our people to go out and take part in or become victims of a bloodbath. I held firm because I truly believed I was right. Eldridge didn't know the objective conditions here. He was over 3,000 miles away, in Algeria.
>
> When he saw he was getting nowhere with me he put Cetawayo [Michael Tabor, one of the *Panther 21,* who fled to Algiers rather than face trial or reprisal] on the phone. Cet told me I should do as Eldridge requested. I asked, *Cet, do you remember what you taught me? To deal with the principle and not the personality?* Cet said in that deep, deep, melodious voice, that he possessed, *Yes.* He was silent for a moment and then made no further attempt to get me to do what Eldridge wished.[4]

Although Bukhari felt tremendously empowered by her stand off with the influential and charismatic information minister, Cleaver's voice remained the dominant one heard through the East Coast's main organs, *Right On!* and *Babylon!* These papers documented the growing splits and countersplits severing the Party. To the people not intimately involved with the various feuding factions this was but a recipe for confusion and did not serve any faction well.

It served the interests of the State.

The second split, marked by the journal *Babylon!,* meant far more than a third Black revolutionary paper. It meant, for some, their final leave from the party of their dreams and hopes and the leap into the uncertainty of small, revolutionary collectives like the clandestine Black Liberation Army, unaffiliated with known, above-ground radical organizations.

From his penthouse in Alameda County, Newton would decry the revolutionary cultism of the early Black Panther days and, by clear implication, criticize Cleaver for what Newton termed his defection from the Party and, more importantly, the Party's defection from the very people it was sworn to defend and serve:

> [A]nything said or done by a revolutionist that does not spur or give the forward thrust to the process (of revolution) is wrong. Remember that the people are the makers of history, the people make everything in their society. They are the architects of the society and if you don't spur them on, then I don't care what phrases you use or whether they are political or religious, you cannot be classified as being relevant to that process. If you know you're wrong and do certain things anyway, then you're reactionary because you're very guilty.

> …[T]he revolutionary cultists use words of social change; he uses words about being interested in the development of society. He uses that terminology, you see; but his actions are so far divorced from the process of revolution and organizing the community that he is living in a fantasy world. So we talk to each other on the campuses, or we talk to each other in the secrecy of night, concentrating on weapons, thinking these things will produce change without the people themselves. Of course people do dangerous things and call themselves the vanguard, but the people who do things like that are either heroes or criminals. They are not the vanguard because the vanguard means spearhead, and the spearhead has to spear something. If nothing is behind it, then it is divorced from the masses and is not the vanguard.[5]

As Newton's remarks suggest, the Black Panther Party, like any living, sentient organism, changed, developed, and transformed itself over time. Indeed, even before the split in its very insular, organizational history, it was "one, two, many parties."

As we have seen, at its inception under the name of the Black Panther Party for Self-Defense, the Party was deeply nationalist and was influenced by the ideas of the late Malcolm X. Shortly thereafter, the dropping of the "for Self-Defense" from the group's name signified the broadening of the Party's vision, and it began to view itself as a "revolutionary nationalist" formation and opposed the cultural nationalism of groups like the US organization.[6]

During this period, the Party's internal organization took the form of revolutionary cultism. Inspired by the explosion of national liberation movements and armed revolutions in the 1960s, the model of the revolutionary *foco*, a relatively small group of men (and occasionally women) staging antistate, or anticolonial actions, had tremendous appeal to young African American revolutionaries who, like all Americans, were notoriously impatient. Newton condemned this period for its concentration on weapons and revolutionary dialogue; for ignoring the hard necessity of popular organizing.[7]

As members studied the struggles raging around the world, they saw so many similarities between those waged internationally and domestically that solidarity with the world's people seemed only logical. The Party used the term intercommunalism to describe this development. This term referred to the interaction of global communities and was based in Newton's analysis that US imperialism precluded nationhood and recognized that independent nations couldn't exist.

The Party, reeling from repression and accumulated death and loss, ended its days operating in a reformist/electoral mode that left it isolated from its core community as it focused its efforts on the mayoral campaign of Bobby Seale and the City Council campaign of Elaine Brown.

The year 1982 marks the official death of the Black Panther Party, since that was when many of the Party's programs, like the once-acclaimed Intercommunal Youth Institute (or primary school), and the publication of the BPP newspaper ceased, though, for many, it had died years before.

At each phase, the Party evolved (or devolved) into something quite distinct from what it had been before. The Party, like the proverbial cat, had many lives. At some phases of its life, it ran with grace and purpose, at others, it limped, wounded by external and self-inflicted injuries.

That it survived and functioned at all, in the face of the State's overt and covert repression, especially for the extended period that it did, is a startling testament to the vision of its founders and the gritty will of its membership.

## After the Party?

Organizations such as the Black Panther Party, which have appreciable impacts on community consciousness and political development, do not simply fade into the ether. Throughout African American history, we have seen the demise of one group presage the rise and development of another. The quasi-nationalist Moorish Science Temple movement of the 1930s gave rise to the Nation of Islam and other Black Muslim movements.

Similarly, the Black Panther Party's formal and informal demise as a national revolutionary entity gave rise to a number of localized radical and revolutionary formations. Many of these successor groupings were led by former members of the BPP and sought to recreate the spark of the Party along local, regional, or coastal lines.

In Philadelphia, ex-BPP cadre formed the Black United Liberation Front (BULF), which worked on police brutality issues and ran "a free breakfast for children program, a free clothing program, a bus ... to take people to visit relatives and friends in prison.... [It] organized all the gangs on this side of Broad Street at one point in 1971–72 and got them instead of fighting each other, to start turning over abandoned cars, throwing trash and garbage that the city wouldn't collect, and blocking up the street demanding that the city turn over abandoned houses in the Black community..."[8] Within a decade, through declining membership and lack of resources, BULF was largely defunct. In Kansas City, Missouri, a militant, aggressive cadre of ex-BPP personnel transformed their chapter into a group called the Sons of Malcolm. They, too, after several years, ceased to exist.

While the African People's Socialist Party (APSP) was more a contemporary competitor than a successor, the St. Petersburg, Florida–based nationalist organization utilized ex-BPP talent like Akua Njeri (née Deborah Johnson) to preside over the APSP-led National People's Democratic Uhuru Movement. Njeri was the fiancée of Fred Hampton, and narrowly escaped death in the government attack that left Hampton dead. In addition to using key ex-Panthers in their APSP apparatus, the organization created propaganda that made frequent references to BPP personnel. Njeri has spoken of her current political role as a "continuation of the Panther legacy."[9]

What began in 1990 as the New Black Panther Party (NBPP) in Dallas, Texas, took root from a call by Michael McGee, a city councillor and former Panther, for the establishment and arming of what he termed the Black Panther Militia of Milwaukee, Wisconsin. McGee's 1990 talk show appearance in Dallas would inspire radio producer Aaron Michaels to launch a local chapter.

Although there are indications that the Dallas group initially began community programs, notably a breakfast program,[10] by 1991, when the NBPP name was formally registered, Michaels seemed to have soured on this idea. He is quoted opining, "Survival programs are good, but they don't make us free."[11]

This suggests the NBPP has traveled some distance from its namesake. The rise of Dr. Khallid Abdul Muhammad, the former NOI national spokesman, to the group's leadership perhaps best marks the change. While Michaels took the rank of Defense Minister, Dr. Muhammad, with his penchant for angry, anti-white and anti-Jewish speech, emerged as de facto leader of the NBPP until his sudden death, due to a brain aneurism, on February 17, 2001.

His successor, the Howard University–trained attorney, Malik Zulu Shabazz, has tried to emulate Muhammad in style and speech. Under Shabazz, the NBPP sounds themes that sound closer to NOI ideology than to the original BPP. When David Hilliard critiqued the NBPP for having "totally abandoned our survival programs," Shabazz claimed that the original BPP "are really working with the Zionists,"[12] and suggested that they may be engaged in counterintelligence for the FBI.

That Shabazz could suggest that the "originals" were somehow "Zionist" supporters reflects the dearth of study engaged in by the NBPP on those whose name they now bear. It was the original BPP who announced that "Zionism=Racism" and took the largely unique stance among Black nationalist-oriented groups of the era in support of Palestinian liberation.

In the NBPP Newton's writings are rarely, if ever, read, and although its imagery and uniform may have been adopted—few original ideas have been. The NBPP seems to be an emergence of the NOI under a different name.

In 1994, the New African American Vanguard Movement (NAAVM) emerged in Los Angeles, California. The organization was founded by, and its collective leadership was partly composed of, former members of the original BPP. The group formulated an eight-point platform and program as an updated version of the original Ten-Point Program.[13]

This group has continued to develop, changing its name to the New Panther Vanguard Movement (NPVM), expanding the original eight points to its present ten, and publishing a newspaper that bears a striking similarity to the original Panther newspaper. According to a recent edition of the NPVM quarterly, NPVM collectives are active in Indianapolis, Indiana, and Decatur, Georgia.

In New York City, a group partly composed of former BPP people formed the Black Panther Collective (BPC) in 1994. They have described their objectives thusly:

(1) to continue the revolutionary legacy of the Black Panther Party; (2) to put forth a vision of a new and just society; (3) to build a revolutionary infrastructure; and (4) to engage in protracted revolutionary struggle.[14]

In language at least, the BPC's objectives can hardly be distinguished from the early Party.

Anarchist organizations are also looking to the Black Panther Party as they formulate their positions. Ashanti Alston, a former member of the BPP and the BLA, and a political prisoner for over twelve years, publishes the magazine *Anarchist Panther* and was active in organizing the Anarchist People of Color conference. Revolutionary Active Communities Uprising in Numbers (RACUN) developed a version of a ten-point plan and is developing survival programs and a self-defense program.

Such groups as these demonstrate the wish to utilize the original BPP as a potent symbol of radical social change. They continue to look to the Party's remarkable example for sustenance and as a source of strength for the struggles yet to come.

In that sense, it may be said that the Party continues to exist—if only in the hearts and minds of many.

## Legacies

There are many legacies of the Black Panther Party. They are, as all else in life, both positive and negative and vary depending upon where one looks for them.

What remains in Black youth consciousness (and youth consciousness in general) is the Black Panther Party as a symbol of resistance. The image and ideas of the Black Panther Party, and Huey P. Newton, still attract interest and attention. This may be traced to the frequent mention of the Black Panthers in hip hop. The relative success of the 1994 film *Panther,* by popular Black filmmakers and actors Mario and Melvin Van Peebles, while hardly a blockbuster, became for many young people their eye-opening introduction to an aspect of Black contemporary history they were never told about in school.

Another measure of the continuing vitality of the Black Panther Party in Black consciousness may be seen in the continued publication of writings by and about the Panthers. Seven Stories *Huey P. Newton Reader* collected Newton's writings and Black Classics Press (whose publisher, Paul Coates, was a Baltimore Panther) reissued Bobby Seale's *Seize the Time* and George Jackson's *Blood in My Eye*. Philip Foner's *The Black Panthers Speak* has also been reissued, and Assata Shakur's autobiography and Elaine Brown's *A Taste of Power* remain popular. More recently, The Feminist Press published Safiya Bukhari's memoir *The War Before*; *The Revolutionary Art of Emory Douglas* showcases the former Minister of Culture's profound work; and former Panther 21 member and political prisoner, Jamal Joseph published a deeply engaging memoir, *Panther Baby*, covering his Panther, prison, personal, and scholarly histories.

At the same time, there has been invaluable work from a new generation of scholars of Black consciousness by historians such as Peniel E. Joseph and Robyn C. Spencer, who have made vital contributions to new understandings of the Party as well as the emerging field of "Black Power studies." Recent titles include *Black Against Empire: The History and Politics of the Black Panther Party* by Joshua Bloom and Waldo E. Martin Jr.; *Living for the City: Migration, Education, and the Rise of the Black Panther Party in Oakland, California* by Donna Jean Murch; as well as Alondra Nelson's *Body and Soul: The Black Panther Party and the Fight against Medical Discrimination*. Judson L. Jeffries outstanding *Comrades* and *On the Ground* provide invaluable insight into how Panthers lived, struggled, and died in various chapters across the country. In *Party Music,* musicologist Rickey Vincent writes about the Black Panther Party's funk/rock band The Lumpen.

Of course, it would be disingenuous to ignore some other legacies, even if they are negative ones. *Forrest Gump,* a somewhat more successful film venture than *Panther,* starred Tom Hanks as a mentally challenged individual who makes improbable friends with people, with unforeseen historical effects. In order to lend the film a sense of authenticity reflective of the period of social upheaval, the Hanks character encounters a uniformed Panther figure who is so overcome with rage that what he says sounds like barely intelligible nonsense. The clear inference of the movie is that the Panthers largely spoke incoherently to people. It also perpetuated the impression of the BPP as an armed group of outlaws. The two film treatments demonstrate that the legacy and meaning of the Black Panther Party continues to be a contested one.

This is not only so in the realm of American popular culture, but in an area that impacts African American life in dozens of ghettos and inner cities every day.

Urban gangs have become a national phenomenon since the passing of the BPP. This was not unforeseen as former BPP political prisoner Geronimo ji-Jaga told a German reporter in 1993:

> Huey Newton gave a lecture on that one time and we had foreseen that this was gonna happen. After the leadership of the BPP was attacked at the end of the '60s and the early '70s, throughout the Black and other oppressed communities, the role models for up-coming generations became the pimps, the drug dealers, etc. This is what the government wanted to happen. The next result was that the gangs were being formed, coming together with a gangster mentality, as opposed to the revolutionary progressive mentality we would have given them.[15]

Given this ruinous social dynamic, it is telling that even under these conditions the ethos of the BPP, perhaps through remnants of the organization or perhaps through the power of example, seemed to seep into the origins of the notorious Crips and the Bloods.

This influence may be seen in the gangs' names. CRIP originally stood for Community Resource Independent Project.[16] Their adversaries were originally Brotherly Love Overrides Oppression Daily (BLOOD).[17] The former Crip turned New Afrikan nationalist Sanyika Shakur (formerly "Monster" Kody Scott) cites prison sources for an attempted reorganization of Crips under the name Clandestine Revolutionary Internationalist Party Soldiers.[18]

Clearly, at some level, the rhetoric of the BPP has resonance in the psyches of the originators and reorganizers of Black youth gangs. That it did not go further may be ascribed to the loss of a living model.

## Public Service

To a generation living in an era of market ascendacy and cultural commodification, one lesson the Party teaches is the importance of public service as an organizing focus. The Party stood for social service to one's community that was unremunerated and was one's collective, communal duty. Integral to this idea was the secular mission of the Party to reclaim and redeem Black men who were engaged in antisocial, lumpen-type criminal activities.

The very process of politicization served to provide members an analytical framework through which they could perceive the function of the State, and its "security" apparatus, as a protector not of the people, but of a privileged class. It also illuminated how the acts of petty, antisocial criminals contributed to the continued powerlessness and political subordination of their communities. While the Party did not actively promote the redemptive side of itself, the lived experiences of members were telling reflections of a deeply held and socially acceptable conversion experience, not to a religion, but to a political perspective. Shaba Om (né Lee Roper) recalled reading an issue of *Ramparts* magazine that featured an article on the Black Panther Party. The article impressed him so much that he began searching for members of the BPP in Harlem. When a member provided him with a copy of *The Black Panther,* he found himself deeply moved and deeply motivated to renounce and distance himself from his criminal past. This tactic was also a popular organizing strategy of the Nation of Islam and was a well-known element in the transformation of Malcolm X. Om recalls:

> I began to go to political education classes—but I was still hung up on the bag of pimping. What really got me out of that madness was political education, me digging on my true self as a black man, and the Honorable John Coltrane's music. I dug what I was doing to my people and myself. In 1968, I had got myself together and stopped jiving. Began to go to political

education classes every night after slave. After political education classes, I would go to my pad and try to hide from the jive niggers I knew.

It was past time for me to come forward and correct the wrong I'd done. I knew all the madness I was doing on the streets was wrong as two right shoes, dig.... [T]he only thing left was to become a true helper and servant of my beautiful people.... This is when I really became a Black Panther, warrior of my people.[19]

This can only be seen as a profound conversion experience—a redefinition of the self, one's true self; one's becoming. What pushed Om and others across the divide, from a life of crime to a life of service and sacrifice, was personal tragedy, a shattering event that forced one to confront one's place in the world, especially one's racial identity, and one's political place in the universe.[20] Om, and many young people like him, was undergoing a profound psychological metamorphosis; the cracking of the egg of the old self, and the emergence of the new. To Om, as a pimp, drug pusher, and user, death became the doorway to this new life:

And this sister I was relating to as my main love died from skag. Man ... like this blew my mind, because she had quit skag once, and come to me for help because she dug me and my way of thinking—and I turned my back on her; this really blew my mind when she died. I was going to political education classes then, too, when she died. The first thing that came into my mind was, I helped the pigs kill one of my sisters.[21]

Love and loss brought him to the Black Panther Party and compelled him to find his better self—a servant of the people, rather than as a predator against the people.

Many former Panthers continue the legacy of social service by working as drug counselors, antigang coordinators, and teachers. Former Panther and the Illinois Deputy Minister of Defense Bobby Rush serves in the nation's House of Representatives.

## Women of the Party

Many female Panthers went on to lead or staff community organizations and social help groups. Some have become scholars. Some have become lawyers. Some, like Kathleen Neal Cleaver, have merged both practices into one. Cleaver, a law professor, has worked on cases such as the infamous frame-up of former political prisoner Geronimo ji-Jaga. Joan Gibbs, a former political prisoner, has worked for years as a legal scholar, activist, and administrator at Medgar Evers College in Brooklyn, New York.

The Black Panther Party was a distinct training ground for young radical women and instilled in many a certain "can do" attitude that has transcended their years of service in the BPP. Their experiences in the Party prepared them for lives of activism and service. Joan Kelly (now Joan Kelly Williams), who headed the LA chapter's Free Breakfast Program for a time reports:

> It's hard to describe what I did. I think all of us did so many different things. When I was in Los Angeles … your focus could change daily. "So and so is in jail, you've got to run the Breakfast Program." … men did do program work, I think that's the other illusion that people have is that we had a paramilitary underground and went off and offed pigs at night and the women got up and served breakfast and helped care for people. It is a little more comprehensive than that [audience and panelist laugh]. So, I remember somebody went to jail and I got responsibility in LA for the Breakfast Programs.…The clearest thing we could do was our programs. And if [the police] could keep enough people who serve breakfast in jail in the morning, and the kids got there and there was nobody serving breakfast, then the media could go on the 7 o'clock news and say, That Panther Breakfast Program doesn't work, it's all a fluke. Or whatever, or hoax. So we became very sophisticated. We could come back at you real quick in terms of strategies and ways to meet the challenges that we faced.… The conditions thrust women into roles of leadership early.[22]

Women like Kelly Williams functioned, from sheer necessity, as captains, field secretaries, section leaders, lieutenants, communications officers, and, with Elaine Brown's ascension after the self-imposed exile of Newton in 1974, as head of the entire organization. No other radical or revolutionary formation of that period could boast of such a pronounced range of female prominence.

This depth of revolutionary activist experience and leadership equipped a generation of women with a kind of palpable knowledge; informed and steeled a cadre of women; and prepared them well for the tasks that lay ahead. For example, the revered former political prisoner Ericka Huggins, who supervised the Intercommunal Youth Institute for nearly a decade, continues to work in the field of education as a professor at San Francisco State University and other institutions. She also works with HIV-exposed persons in her community. JoNina Abron, who was an editor of *The Black Panther*, later became managing editor of *The Black Scholar*, and is a tenured English professor at Western Michigan University. Regina B. Jennings, who was with the Oakland and Philadelphia branches, earned a doctorate in African American studies and now teaches at Franklin and Marshall College.[23]

Safiya A. Bukhari, a licensed paralegal, worked on behalf of ex-BPP political prisoners until her death in 2003. Kiilu Nyasha of the New Haven chapter is a brilliant artist who addresses political and cultural themes and hosts a popular radio program on Black and radical politics in San Francisco. Rosemari Mealy, who worked in the Philadelphia and New Haven branches, worked as a broadcaster on public radio, has earned her law degree, and later, her Ph.D. Rita Gaye Sisk of the Philadelphia branch is a prominent member of the Temple of the Black Messiah in Philadelphia. Cleo Silvers who was with the New York chapter and Young Lords Party is a community organizer and labor activist, who, like Bukhari, has done work on behalf of Black political prisoners. She is a member of the United Auto Workers (UAW) and is active in the League of Revolutionary Black Workers. She also co-chairs the Health Revolutionary Unity Movement (HRUM) and heads the Peace and Justice Anti-War Caucus of New York Local 1199C.

These women, and many unknown soldiers like them, the local Party defunct or in shambles, went back to their homes or adopted communities and continued to serve the needs of the people. They remain remarkable legacies of the Party.

## International Impacts and Inspirations

Because the BPP inspired so much media coverage, it assumed an international profile that sparked imitators and admirers around the world. Political scientists Charles E. Jones and Judson L. Jeffries have examined the Party's impressive global reach:

> The impact of the BPP transcended the borders of the United States. Panther activities served as a revolutionary exemplar for various oppressed indigenous groups in several foreign countries. Left-wing political formations in England (Black Panther Movement), Israel (Black Panther Party of Israel), Bermuda (Black Beret Cadre), Australia (Black Panther Party), and India (Dalit Panthers) drew from the organization founded by Huey P. Newton and Bobby Seale in the United States. Members of the Black Beret Cadre formed in Bermuda in 1969 adopted the Panthers' signature black beret and sponsored liberation schools and political education classes. Similarly, the Black Panther Party of Israel created by Jews of Moroccan descent in 1971 implemented community services for the children in the slums of West Jerusalem.[24]

That so many radical and nationalist-type groups could borrow the imagery, name, and format of the BPP bespeaks the power and potency of the original organization. While few of these overseas groups had formal organizational ties to BPP headquarters in Oakland, California, by their very existence they helped project the Party's image and message of militant resistance and community service to the poor and oppressed deep into international consciousness. The BPP, perhaps proving the veracity of the old adage that imitation is the sincerest form of flattery, had a global impact that moved radicals, nationalists, and revolutionaries worldwide to emulate some of their more positive attributes.

## From Losers to Legends

If there is one unavoidable historical truth about the Black Panther Party, it is this: it lost its long battle for institutionalization and the primary realization of its revolutionary political objectives. It did not establish Black revolutionary power, due to reasons both internal and external.

That said, it experienced a somewhat curious transformation over the course of time, from loser into legend. The very existence of the Party seems to strengthen those who learn of it for the first time. This introduction usually comes not through popular sources of indoctrination—schools and parents—but through one's own effort.

This transformation has historical precedent. Consider the case of the Pan-Indian warrior Tecumseh. History concluded that the Shawnee warrior lost, and lost decisively, to the American "Long Knives." Of that, there can be little question. It is also true to say that he is remembered and respected today for the purity of his vision and his attempt to protect traditional, indigenous lands from Western, white domination. His lost struggle was against white *lebensraum*. Tecumseh and his valiant struggle have joined the annals of legend for generations of Native American, African American, and, indeed, American youth.

As evidence of the transcendence of Native American resistance and how it often finds home in the souls of Black folk, one need look no further than the late but explosively popular rap artist Tupac Shakur. The son of Afeni Shakur, a Black Panther and a veteran of the *Panther 21,* Tupac was named for an Amerindian warrior who fought against the Spanish colonizers of Peru, Tupac Amaru.

A son of a Panther, he was born to let millions know of the unfairness and indignity of the life of his people, and he did so, with great talent and boundless passion.

Before his birth, his pregnant mother was esconced in the city jail called the Tombs. As she awaited a trial that could send her to prison for decades, she composed a gentle, heartfelt letter to her family. I do not know if Tupac ever got around to reading it. But a teenaged Panther in New York on loan from Philadelphia read it, and it made his heart weep with its beauty, its love, and its profound courage. Afeni Shakur wrote:

A Letter to Jamala, Lil Afeni, Sekwiya, and the unborn baby (babies) within my womb.

First let me tell you that this book [a collective autobiography of the *Panther 21*] was not my idea at all (as a matter of fact I was hardly cooperative). But I suppose one day you're going to wonder about all this mess that's been going on now and I just had to make sure you understood a few things.

I've learned a lot in two years about being a woman and it's for this reason that I want to talk to you. Joan [Bird—another *Panther 21* captive] and I, and all the brothers in jail, are caught up in this funny situation where everyone seems to be attacking everyone else and we're sort of in the middle looking dumb. I've seen a lot of people I knew and loved die in the past year or so and it's really been a struggle to remain unbitter.

February 8th when Joan and I came back to jail I was full of distrust, disappointment and disillusionment. But now the edges are rounded off a bit and I think I can understand why some things happened. I don't like most of it, but I *do* understand. I've discovered what I should have known a long time ago—that change has to begin within ourselves—whether there is a revolution today or tomorrow—we still must face the problem of purging ourselves of the larceny that we have all inherited. I hope we do not pass it on to you because you are our only hope.

You must weigh our actions and decide for yourselves what was good and what was bad. It is obvious that somewhere we failed but I know it will not—it cannot end here. There is too much evilness left. I cannot get rid of my dream of peace and harmony. It is for that dream that most of us have fought—some bravely, some as cowards, some as heroes, and some as plain old crooks. Forgive us our mistakes because mostly they were mistakes which were made out of blind ignorance (sometimes arrogance). Judge us with empathy for we were (are) idealists and sometimes we're young and foolish.

I do not regret any of it—for it taught me to be something that some people will never learn—for the first time in my life I feel like a woman—beaten, battered and scarred maybe, but isn't that what wisdom is truly made of. Help me to continue to learn—only this time with a bit more grace for I am a poor example for anyone to follow because I have deviated from the revolutionary principles which I know to be correct. I wish you love.

Afeni Shakur (Mar. 20, 1971)[25]

There are, indeed, many legacies of the Black Panther Party. Perhaps the best of them are expressed in Afeni's letter to her unborn child: hope, empathy, knowledge of our imperfections, knowledge of our shortcomings, the continued will to resist—and love.

## AFTERWORD

**FOR ME, POLITICAL** life began with the Black Panther Party.

When an older sister named Audrea handed me a copy of *The Black Panther* newspaper around the spring of 1968 my mind was promptly blown. It was as if my dreams had awakened and strolled into my reality.

I read and reread the issue, tenderly fingering each page as if it were the onion-skinned, tissue-like leaf of a holy book. My eyes drank in the images of young Black men and women, their slim and splendid bodies clothed in black leather, their breasts bedecked with buttons proclaiming rebellion, resistance, and revolution.

I almost couldn't believe my eyes as I scanned photos of armed Black folks proclaiming their determination to fight or die for the Black Revolution.

It would be some months before I would formally join something called the Black Panther Party, but, in truth, I joined it months before, when I saw my first *Black Panther* newspaper.

I joined it in my heart.

I was all of fourteen years old.

A downtown bookstore, Robin's, squeezed between a restaurant and a discount clothing shop, became my Mecca, for there every week, like clockwork, the "holy book" would descend, like manna from a Black, revolutionary heaven—the latest issue of *The Black Panther!*

I would buy a copy and then scrounge the shelves for books; Black books, radical books, all kinds of books. The guy at the cash register would occasionally growl (or bellow), "This ain't a library, kid! Ya gonna buy sumpin' or what?" I usually ignored him, and went back to my reading.

Here I found the writings of Frantz Fanon, of Malcolm X, of Kwame Nkrumah; the poetry of Langston Hughes; the prose of Richard Wright; and the magnificent example of Paul Robeson. I also found several other young men (although most were older than I) who would be among the first to join the organization that had set my heart aflame.

In many ways, it is fitting that the first quasi-"office" of the Black Panther Party in Philadelphia was neither a tenement apartment, nor a basement, nor a bar, but a bookstore, a realm for the exchange of ideas. For there our minds first met.

It is striking that the present age offers scant opportunities for young rebels (and the young are ever innately rebellious!) to meet, to talk, to think, to exchange. For one thing, some bookstores, though certainly not all, are part of larger, often times global, commercial networks—they are not so much meeting places as buying places.

The internet, while pervasive in its reach, diminishes, rather than enhances social contact. One never really knows who is the recipient of a communication. Moreover, the internet is interlaced with snoops of the ubiquitous State, sniffing for any hint of rebellion as demonstrated by Project Echelon. This official paranoia is, in a sense, a reflection of a cultural change wrought by time.

The age of rebellion was succeeded by an age of conservatism; Huey the rebel devolves into Huggy Bear, the snitch character of popular (white, corporate) culture.

And yet. And yet... There are cycles in history.

No empire foresees its tumble into time's abyss. The Roman Empire didn't. The British Empire once boasted that "the sun will never set on our glorious empire." It has set now, hasn't it? I recently read a remarkable book about the six hundred years of the vast Ottoman Empire. At its apogee it stood as the mightiest empire on Earth; it conquered the eastern home of the Roman Empire, the Byzantine capital of Constantinople with relative ease, and renamed it as Istanbul. Yet, this empire went out with a whimper, in a burst of familial madness, of men who became deadly to their families, and became, finally, irrelevant.

The lesson of history is inescapable—empires rise; empires fall. No empire lasts forever. Mahatma Gandhi once noted:

> It is possible for a single individual to defy the whole might of an unjust empire to save his honour, his religion, his soul and lay the foundation for that empire's fall or its regeneration.[1]

At its heart, the Black Panther Party was a profoundly anti-imperial project, a reflection of the deep ambivalence that dwells in Black hearts and arises from African American experience. It was but a reflection of a consciousness that had been active in Black communal life for several generations. Given the common roots of Black communities in the Americas, that is, despite the shading of Spanish-, Dutch-, Portuguese-, or English-speaking cultures they all can be traced to the Atlantic slave trade, it would be surprising if there were not solidarity between these communities.

Thus, in the 1930s, US Black newspapers reported on the lives and struggles of Afro-Cubans (then called *la raza de color*—the colored race).[2] Thus, the Black press wrote of the lives and achievements of people like Antonio Maceo, the celebrated mulatto general who fought in the Cuban War of Independence against Spain. The work of the great poet Nicholas Guillén was also translated and circulated there. African Americans of distinction, like Mary McLeod Bethune and Langston Hughes, visited Cuba to see how Black folks lived under a different regime.

254 | WE WANT FREEDOM

This internationalism reached perhaps its highest point in the life of the Black Panther Party with the establishment of a virtual embassy in Algiers.

The Black Panther Party didn't create international solidarity, but tried to do its best to extend it.

Yet internationalism didn't define the Party—internal resistance to the status quo did.

Nor does it seem accidental that this resistance emerged when the Empire was engaged in an external war against Vietnam.

This timing, too, had a historical precedent in Black life. For, during World War II, Black Americans engaged in what was called the Double V campaign, which demanded victory on two fronts: at home and abroad. Thus, a previous generation utilized the language of war to symbolize the battles Black Americans faced inside imperial space.

The Black Panther Party took that language further—enriched by anticolonial and anti-imperialist struggles abroad.

These impulses, it is important to note, while enriched and, perhaps, informed by external events, did not proceed from them. These were internal responses to the lived experiences of Black Americans in a land where life seemed that of the eternal alien.

Moreover, that deep feeling, that certain sense of alienation lives still in millions of Black hearts at this hour, in every ghetto in America—and elsewhere. The repression of the State muted that expression, driving some of it underground.

Yet, as Freud has often argued, writing on another kind of repression to be sure, that which is repressed will eventually find expression.

The Black Panther Party may indeed be history, but the forces that gave rise to it are not.

They wait, for the proper season, to arise again.

## PHOTOS AND DOCUMENTS

Mumia Abu-Jamal speaking at the memorial for Chairman Fred Hampton, December 1969, in the Church of the Advocate, Philadelphia.

Jon Pinkett, Barbara Easley Cox, and Kentu share a frame (top). Barbara Cox reads to a child during a BPP function (bottom).

BPP member Rene Johnson raps with community in front of the office (top). Black Panther meeting in Philadelphia, summer 1970, at center are Sister Love and Barbara Easley Cox. (bottom).

Photos of the "Pilots for Panthers" demonstration in Philadelphia supporting Eldridge Cleaver's call to exchange imprisoned Panthers for US POWs held in Vietnam by the NLF (see p. 107).

Rolando "Montae" Hearn and Gladys are married in the BPP office. Captain Reggie Schell in background (top). Montae and Billy O. in the office (bottom).

Captain Reggie Schell speaking at the memorial for Fred Hampton (top). Black Panther Milt McGriff raps to a brother in a record shop (bottom).

Two Philadelphis Panthers pore over the latest copy of *The Black Panther* (top). Two photos of Mumia Abu-Jamal, Lieutenant of Information, working in the BPP office typing up a leaflet for the Philadelphia branch (bottom).

Michael "Cetewayo" Tabor of the *New York 21* sitting and watching at the Revolutionary People's Constitutional Convention in Philadelphia, September 1970 (top). Sam Napier, the late, martyred Distribution Manager of *The Black Panther;* former *Black Panther* editor "Big Man" Howard; and Philadelphia Panther Jon Pinkett (bottom).

Black Panther Madelyn Coleman catches up on some reading (top). Philadelphia Black Panther member "Fish" shows bruises on his face after being beaten at the 55th and Pine Street police station (bottom).

Mumia Abu-Jamal on the phone in the Philadelphia Black Panther office. This picture originally ran on the front page of the *Philadelphia Inquirer,* January 4, 1970. All other photographs taken from contact sheets by Philadelphia Black Panther Party photographer Steve Wilson (1969–70).

Airtel to SAC, Albany
RE: COUNTERINTELLIGENCE PROGRAM
BLACK NATIONALIST-HATE GROUPS

nationalist activity, and interested in counterintelligence,
to coordinate this program. This Agent will be responsible
for the periodic progress letters being requested, but each
Agent working this type of case should participate in the
formulation of counterintelligence operations.

GOALS

For maximum effectiveness of the Counterintelligence
Program, and to prevent wasted effort, long-range goals are
being set.

1. Prevent the coalition of militant black
nationalist groups. In unity there is strength; a truism
that is no less valid for all its triteness. An effective
coalition of black nationalist groups might be the first
step toward a real "Mau Mau" in America, the beginning of
a true black revolution.

2. Prevent the rise of a "messiah" who could
unify, and electrify, the militant black nationalist movement.
_____ might have been such a "messiah;" he is the martyr
of the movement today.
and _____ ____ all aspire to this position.
_____ is less of a threat because of his age. ____ could
be a very real contender for this position should he abandon
his supposed "obedience" to "white, liberal doctrines"
(nonviolence) and embrace black nationalism. ___.
has the necessary charisma to be a real threat in this way.

3. Prevent violence on the part of black
nationalist groups. This is of primary importance, and is,
of course, a goal of our investigative activity; it should
also be a goal of the Counterintelligence Program. Through
counterintelligence it should be possible to pinpoint potential
troublemakers and neutralize them before they exercise their
potential for violence.

4. Prevent militant black nationalist groups and
leaders from gaining respectability, by discrediting them
to three separate segments of the community. The goal of
discrediting black nationalists must be handled tactically
in three ways. You must discredit these groups and
individuals to, first, the responsible Negro community.
Second, they must be discredited to the white community,

- 3 -

FBI memo of February 29 and May 4, 1968: The infamous
"prevent the rise of a 'messiah'" memorandum.

Airtel to SAC, Albany
RE: COUNTERINTELLIGENCE PROGRAM
BLACK NATIONALIST-HATE GROUPS

both the responsible community and to "liberals" who have
vestiges of sympathy for militant black nationalist simply
because they are Negroes. Third, these groups must be
discredited in the eyes of Negro radicals, the followers
of the movement. This last area requires entirely different
tactics from the first two. Publicity about violent tendencies
and radical statements merely enhances black nationalists
to the last group; it adds "respectability" in a different
way.

5. A final goal should be to prevent the long-
range growth of militant black nationalist organizations,
especially among youth. Specific tactics to prevent these
groups from converting young people must be developed.

Besides these five goals counterintelligence is
a valuable part of our regular investigative program as it
often produces positive information.

TARGETS

Primary targets of the Counterintelligence Program,
Black Nationalist-Hate Groups, should be the most violent
and radical groups and their leaders. We should emphasize
those leaders and organizations that are nationwide in scope
and are most capable of disrupting this country. These
targets should include the radical and violence-prone
leaders, members, and followers of the:

[Below] FBI memo of February 14, 1969: Valentine's Day
memo detailing a COINTELPRO against the Black Liberators
of St. Louis (see p. 107) and noting anticipated results.

UNITED STATES GOVERNMENT

*Memorandum*

DIRECTOR, FBI                           DATE: 2-14-69

SAC, ST. LOUIS

SUBJECT: COUNTER-INTELLIGENCE PROGRAM
BLACK NATIONALIST - HATE GROUPS
(BLACK LIBERATORS)

Enclosed for the Bureau are two copies and for Springfield
one copy of a letter to "SISTER"

The following counter-intelligence activity is being proposed
by the St. Louis Division to be directed against        He is
former            of the BLACK LIBERATORS (Bufile 157-10356),
The activity attempts to alienate
him from his wife and cause suspicion among the BLACK LIBERATORS that
they have a dangerous troublemaker in their midst.

BACKGROUND:

                        is currently separated from his wife,
      who lives with their two daughters in        He occasionally
     ds her money and she appears to be a faithful, loving wife, who is
a    arently convinced that her husband is performing a vital service to
the Black world and, therefore, she must endure this separation without
bothering him. She is, to all indications, an intelligent, respectable
young mother, who is active in the AME Methodist Church in

EXPLANATION OF LETTER:

The enclosed letter was prepared from a penmanship, spelling, and vocabulary style to imitate that of the average Black Liberator member. It contains several accusations which should cause wife great concern. The letter is to be mailed in a cheap, unmarked envelope with no return address and sent from St. Louis to
Since her letters to _____ are usually sent via the Black Liberator Headquarters, any member would have access to getting her address from one of her envelopes. This address is available to the St. Louis Division.

Her response, upon receipt of this letter, is difficult to predict and the counter-intelligence effect will be nullified if she does not discuss it with him. Therefore, to insure tha ____ and the Black Liberators are made aware that the letter was sent, the below follow-up action is necessary:

St. Louis will furnish _____ with a machine copy of the actual letter that is sent. Attached to this copy will be a neat typed note saying:

> "A mutual friend made this available without
> knowledge. I understand she recently
> recieved this letter from St. Louis. I suggest
> you look into this matter.
>
> God Bless You! "

This note would give the impression that somehow one of close friends, probably a minister, obtained a copy of the letter and made it available to ____. The above material is to be mailed by the _____ Division at _____ anonymously in a suitable envelope with no return address to:

ANTICIPATED RESULTS:

The following results are anticipated following the execution of the above-counter-intelligence activity:

1. Ill feeling and possibly a lasting distrust will be brought about between ____ and his wife. The concern over what to do about it may detract from his time spent in the plots and plans of ____. He may even decide to spend more time with his wife and children and less time in Black Nationalist activity.

2. The Black Liberators will waste a great deal of time trying to discover the writer of the letter. It is possible that their not-too subtle investigation ____ will lose present members and alienate potential ones.

3. Inasmuch as Black Liberator strength is ebbing at its lowest level, this action may well be the "death-blow."

RECOMMENDATION:

Bureau authority is requested to initiate the above-described activity.

Sister,

Us Black Liberators are tried to respect Black Women and special are wifes and girls. Brother ___ keeps tellen the Brothers this but he dont treet you that way. I only been in the organisatoin 2 months but ___ been maken it here with Sister Marva Bass & Sister Tony and than he gines ___ bout their better in bed then you ___ and ___ how he keeps you off his back. J senden you a little dittey even now an then — He says he gotta send ___ you moniy the Draft boarde gonna chuck him in the army somethen. This aint rite and were sayen that ___ is treeten you wrong —

A Black Liberator

Photocopy of the letter to the head of the Black Liberator's wife prepared in the "penmanship, spelling, and vocabulary style to imitate that of the average Black Liberator member."

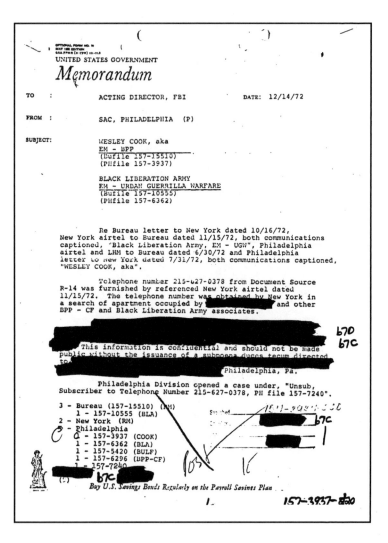

Two pages of FBI memo of December 14, 1972, apparently linking Mumia Abu-Jamal to the Black Liberation Army (BLA) as a result of his home phone number being found in a search of an apartment occupied by BPP and BLA "associates."

PH 157-3937
: 157-6362

      EDITH L. COOK, 718 Wallace Street, Philadelphia,
is the mother of WESLEY COOK, aka. COOK is an ADEX subject
from Philadelphia, who has been associated with the BPP and
in the past has written articles for the BPP - CF newspaper,
"Babylon". 718 Wallace Street has been the address utilized
by the subject in the past.

      On 11/24/72, [ ] Civil Disobedience b7C
Unit, Philadelphia Police Department, advised that on 10/13/72
during the trial of RUSSELL SHOATZ, COOK was arrested while
in the possession of a six inch bladed Exacto knife. SHOATZ
was on trial on charges of homicide of Philadelphia Police
park guard Sergeant FRANK VON COLLN. COOK attempted to
attend the above trial and prior to entering the court room
he was found to be in possession of the Exacto knife. COOK
insisted that his address was 1928 West Columbia Avenue,
the headquarters address of the BULF. BULF, an organization
with aims similar to those of the BPP, is headed by RICHARD
REGINALD SCHELL, former Defense Captain of the BPP in Philadelphia. COOK was arrested by the Philadelphia Police Department and charged with Carrying a Concealed Deadly Weapon.

      [ ] a source who is familiar with BPP b2,
activities in Philadelphia, has continually advised that COOK b7D
is unknown, and he has never been known to associate with
the BPP in Philadelphia. The source has also been unable to
link COOK with the BULF, BPP - CF or the BLA.

      In January 1971 COOK refused to be interviewed by
Bureau Agents and further attempts have not been made to
interview him since that time.

      Philadelphia has a pending case on the subject and
further efforts will be made to determine subject's associates
and extent of alliance with BULF, BPP - CF and BLA. Results
of investigation will be reported under individual caption.

      ARMED AND DANGEROUS.

-2-

157-3937-130

Page two of the memo notes his arrest while trying to attend
the trial of Russell Shoatz. A third page (not reproduced here)
referring to his arrest at the trial is almost entirely blacked out.

# ENDNOTES

## CHAPTER ONE

1. Seale, *Seize the Time*, 13–14.

2. Seale, *Seize the Time*, 14.

3. Seale, *Seize the Time*, 25.

4. Fanon, *Wretched of the Earth,* 96.

5. Newton, *Revolutionary Suicide*, 113.

6. Newton, *Revolutionary Suicide*, 71.

7. Newton, *Revolutionary Suicide*, 71.

8. Newton, *Revolutionary Suicide*, 113.

9. Seale, *Seize the Time*, 4; Marine, *The Black Panthers*, 12; Hilliard, *This Side of Glory*, 26.

10. Hilliard, *This Side of Glory*, 20.

11. Segal, *The Black Diaspora*, 142.

12. Moses, *Classic Black Nationalism*, 114.

13. Foner, E., *Reconstruction*, 285.

14. Foner, E., *Reconstruction*, 285.

15. Moses, *Classic Black Nationalism*, 9.

16. Jefferson, *Notes on the State of Virginia (1781–32)*. Quoted in Moses, *Classic Black Nationalism*, 46.

17. Moses, *Classic Black Nationalism*, 210 (emphasis added).

18. Moses, *Classic Black Nationalism*, 212.

19. Moses, *Classic Black Nationalism*, 209.

20. Foner, E., *Reconstruction*, 45.

21. Foner, E., *Reconstruction*, 598–99.

22. A briefly attempted appellation of the post–Nation of Islam formation, the World Community of Islam in the West, led by the son of Elijah Muhammad, known as Warith Deen Muhammad.

23. Equiano, *Life of Olaudah Equiano*, 31.

24. Katz, *Breaking the Chains*, 11–12.

25. Linebaugh and Rediker, *Many-Headed Hydra*, 194.

26. Aptheker, *American Negro Slave Revolts*, 180–92. Quoted in Linebaugh and Rediker, *Many-Headed Hydra*, 194.

27. Frass, Matthew. "The First Rhode Island Regiment," www.nps.gov/colo/Ythanout/firstri.html; Wiencek, *Imperfect God*, as discussed on Booknotes, CSPAN II November 2003.

28. Lee, Butch. *Jailbreak Out of History*, 21–22.

29. Kelley and Lewis, *To Make Our World Anew*, 120.

30. Wright, *Creeks and Seminoles*, 86–87.

31. The term *buckra* was common in Black speech in the US South and in Jamaica to denote whites. Although its derivation is unclear, some suggest it arose during slavery days to reflect how brutal treatments and whippings made one's "back raw." Harriet Tubman is quoted in McPherson's *The Negro's Civil War* as using the term to describe the Southern secessionists

(she uses the word "Sesh") during the Civil War: "Den I heard 'twas the Yankee ship [the *Wabash*] firin, out de big eggs, and dey had come to set us free. Den I praised the Lord. He come an, put he little finger in de work, an, dey Sesh Buckra all go ..." (58–59).

32. Fresia, *Toward an American Revolution*, 25.

33. Aptheker, *American Negro Slave Revolts*, 22.

34. Aptheker, *American Negro Slave Revolts*, 213.

35. Judges 15:14–15, 20 (AV).

36. Wilmore, *Black Religion and Black Radicalism*, 77–78.

37. Segal, *The Black Diaspora*, 144.

38. Aptheker, *American Negro Slave Revolts*, 222. Quoted in Segal, *The Black Diaspora*, 144.

39. McReynolds, *The Seminoles*, 75 (emphasis added).

40. McReynolds, *The Seminoles*, 75.

41. Aptheker, *American Negro Slave Revolts*, 259.

42. Kelley and Lewis, *To Make Our World Anew*, 197.

43. McReynolds, *The Seminoles*, 89.

44. McReynolds, *The Seminoles*, 40.

45. Wright, *Creeks and Seminoles*, 5–6.

46. Wright, *Creeks and Seminoles*, 218.

47. DuBois, *John Brown*, 131.

48. DuBois, *John Brown*, 131.

49. Anderson, *Voice from Harper's Ferry*, 98.

50. Anderson, *Voice from Harper's Ferry*, 98–99.

51. Faulkner, *Requiem for a Nun* (Act 1, Scene 3).

52. Matthews, *Honoring the Ancestors*, vii–viii (emphasis added).

53. Matthews, *Honoring the Ancestors*, viii.

## CHAPTER TWO

1. Forbes, E., *We Have No Country*, 121.

2. Cone, *Martin and Malcolm*, 222.

3. Cone, *Martin and Malcolm*, 223.

4. Newton, *Revolutionary Suicide*, 48.

5. I have used the term mass violence rather than the elite's preferred, and more projected, term, riot, because this term is usually given a somewhat pejorative connotation, attempting to mask the political objections and objectives of the agents involved in such acts.

6. Feagin, *Racist America*, 63.

7. http://www.pbs.org/wnet/aaworld/reference/articles/red_summer.html

8. Forbes, E., *We Have No Country*, 9.

9. Forbes, E., *We Have No Country*, 134.

10. Forbes, E., *We Have No Country*, 304.

11. Forbes, E., *We Have No Country*, 305.

12. Forbes, E., *We Have No Country*, 51–52.

13. Forbes, E., *We Have No Country*, 142.

14. Moses, *Classical Black Nationalism*, 108–9.

15. Forbes, E., *We Have No Country*, 114–15.

16. Forbes, E., *We Have No Country*, 51–52.

17. Forbes, E., *We Have No Country*, 150 (emphasis added).

18. Quoted in Forbes, E., *We Have No Country*, 114.

19. Forbes, E., *We Have No Country*, 114.

20. Zinn, *People's History*, 449. Malcolm was not being merely rhetorical in his denunciation; young SNCC leader John Lewis wanted to deliver an equally biting speech, but older civil rights leaders urged him to "tone it down." His full, suppressed text can be found in Zinn and Arnove, *Voices of a People's History of the United States*, 398–99.

21. Zinn, *People's History*, 450.

22. Zinn, *People's History*, 451.

23. Seale, *Seize the Times*, 80. It is worth noting that several formations adopted the imagery of the black panther including one formed with the assistance of Stokely Carmichael in New York City as early as August

1966. Led by SNCC and RAM activists, these radicals later joined the Newton-led formation when it was established in New York. (Ahmad, *We Will Return in the Whirlwind*, 167-70.)

24. Seale, *Seize the Times*, 139.

25. Seale, *Seize the Times*, 139.

26. Seale, *Seize the Times*, 136.

27. Seale, *Seize the Times*, 139.

28. Smith, William Gardner, *Return to Black America*, 173. Quoted in Singh, "'Undeveloped Country' of the Left," 63.

29. Newton, *To Die For the People*, 8.

30. This passage was written from memory. Years later it was learned that Frankhouser was, in fact, an informant for the ATF (Alcohol, Tobacco & Firearms Division of the Treasury Department) and, as such, had snitched on the Klan, the Minutemen, and various other right-wing groups with which he was affiliated (Donner, *Age of Surveillance*, 346).

### CHAPTER THREE

1. McPherson, *The Negro's Civil War*, 259.

2. Zinn, *People's History*, 248.

3. Zinn, *People's History*, 49–50.

4. Zinn, *People's History*, 213.

5. Forbes, E., *We Have No Country*, 191.

6. Abdy, Edward. *Journal of Residence and Tour in the United States*. Quoted in Forbes, E., *But We Have No Country*, 191.

7. Ignatiev, *How the Irish*, 124.

8. Ignatiev, *How the Irish*, 125–26.

9. Ignatiev, *How the Irish*, 155.

10. Ignatiev, *How the Irish*, 134.

11. Ignatiev, *How the Irish*, 134.

12. Ignatiev, *How the Irish*, 144.

13. Forbes, E., *We Have No Country*, 150–51.

14. Irons, *People's History of the Supreme Court*, 152 (emphasis added).

15. *Prigg v. PA*, 41 US 536, 625–26 (1842).

16. Newton, *Revolutionary Suicide*, 90–91.

17. *The Black Panther*, April 6, 1970, 17.

### CHAPTER FOUR

1. Newton, *Revolutionary Suicide*, 110.

2. Cleaver, *Soul On Ice*, 27.

3. Hilliard, *Huey Newton Reader*, 51–52.

4. Newton, *Revolutionary Suicide* 120–21.

5. Seale, *A Lonely Rage*, 153, 154.

6. Seale, *A Lonely Rage*, 154.

7. Hilliard, *Huey Newton Reader*, 67.

8. Neal, "Church and Survival Programs," 11.

9. Newton, *To Die For the People*, 89.

10. Newton, *To Die For the People*, 89.

11. Abron, "Serving the People," 184.

12. Washington, *Other Sheep*, 128.

13. Washington, *Other Sheep*, 134.

14. Latinx is a gender-neutral alternative to Latino, Latina, and Latin@ that goes beyond gender binaries. Latinx and Black are both terms that rose out of struggle and are not mutually exclusive categories.

15. Freed, *Agony in New Haven*, 113–14.

16. Newton, *Revolutionary Suicide*, 296.

17. Cluster, *Should Have Served*, 61.

18. Singh, "Black Panther Party," 32.

19. Singh, "Black Panther Party," 84–85.

20. Fresia, *Toward an American Revolution*, 28.

21. Fresia, *Toward an American Revolution*, 50.

22. "The People and the People Alone Were the Motive Power in the Making of the History of the People's Revolutionary Constitutional Convention Plenery Session!" *The Black Panther*, September 12, 1970, 3.

23. Newton, *To Die For the People*, 90–91.

24. Newton, *To Die For the People*, 31.

25. Newton, *To Die For the People*, 31 (emphasis added).

26. Hilliard, *Huey Newton Reader*, 253.

27. Fredrickson, *White Supremacy*, xi.

28. Fredrickson, *White Supremacy*, 4–5.

29. Hilliard, *Huey Newton Reader*, 206.

30. Hilliard, *Huey Newton Reader*, 260–61.

31. Hilliard, *Huey Newton Reader*, 259.

32. Hilliard, *Huey Newton Reader*, 259.

33. This passage written from memory.

## CHAPTER FIVE

1. Newton, *The Black Panther*, July 20, 1967, 5.

2. Brown, *Taste of Power*, 252. Soul Breaker was the prisoner's name for the solitary confinement cell in Alameda County Jail, California.

3. Brown, *Taste of Power*, 252.

4. Brown, *Taste of Power*, 252.

5. Brown, *Taste of Power*, 253.

6. Seale, *Seize the Times*, 59 (emphasis added).

7. Mao, *Quotations*, 58.

8. Hayes, "All Power to the People," 168.

9. Anthony, *Picking Up the Gun*, 21.

10. Hayes, "All Power to the People," 167.

11. Swearingen, *FBI Secrets*, 83.

12. Newton, *To Die For the People*, 92.

13. Singh, "Black Panther Party," 56.

14. Eldridge Cleaver, "Letter to My Black Brother in Vietnam," *The Black Panther*, May 2, 1970. This long article was reprinted as a pamphlet and sent to Black veterans and soldiers fighting in Vietnam. (Cleaver, K. "Back to Africa," 233.)

15. *The Black Panther*, November 1, 1969, 12–13.

16. *The Black Panther*, January 19, 1971, 10–11. That said, there were Black Panthers in Vietnam. They organized branches by themselves and wore Panther buttons on their US uniforms. They didn't care whether they were "officially" recognized by California, they just did what they thought was right.

17. *The Black Panther*, August 23, 1969.

18. *Washington Post* December 28, 1969, A-18.

19. *Washington Post*, February 1, 1970, A-13.

20. Cleaver, K., "Back to Africa," 214.

21. Cleaver, K., "Back to Africa," 214.

22. Kelley and Lewis, *To Make Our World Anew (vol. 2)*, 271-72 and Grady-Willis, "Black Panther Party," 377.

23. This section based on materials sent to the author by the Angola Support Committee and a filmmaker from Texas doing their story.

24. Zinn, *People's History*, 593.

25. Donner, *Age of Surveillance*, 178.

26. This passage was written from memory.

27. Cleaver, K., "Back to Africa," 235.

28. U.S. Dept. of Justice, FBI report to Attorney General, July 15, 1969:4.

29. Donner, *Age of Surveillance*, 83.

## CHAPTER SIX

1. Barenblatt v. U.S. 360 U.S. 109; dissent, 150 (1959). In light of the revelation that Black was a member of the Ku Klux Klan in his younger manhood, one might wonder at the extent of his knowledge of "groups which advocate extremely unpopular social or government innovations." Despite his KKK membership, Black's nomination was opposed for being too "radical," that is, too much in favor of the causes of the poor. The *Chicago Tribune* would denounce Roosevelt for the nomination, calling it "the worst he could find." Irons, *People's History of the Supreme Court*, 326.

2. *Newsweek*, February, 1969.

3. US Dept. of Justice, FBI Report to Attorney General, July 15, 1969:4.

4. Hoover, House Subcom. Testimony; April 17, 1969:68–70, 99.

5. Aoki didn't just furnish Newton and Seale with weapons, he later joined the BPP and helped it interact with the Asian-American anti-imperialist community. In recent years author Seth Rosenfeld has raised the question of whether Aoki was also acting as an informant to the FBI.

6. Brown, *Taste of Power*, 200.

7. Grady-Willis, "Black Panther Party," 372. Interestingly, another US Senate document, published in 1976, displays exhibits which feature other misspellings, at least in the proposed letter sent to FBI HQ on January 12, 1969. The document, of several pages, includes the following interesting language: "Consequently, Chicago now recommends the following letter be sent [Blank] handwritten, on plain paper: 'Brother....I think you ought to know what I'd do if I was you. You might hear from me again.'" We need not be psychic to intuit the intentions of the FBI. The document itself makes these clear. "It is believed the above may intensify the degree of animosity between the two groups and occasion [Blank] to take retalitory[sic] action which could disrupt the BPP or lead to reprisals against its leadership." The FBI, then, under the claimed objective of "preventing black militant violence," wrote to the Rangers, telling them the Panthers were trying to "hit" them, in a very bald attempt to spark "retaliatory action" against the BPP, or, at the very least, "reprisals" from disgruntled BPP members against their own leadership. (Sen. Sel. Com. Hearing, vol. 6, 433).

8. Churchill, *Agents of Repression*, 58.(emphasis added).

9. Zinn, *People's History*, 455.

10. Swearingen, *FBI Secrets*, 29.

11. Swearingen, *FBI Secrets*, 29 (emphasis added).

12. Sen. Sel. Com. Hearings, vol. 6, 9 (emphasis added).

13. Each of the following case studies appears in documents that the author has studied, either a true and correct copy of a government file, testimony before a Senate subcommittee, or a published artifact that survives from the period.

14. Churchill, *Agents of Repression*, 25.

15. Perkus, *COINTELPRO*, 161–62.

16. Perkus, *COINTELPRO*, 162.

17. Perkus, *COINTELPRO*, 163.

18. Perkus, *COINTELPRO*, 154.

19. Perkus, *COINTELPRO*, 164.

20. Perkus, *COINTELPRO*, 165.

21. Perkus, *COINTELPRO*, 165.

22. Perkus, *COINTELPRO*, 70.

23. Perkus, *COINTELPRO*, 77–78.

24. Sen. Sel. Com. Hearing, vol. 6, 617–21 (emphasis added).

25. Sen. Sel. Com. Hearing, vol. 6, 617–19.

26. Sen. Sel. Com. Hearing, vol. 6, 621.

27. The full name of the Church Committee is the Senate Select Committee to Study Governmental Operations with Respect to Intelligence Activities: Frank Church, Idaho, Chairman.

28. Sen. Sel. Com. Hearing, vol. 6, 23.

29. Sen. Sel. Com. Hearings, vol. 6, 24.

30. Sen. Sel. Com. Hearing, vol. 6, 24.

31. Sen. Sel. Com. Hearing, vol. 6, 49–50 (emphasis added).

32. Sen. Sel. Com. Hearing, vol. 6, 411–12.

33. Perkus, *COINTELPRO*, 28.

34. Perkus, *COINTELPRO*, 23.

35. Sen. Sel. Com. Hearing, vol. 6, 25.

36. Swearingen, *FBI Secrets*, 82–83. In Swearingen's text, the names of fellow agents are aliases, which he italicized.

37. Swearingen, *FBI Secrets*, 82–83.

38. Anthony, *Spitting in the Wind*, 37.

39. Anthony, *Spitting in the Wind*, 37.

40. Anthony, *Spitting in the Wind*, 38.

41. Anthony, *Spitting in the Wind*, 38 (emphasis added).

42. "8 Panthers Held in Murder Plot," *New Haven Register*, May 22, 1969.

43. Freed, *Agony in New Haven*, 25.

44. Freed, *Agony in New Haven*, 251–53.

45. Among the names Sams claimed was Dingiswayo, the name of the eighteenth-century Chief of the Mthethwa Confederacy in Southern

Africa (where a young Shaka learned the arts of war leading to the rise of the Zulus).

46. Freed, *Agony in New Haven*, 255.

47. Freed, *Agony in New Haven*, 253.

48. Freed, *Agony in New Haven*, 25. Much of the information in this section stemmed from personal correspondence between the author and former New Haven Black Panther Kiilu Nyasha.

49. Tackwood, *Glass House Tapes*, 30.

50. Tackwood, *Glass House Tapes*, 30 (emphasis added).

51. Tackwood, *Glass House Tapes*, 46–48.

52. Tackwood, *Glass House Tapes*, 48.

53. Churchill, *Agents of Repression*, 65.

54. Churchill, *Agents of Repression*, 66.

55. Churchill, *Agents of Repression*, 66.

56. Churchill, *Agents of Repression*, 68.

57. Austin, *Up Against the Wall*, 197-98

58. Churchill, *Agents of Repression*, 403.

59. Churchill, *Agents of Repression*, 58.

60. Shakur, *Assata*, 222.

61. Zinn, *People's History*, 455.

62 *The Harris Survey Yearbook of Public Opinion*, 1970.

63. James, *Shadow Boxing,* 112.

64. James, *Shadow Boxing,* 112.

65. This figure is provided by long-time Party member Forbes, F., "Why I Joined the Black Panther Party," 237. Forbes counts from 1966–1970.

66. Lule, *Eternal Stories,* 65–66. See notes 13 and 15 in Lule's text for extensive sources.

67. Reed, "Another Day at the Front," 193.

68. Churchill, *COINTELPRO Papers*, 215.

69. Citizen's Commission to Investigate the FBI, "Complete Collection," 8–9.

70. Churchill, *Agents of Repression*, 60.

71. Churchill, *Agents of Repression*, 60.

72. Sen. Sel. Com. Hear., vol. 6, 61–2 (emphasis added).

## CHAPTER SEVEN

1. Eugene, "Moral Values," 317.

2. Pearson, *Shadow of the Panther*, 179.

3. Pearson, *Shadow of the Panther*, 344.

4. Henderson, "Lumpenproletariat as Vanguard," 188.

5. Jones, *Black Panther Party Reconsidered*, 4.

6. Jones, *Black Panther Party Reconsidered*, 11.

7. Cleaver, K., "Women, Power, and Revolution," 125–26.

8. Cleaver, E., "Message to Sister Erica Huggins," *The Black Panther*, July 5, 1969. In the article Cleaver spells Ericka's name without the *k*.

9. Cleaver, E., "Message to Sister Erica Huggins."

10. Foner, P., *Black Panthers* Speak, 6.

11. Cleaver, K., "Women, Power, and Revolution," 126.

12. Balagoon, *Look For Me*, 293.

13. Bukhari, "Reflections, Musings," 84.

14. Bukhari, "Reflections, Musings," 84.

15. Balagoon, *Look For Me*, 293.

16. Matthews, "No One Ever Asks," 289.

17. Balagoon, *Look For Me*, 287.

18. Balagoon, *Look For Me*, 292 (emphasis added).

19. Matthews, "No One Ever Asks," 291.

20. Pearson, *Shadow of the Panther*, 179.

21. LeBlanc-Ernest, "The Most Qualified Person," 307–78.

22. Seale, *A Lonely Rage,* Quoted in LeBlanc-Ernest, "The Most Qualified Person," 309.

23. Jennings, "Why I Joined the Party," 262–63.

24. Jennings, "Why I Joined the Party," 255.

25. Jennings, "Why I Joined the Party," 260.

26. Jennings, "Why I Joined the Party," 263.

27. Brown, *Taste of Power*, 368–70.

28. Brown, *Taste of Power*, 371.

29. Bukhari, "Reflections, Musings."44–5. Bukhari's account is drawn from an unpublished manuscript of her

"Reflections, Musings, and Political Opinions," ca. 1997.

30. Bukhari, "Reflections, Musings," 5, 6.

31. Bukhari, "Reflections, Musings," 6.

32. Bukhari, "Reflections, Musings," 6.

33. Bukhari, "Reflections, Musings," 7.

34. Bukhari, "Reflections, Musings," 9.

35. Bukhari, "Reflections, Musings," 36–52.

36. Bukhari, "Reflections, Musings," 37, 42.

37. Bukhari, "Reflections, Musings," 43.

38. Bukhari's original footnote text reads: "The Black Panthers split in 1971. From that time until 1976 there existed an East Coast and West Coast Black Panther Party. For purposes of this writing, the Black Panther Party was destroyed in 1971."

39. Bukhari, "Reflections, Musings," 44, 45.

40. Bukhari, "Reflections, Musings," 47, 48.

41. Singh, "Black Panther Party," 87.

42. Barbara Easley Cox, personal communication with the author, 2003.

43. Barbara Easley Cox, personal communication with the author, 2003.

44. Cleaver, E., "Message to Sister Erica Huggins."

45. Naima Major, personal communication with the author, 2003.

46. Rosemari Mealy, from four page letter to the author, December 28, 2003.

47. Personal conversation with the author, August 11, 2016.

48. This section is drawn from memory. It has been uncovered in recent years that "Bro. Mojo" was also, alas, a police informant. This revelation makes my loss far more than ironic.

49. Brown, *Taste of Power*, 260.

50. Cleaver, E., *Soul On Ice*, 282; Cleaver, E., "Message to Sister Erica Huggins."

51. Cleaver, E., "Message to Sister Erica Huggins."

## CHAPTER EIGHT

1. Newton, *Revolutionary Suicide*, 51.

2. Jennings, "Why I Joined the Party," 240.

3. Forbes, F., "Point No. 7," 231.

4. Forbes, F., "Point No. 7," 232–33.

5. Forbes, F., "Point No. 7," 233.

6. Forbes, F., "Point No. 7," 224–25.

7. Forbes, F., "Point No. 7," 226–27.

8. Cluster, *Should Have Served That Cup*, 65.

9. Washington, *Other Sheep I Have*, 126–27.

10. Freed, *Agony in New Haven*, 34–35.

11. This passage was written from memory.

## CHAPTER NINE

1. Thomas Paine, *Common Sense*, 3 (emphasis in original).

2. Hilliard, *Huey Newton Reader*, 346–47.

3. Grady-Willis, "The Black Panther Party," 366; Fletcher *et al.*, *Still Black, Still Strong*, 18.

4. Exhibit 5 in *Black Panther Party, Pt.1: Investigation of Kansas City Chapter; National Organization Data,* Hearings Before Committee on Internal Security, Mar. 4–5, 10, 1970 (Wash., DC: US Gov't Print Off., 1970), p. 2805) emphasis added.

5. Papke, *Heretics in the Temple*, 120.

6. Shakur, *Assata*, 232.

7. Kleffner, "Interview with Geronimo."

8. Lapham, "Notebook: Power Points."

9. From FBI Memo from HQ to San Francisco field office, February 24, 1971. Quoted in Newton, *War Against the Panthers*, 68–69.

10. Newton, *Revolutionary Suicide*, 296.

11. Hilliard, *Huey Newton Reader*, 355.

12. Cleaver, K., "Back to Africa," 237.

13. On the Purge of Geronimo from the Black Panther Party," *The Black Panther*, January 23, 1971, 7.

14. Hilliard, *Huey Newton Reader*, 355 (emphasis added).

15. Hilliard, *Huey Newton Reader*, 356.

16. Hilliard, *Huey Newton Reader*, 356.

17. FBI Memo from HQs to Philadelphia field office; August 19, 1970. Quoted in Newton, *War Against the Panthers*, 58.

18. Hilliard, *Huey Newton Reader*, 356.

19. Shakur, *Assata*, 231.

20. Shakur, *Assata*, 231–32.

21. Hilliard, *Huey Newton Reader*, 358–59.

22. Brown, *Taste of Power*, 252.

23. Hilliard, *This Side of Glory*, 180.

24. Hilliard, *This Side of Glory*, 120–22.

25. Johnson, "Explaining the Demise," 404.

26. Johnson, "Explaining the Demise," 404.

## CHAPTER TEN

1. Carmichael, *Black Power*, 58–59.

2. Hilliard, *Huey Newton Reader*, 277.

3. Hilliard, *Huey Newton Reader*, 358.

4. Bukhari, "Reflections, Musings," 86–88 (emphasis added).

5. Hilliard, *Huey Newton Reader*, 222–23.

6. Hilliard, *Huey Newton Reader*, 169.

7. Hilliard, *Huey Newton Reader*, 222–23.

8. Schell, 67; I left the Black Panther Party in late 1971–early 1972 and participated in this collective—MAJ.

9. LeBlanc-Ernest, "The Most Qualified Person," 326. Njeri's son, Fred Hampton, Jr., did time as a political prisoner. An outstanding speaker like his father, "Young Chairman Fred" is known to many as a hip-hop activist and through the Dead Prez song "Behind Enemy Lines."

10. Jones, *Black Panther Party Reconsidered*, 6.

11. www.adl.org/learn/Ext_US/Black_Panther.asp; www.newblackpantherparty.com

12. www.adl.org/learn/Ext_US/Black_Panther.asp; www.newblackpanther-party.com

13. Jones, *Black Panther Party Reconsidered*, 6.

14. The Black Panther Collective*The Black Panther International News Service*, 1:5 (1998), 12. .

15. Heike Kleffner, "Interview with Geronimo," *Race and Class* [35:1] 1993.

16. Carr, *Bad*, 233. Citation is to an unsigned afterword completed in 1993.

17. CRIP informant (Br. Amir) to author, December 2003.

18. Shakur, S., *Monster*, 304.

19. Balagoon, *Look For Me*, 285–86.

20. Cross, "Stages of Black Identity," 324.

21. Balagoon, *Look For Me*, 286.

22. Williams, J., "The Black Panthers of Oakland."

23. LeBlanc-Ernest, "The Most Qualified Person," 325–26.

24. Jones, "Don't Believe the Hype," 37.

25. Balagoon, *Look For Me*, 360–61.

## AFTERWORD

1. Roberston, *Wordsworth Dictionary of Quotations*, 167.

2. Frank A. Guridy, "From Solidarity to Cross-Fertilization: Afro-Cuban/African American Interaction during the 1930s and 1940s," *Radical History Review* (Fall 2003), 20.

# BIBLIOGRAPHY

Abdy, Edward. *Journal of Residence and Tour in the United States of Northern America from April, 1833 to October, 1834*. London: J. Murray, 1835.

Abron, JoNina M., "'Serving the People:' The Survival Programs of the Black Panther Party." In Jones, ed., *Black Panther Party Reconsidered*, 177–192.

Ahmad, Muhammad (Maxwell Stanford, Jr.) *We Will Return in the Whirlwind: Black Radical Organizations 1960-1975*. Chicago: Charles H. Kerr, 2007.

Anderson, Osbourne P. *A Voice From Harper's Ferry*. New York: World View, 1974.

Anthony, Earl. *Picking Up the Gun: A Report on the Black Panthers*. New York: Dial, 1970.

———. *Spitting in the Wind: The True Story Behind the Violent Legacy of the Black Panther Party*. Mailibu, CA: Roundtable, 1990.

Aptheker, Herbert. *American Negro Slave Revolts*. New York: International, 1943.

Austin, Curtis J. *Up Against the Wall: Violence In the Making and Unmaking of the Black Panther Party*. Fayetteville: Univ. of Arkansas Press, 2006.

Balagoon, Kuwasi, et al. *Look For Me in the Whirlwind: The Collective Autobiography of the New York 21*. New York: Vintage, 1971.

Booker, Chris. "Lumpenization: A Critical Error of the Black Panther Party." In Jones, ed., *Black Panther Party Reconsidered*, 337–362.

Brown, Elaine. *A Taste of Power: A Black Woman's Story*. New York: Anchor, 1992.

Bukhari, Safiya Asya. "Reflections, Musing, and Political Opinions." Unpublished Manuscript, ca. 1997.

Carmichael, Stokely (Kwame Turé) and Charles V. Hamilton. *Black Power: The Politics of Liberation in America*. New York: Vintage, 1967.

Carr, James. *Bad: The Autobiography of James Carr*. Oakland, CA: AK Press, 2002.

282 | WE WANT FREEDOM

Churchill, Ward and Jim Vander Wall. *Agents of Repression: The FBI's Secret Wars Against the Black Panther Party and the American Indian Movement.* Cambridge, MA: South End, 1990.

———. *The COINTELPRO Papers: Documents from the FBI's Secret Wars Against Dissent in the United States.* Cambridge, MA: South End, 1990.

Citizens' Commission to Investigate the FBI. 1972. "The Complete Collection of Political Documents Ripped-Off From the F.B.I. Office in Media, PA, March 8, 1971." *WIN.*

Cleaver, Eldridge. "Message to Sister Erica Huggins of the Black Panther Party," *The Black Panther,* July 5, 1969.

———. *Soul on Ice.* New York: Dell, 1970.

Cleaver, Kathleen Neal. "Back to Africa: The Evolution of the International Section of the Black Panther Party (1969–1970)." In Jones, ed., *Black Panther Party Reconsidered,* 211–254.

———. "Women, Power, and Revolution." In Cleaver, K., ed., *Liberation, Imagination,* 123–127.

Cleaver, Kathleen and George Katsiaficas, eds. *Liberation, Imagination, and the Black Panther Party: A New Look at the Panthers and Their Legacy.* New York: Routledge, 2001.

Cluster, Dick, ed. *They Should Have Served that Cup of Coffee: 7 Radicals Remember the '60s.* Boston: South End, 1979.

Cone, James H. *Black Theology,* vol. 3. Maryknoll, NY: Orbis, 1993.

———. *Martin and Malcolm and America: A Dream or a Nightmare.* Maryknoll, NY: Orbis, 1991.

Cross, Jr., W.E., Thos. Parham and J.E. Helms. "The Stages of Black Identity Development: Nigrescence Models." In Jones, ed., *Black Psychology,* 319–338.

Donner, Frank. *The Age of Surveillance: The Aims and Methods of America's Political Intelligence System.* New York: Vintage, 1981.

DuBois, W.E.B. *John Brown.* Armonk, NY and London: M.E. Sharpe, 1997.

Equiano, Olaudah. *The Life of Olaudah Eqiano, or Gustavus Vassa, the African.* Mineola, NY: Dover, 1999.

Eugene, Toinette M., "Moral Values and Black Womanists." In Cone, *Black Theology,* 309–320.

Fanon, Frantz. *The Wretched of the Earth.* Translated by Constance Farrington. New York: Grove, 1966.

Feagin, Joe R. *Racist America: Roots, Current Realities and Future Reparations.* New York: Routledge, 2000.

Faulkner, William, *Requiem for a Nun.* New York: Random House, 1951.

Fletcher, Jim, Tanaquil Jones, and Sylvere Lotringer, eds. *Still Black, Still Strong: Survivors of the U.S. War Against Black Revolutionaries—Dhoruba bin Wahad, Mumia Abu-Jamal, Assata Shakur.* New York: Semiotext(e), 1993.

Foner, Eric. *Reconstruction: America's Unfinished Revolution: 1963–1877.* New York: Harper & Row, 1988.

Foner, Phillip S., ed. *The Black Panthers Speak.* Philadelphia: Lippincott, 1970. Reprinted New York: Da Capo, 1995. Page references are to the 1995 edition.

Forbes, Ella. *"But We Have No Country": The 1851 Christiana Pennsylvania Resistance.* Cherry Hill, NJ: African Legacy Homestead, 1998.

Forbes, Flores Alexander. "Point No. 7: We Want an Immediate End to Police Brutality and the Murder of Black People: Why I Joined the Black Panther Party." In Nelson, ed., *Police Brutality,* 225–239.

Frederickson, George M. *White Supremacy: A Comparative Study in American and South African History.* New York: Oxford University, 1981.

Freed, Donald. *Agony in New Haven: The Trial of Bobby Seale, Ericka Huggins and the Black Panther Party.* New York: Simon & Schuster, 1973.

Fresia, Jerry. *Toward an American Revolution: Exposing the Constitution and Other Illusions.* Boston: South End, 1988.

Grady-Willis, Winston A. "The Black Panther Party: State Repression and Political Prisoners." In Jones, ed., *The Black Panther Party Reconsidered,* 363–389.

*Harris Survey Yearbook of Public Opinion, 1970.* New York: Louis Harris and Associates, 1971.

Hayes III, Floyd W., and Francis A. Kleine III. "'All Power to the People': The Political Thought of Huey P. Newton and the Black Panther Party." In Jones, ed., *The Black Panther Party Reconsidered,* 158–175.

Henderson, Errol A. 1997. "The Lumpenproletariat as Vanguard? The Black Panther Party, Social Transformation, and Pearson's Analysis of Huey Newton." *Journal of Black Studies* 28(2): 171–199.

Hilliard, David and Lewis Cole. *This Side of Glory: The Autobiography of David Hilliard and the Story of the Black Panther Party.* Boston: Little, Brown, 1993.

Hilliard, David and Donald Weise, eds. *The Huey P. Newton Reader.* New York: Seven Stories, 2002.

*The Holy Bible (King James Version).* Dallas, TX: International Prison Ministry, 1988.

Ignatiev, Noel. *How the Irish Became White.* New York: Routledge, 1995.

Irons, Peter. *A People's History of the Supreme Court.* New York: Viking, 1999.

James, Joy. *Shadow Boxing: Representations of Black Feminist Politics.* New York: St. Martin's Press, 1999.

Jayko, Margaret, ed. *FBI on Trial: The Victory of the Socialist Workers Party Suit Against Government Spying.* New York: Pathfinder, 1988.

Jennings, Regina. "Why I Joined the Party: An Africana Womanist Reflection." In Jones, ed., *The Black Panther Party Reconsidered,* 258–265.

Johnson III, Ollie A. "Explaining the Demise of the Black Panther Party: The Role of Internal Factors." In Jones, ed., *The Black Panther Party Reconsidered,* 391–414.

Jones, Charles E., ed. *The Black Panther Party Reconsidered*. Baltimore, MD: Black Classic, 1998.

Jones, Charles E. and Judean L. Jeffries. "'Don't Believe the Hype:' Debunking the Panther Mythology." In Jones, ed., *The Black Panther Party Reconsidered*, 25–56.

Jones, R.L., ed. *Black Psychology*. 3rd ed. Hampton, VA: Cobb & Henry, 1991.

The Journal of American History 64(64): June 1977–March 1978.

Katz, William L. *Breaking the Chains: African-American Slave Resistance*. New York: Aladdin, 1990. Page references are to the 1998 edition.

Kelley, Robin D.G. and Earl Lewis, eds. *To Make Our World Anew: A History of African Americans, Vols. 1 and 2*. New York: Oxford University, 2000.

Kleffner, Heike. 1993. "Interview with Geronimo." *Race and Class* 35(1).

Lapham, Lewis. "Notebook: Power Points." *Harper's*, August, 2002.

LeBlanc-Ernest, Angela D. "'The Most Qualified Person to Handle the Job': Black Panther Party Women, 1966–1982." In Jones, ed., *The Black Panther Party Reconsidered*, 305–334.

Lee, Butch. *Jailbreak Out of History: The Re-Biography of Harriet Tubman*. Brooklyn, NY: Stoopsale Books, 2000.

Lee, Chisun. "The NYPD Wants to Watch You: Nation's Largest Law Enforcement Agency Vies for Total Spying Power." *Village Voice*, December 18–24, 2002, 30–36.

Linebaugh, Peter and Marcus Rediker. *The Many Headed Hydra: Sailors, Slaves, Commoners, and the Hidden History of the Revolutionary Atlantic*. Boston: Beacon, 2000.

Lule, Jack. Daily News, *Eternal Stories: The Mythological Role in Journalism*. New York: Guilford Press, 2001.

Mao Tse-Tung. *Quotations from Chairman Mao Tse-Tung*. Peking, China: Foreign Language, 1972.

Marine, Gene. *The Black Panthers*. New York: Signet, 1969.

Matthews, Donald H. *Honoring the Ancient Ancestors: An African Cultural Interpretation of Black Religion and Literature*. Revised. New York: Oxford University, 1998.

Matthews, Tracye. "'No One Ever Asks What a Man's Place in Revolution Is': Gender and the Politics of the Black Panther Party, 1966-1971." In Jones, ed., *The Black Panther Party Reconsidered*, 267–304.

McPherson, James N. *The Negro's Civil War: How American Blacks Felt During the War for the Union*. New York: Ballantine Books, 1965. Page references are to the 1991 edition.

McReynolds, Edwin C. *The Seminoles*. Norman, OK: University of Oklahoma, 1957.

Monges, Miriam Ma'at-Ka-Re. "'I Got a Right to the Tree of Life:' Reflections of a Former Community Worker." In Jones, ed., *The Black Panther Party Revisited*, 135–145.

Moses, Wilson Jeremiah, ed. *Classical Black Nationalism: From the American Revolution to Marcus Garvey*. New York: New York University Press, 1996.

Neal, Father Earl A. "The Role of the Church and the Survival Program." *The Black Panther*, May 15, 1971, 11.

Nelson, Jill. *Police Brutality: An Anthology*. New York: W.W. Norton, 2000.

Newton, Huey P. *To Die For the People: The Writings of Huey P. Newton*. New York: Random House, 1972. Reprinted New York: Writers and Readers, 1995. Page References are to the 1995 edition.

———. *War Against the Panthers: A Study of Repression in America*. New York: Harlem River, 1996.

Newton, Huey P. with J. Herman Black. *Revolutionary Suicide*. New York: Harcourt, 1973. Reprinted New York: Writers and Readers, 1995. Page references are to the 1995 edition.

Newton, Huey P. and Erik Erikson. *In Search of Common Ground: Conversations with Erik H. Erikson and Huey P. Newton*. New York: Norton, 1973.

Nietzsche, Friedrich. *Beyond Good and Evil*. Translated by Helen Zimmern. Mineola, New York: Dover, 1997.

Nyasha, Kiilu. "A Chapter in the Life of a Panther." *San Francisco Bay View*, October 23, 2002, 1–2, 10.

O'Reilly, Kenneth. *"Racial Matters:" The FBI's Secret File on Black America, 1960-1972*. New York: Free Press, 1989. Page references are to the 1991 edition.

Paine, Thomas. *Common Sense*. 1776.

Papke, David Ray. *Heretics in the Temple: Americans Who Reject the Nation's Legal Faith*. New York: New York University Press, 1998.

Pearson, Hugh. *The Shadow of the Panther: Huey P. Newton and the Price of Black Power in America*. Reading, MA: Addison-Wesley, 1994.

Perkus, Cathy, ed. *COINTELPRO: The FBI's Secret War on Political Freedom*. New York: Monad, 1975.

Reed, Ishmael, "Another Day at the Front: Encounters with the Fuzz on the American Battlefront, in Nelson, Jill, *Police Brutality*, 189–205.

Roberston, Connie, ed. *The Wordsworth Dictionary of Quotations*. Hartfordshire, UK: Wordsworth, 1996.

Schell, Reggie. "A Way to Fight Back: The Black Panther Party—An Interview with Reggie Shell." In Cluster, *They Should Have Served that Cup*, 47–63.

Seale, Bobby. *A Lonely Rage: The Autobiography of Bobby Seale*. New York: Times Books, 1978.

———. *Seize the Time: The Story of the Black Panther Party and Huey P. Newton*. New York: Vintage, 1970.

Segal, Ronald. *The Black Diaspora*. New York: Noonday, 1996.

Shakur, Assata. *Assata: An Autobiography*. London: Zed Books, 1987.

Shakur, Sanyika. *Monster: The Autobiography of an LA Gang Member*. New York: Penguin, 1993.

Singh, Nikhil Pal. "The Black Panther Party and the 'Undeveloped Country' of the Left." In Jones, ed., *The Black Panther Party Reconsidered*, 57–105.

Smith, William Gardner. *Return to Black America*. Englewood Cliffs, NJ: Prentice-Hall Publishers, 1970.

Story, J., *Edward Prigg v. Com. v. Pa* (1842), pp. 625–26. *Prigg v. PA.,* 41 ;US 536, 625-26 (1842).

Swearingen, M. Wesley. *FBI Secrets: An Agent's Expose*. Boston: South End, 1995.

Tackwood, Louis E. and Citizens Research and Investigation Committee. *The Glass House Tapes: The Story of an Agent Provocateur and the New Police Intelligence Complex*. New York: Avon Books, 1973.

U.S. Congress, House. Committee on Internal Security. *Black Panther Party, Part 1: Investigation of Kansas City Chapter; National Organization Data*, 91st Congress, 2nd Session. Washington, DC: U.S. Government Printing Office, 1970.

———. *Black Panther Party, Part 2: Investigation of the Seattle Chapter*. 91st Congress, 2nd Session. Washington, DC: U.S. Government Printing Office, 1970.

———. *Black Panther Party, Part 4: National Office Operations and Investigation of Activities in Des Moines, Iowa, and Omaha, Nebraska*. 91st Congress, 2nd Session. Washington, DC: U.S. Government Printing Office, 1970.

U.S. Senate. Select Committee to Study Governmental Operations with Respect to Intelligence Activities. *Federal Bureau of Investigations, Volume 6;* Senate Resolution 21. November/December 1975) (Washington, DC: U.S. Government Printing Office, 1976.

Washington, Father Paul M. with David M. Gracie. *"Other Sheep I Have:" The Autobiography of Father Paul Washington*. Philadelphia: Temple University Press, 1994.

Wiencek, Henry. *An Imperfect God: George Washington, His Slaves and the Creation of America*. New York: Farrar, Straus & Giroux, 2003.

Williams, Joan Kelly, et al. "The Black Panthers of Oakland: The Dilemmas of 'Radicalism,'" Video Conference, California State University, 1994; California Student Conference (Oakland, CA, February 10–12, 1994).

Williams, Robert F. *Negroes with Guns*. New York: Marzani & Munsell, 1962.

Wilmore, Gayraud S. *Black Religion and Black Radicalism: An Interpretation of the Religious History of African Americans*. 3rd Edition. Maryknoll, NY: Orbis, 1998.

Wright, J. Leitch, Jr. *Creeks and Seminoles: The Destruction and Regeneration of the Musgogulge People*. Lincoln, NE: University of Nebraska Press, 1986.

Zinn, Howard. *A People's History of the United States: 1492-Present*. Updated edition. New York: Harper Perennial, 1995.

Zinn, Howard and Anthony Arnove. *Voice's of a People's History of the United States*. New York: Seven Stories, 2004.

# INDEX

## A

Abdy, Edward, 52–53

Abron, JoNina, 246

Adams, Frankye Malika, 163, 168

Adams, Henry, 11

Adams, John Quincy, 22

African People's Socialist Party (APSP), 238

Africanisms, 104–5

Al Fatah, 107–8

Algiers, Algeria: Cleaver's self-imposed exile in, 116, 217, 219–22, 232–34; international BPP headquarters, 106, 109, 117, 184, 254

Ali, Muhammad (Cassius Clay), 4, 62

Alston, Ashanti, 240

Ambulance Services, 70

La Amistad mutiny, 19

*Anarchist Panther,* 240

Anarchist People of Color, 240

Anderson, Osbourne, 26

Angola Penitentiary, 111

Angola 3, 112

Anthony, Earl, xv, 102, 140–41, 154, 226

anti-Semitism, 115, 118, 239

Aoki, Richard, 121, 276

Aptheker, Herbert, 18, 22

Arafat, Yasser, 107

Arizona State University, 129

armed resistance: Christiana, 34–39, 56; at Harper's Ferry, 24–26; Negro Fort, 17, 21–24; police-monitoring patrols, 43–45, 67–69, 78, 99, 213; Seminole Wars, 22–24; Watts Rebellion, 5–6, 31–34, 40–41, 63, 65–66, 102, 105. *See also* rebellions; riots

Ash, Joel, 138

## B

*Babylon! Revolutionary People's Communication Network,* 233

back-to-Africa movements, 6–11, 20

Baker, Ella, 163

Baldwin, James, 5

Baraka, Amiri, 102

*Barenblatt v. U.S.,* 119

"Baron's Revolt," 17–18

Barth, Karl, 27

Bassem, Abu, 108

Bay, Big Bob, 113

Bennett, Fred, 230

Bernice, Sister, 185–86

Bethune, Mary McLeod, 163, 253

Beyoncé, xix, xx, xxii

Biddle, Francis, 135

"Big Man" (Elbert Howard), 6, 216, 219, 223, 263

bin Wahad, Dhoruba, 211, 221–22

Bird, Joan, 186

# Mumia Abu-Jamal

 Mumia Abu-Jamal was born April 24, 1954, in Philadelphia. At the time of his arrest there on December 9, 1981, on charges of the murder of a police officer, he was a leading broadcast journalist and president of the Philadelphia chapter of the Association of Black Journalists. Widely acclaimed for his award-winning work with NPR, Mutual Black Network, National Black Network, WUHY (now WHYY), and other stations, he was known as Philadelphia's "voice for the voiceless."

At the age of fourteen, Mumia was beaten and arrested for protesting at a presidential rally for George Wallace. In the fall of 1968, he became a founding member and Lieutenant Minister of Information of the Philadelphia chapter of the Black Panther Party. During the summer of 1970, he worked for the Party newspaper in Oakland, California, returning to Philadelphia shortly before the Revolutionary People's Constitutional Convention and the city police raid of all three local offices of the Panther Party.

Throughout the following decade, Mumia's hard-hitting criticism of the Philadelphia Police Department and the Rizzo administration marked him as a journalist "to watch." His unyielding rejection of Mayor Rizzo's version of the city's 1978 siege of the MOVE organization (in the Powelton Village neighborhood of West Philadelphia) particularly incensed the establishment, and eventually cost him his broadcast job. In order to support his growing family, Mumia began to work night shifts as a cabdriver.

In the early morning hours of December 9, 1981, Mumia was critically shot and beaten by police and charged with the murder of officer Daniel Faulkner. Put on trial before Philadelphia's notorious "hanging judge," Albert Sabo, he was convicted and sentenced to death on July 3, 1982.

After years of challenges and international protests, on December 18, 2001, the US District Court overturned the death sentence, but upheld the conviction. Judge Yohn's District Court decision was appealed by both sides, with the prosecution objecting to the overturn of the capital sentence and Mumia's attorneys rejecting the upheld conviction. On April 26, 2011 the decision to vacate the death sentence was upheld and in October of that year the Supreme Court declined to hear the case. On December 7, 2011 the Philadelphia District Attorney announced they would no longer seek the death penalty. In late January 2012 Mumia was moved, for the first time, into the general prison population after almost 30 years on death row. Mumia is currently sentenced to spend the rest of his life in prison without the possibility of parole.

On March 30, 2015, Mumia was rushed to the hospital after losing consciousness and going into diabetic shock. Mumia's diabetic shock came in the midst of an escalating year-long health crisis that began with a rash in August 2014. The skin condition grew in intensity over the course of the next several months, eventually covering most of his body with a painful, severe rash that was resistant to conventional treatments. In August 2015 a lawsuit was filed to demand treatment of Mumia's active Hepatitis C, which has likely been the underlying cause of his health crisis. The lawsuit is progressing and if successful will positively impact thousands of people incarcerated without proper medical treatment, in the meantime Mumia is not receiving the treatment that would cure his Hepatits C and his life remains at risk.

Starting with the Black Panther Party's national newspaper, Mumia has reported on the racism and inequity in our society. He added radio to his portfolio, eventually recording a series of reports from death row for NPR's *All Things Considered*. However, NPR, caving in to political pressure, refused to air the programs. Mumia Abu-Jamal is still fighting for his own freedom from prison, and through his powerful voice, for the freedom of all people.

Mumia Abu-Jamal is the author of *Live from Death Row, All Things Censored, Death Blossoms, Faith of Our Fathers, Jailhouse Lawyers, The Classroom and the Cell,* and *Writing on the Wall*. His audio recordings include *175 Progress Drive* and *All Things Censored*. He holds a BA from Goddard College and an MA from California State University, Dominguez Hills and is currently pursuing his Ph.D. His books have sold more than 100,000 copies and have been translated into seven languages. His commentaries appear in periodicals throughout the world and can be heard on www.prisonradio.org.

# Supporter Information

International Concerned Friends and Family of Mumia Abu-Jamal
P.O. Box 19709, Philadelphia, PA 19143 (267) 760-7344
www.freemumia.com | ICFFMAJ@aol.com

The Mobilization to Free Mumia Abu-Jamal
P.O. Box 10328, Oakland CA 94610 (510) 268-9429
www.free-mumia.org

Prison Radio
P.O. Box 411074
San Francisco, CA 94141 (415) 648-4505
www.prisonradio.org | info@prisonradio.org

Free Mumia Abu-Jamal Coalition (NYC)
P.O. Box 16, College Station
New York, NY 10030 (212) 330-8029
www.freemumia.com | info@freemumia.com

Educators for Mumia
www.emajonline.com | emajmumia@gmail.com

Campaign to Bring Mumia Home
http://www.bringmumiahome.com

Critical Resistance: Beyond the Prison–Industrial Complex
National Office: 1904 Franklin Street, Suite 504
Oakland, CA 94612 (510) 444-0484
www.criticalresistance.org | crnational@criticalresistance.org

Millions for Mumia
www.millions4mumia.org

Libérons Mumia
(Collectif Francais de Soutien a Mumia Abu-Jamal)
43, Bld de Magenta
75010 Paris, France 01 53 38 99 99
www. mumiabujamal.com | contact@mumiabujamal.com

## ABOUT COMMON NOTIONS

Common Notions is a publishing house and programming platform that fosters new formulations of living autonomy. We aim to translate, produce, and circulate timely reflections, clear critiques, and inspiring strategies that may amplify movements for social justice.

Our publications trace a constellation of critical and visionary meditations on the organization of freedom. By any media necessary, we seek to nourish the imagination and generalize common notions about the creation of other worlds beyond state and capital. Inspired by various traditions of autonomism and liberation—in the US and internationally, historical and emerging from contemporary movements—our publications provide resources for a collective reading of struggles past, present, and to come.

Common Notions regularly collaborates with political collectives, militant authors, radical presses, and maverick designers around the world. Our political and aesthetic pursuits are dreamed and realized with Antumbra Designs.

www.commonnotions.org
info@commonnotions.org

# MORE FROM COMMON NOTIONS

*Zapantera Negra: An Artistic Encounter Between the Black Panthers and the Zapatistas*
Marc James Léger and David Tomas (editors)
with Emory Douglas
978-1-942173-05-2

*Wages for Students | Sueldo para estudiantes | Des salaires pours les étudiants*
George Caffentzis, Monty Neill, and John Willshire-Carrera (Introduction)
Jakob Jakobsen, María Berríos, and Malav Kanuga (editors)
978-1-942173-02-1

*Family, Welfare, and the State: Between Progressivism and the New Deal*
Mariarosa Dalla Costa, Silvia Federici (Introduction)
978-1-942173-01-4

*Our Mother Ocean: Enclosure, Commons, and the Global Fishermen's Movement*
Mariarosa Dalla Costa and Monica Chilese
978-1-942173-00-7

*The Debt Resisters' Operations Manual*
Strike Debt
978-1-60486-679-7 (copublished with PM Press)

*Revolution at Point Zero: Housework, Reproduction, and Feminist Struggle*
Silvia Federici
978-1-60486-333-8 (copublished with PM Press)

*In Letters of Blood and Fire: Work, Machines, and the Crisis of Capitalism*
George Caffentzis
978-1-60486-335-2 (copublished with PM Press)

*Sex, Race, and Class: The Perspective of Winning A Selection of Writings 1952–2011*
Selma James
978-1-60486-454-0 (copublished with PM Press)

*19 & 20: Notes for a New Social Protagonism*
Colectivo Situaciones; Nate Holdren and Sebastián Touza (translators); Michael Hardt and Antonio Negri (Introduction)
978-1-942173-03-8

MORE FROM **COMMON NOTIONS**